WITHDRAWN
D0072880

Judgments on History and Historians

JACOB BURCKHARDT

Judgments on History and Historians

Translated by Harry Zohn

WITH A FOREWORD BY ALBERTO R. COLL

CALVIN T. RYAN LIBRARY
U. OF NEBRASKA AT KEARNEY

LIBERTY FUND

Indianapolis

This book is published by Liberty Fund, Inc., a foundation
established to encourage study of the ideal of a society of free and
responsible individuals.

𒂗𒄄

The cuneiform inscription that serves as our logo and as the
design motif for our endpapers is the earliest-known written appearance
of the word "freedom" (*amagi*), or "liberty." It is taken from a clay
document written about 2300 B.C. in the Sumerian
city-state of Lagash.

© 1999 by Liberty Fund, Inc.
All rights reserved
Printed in the United States of America
Originally published in 1958 by Beacon Press

Frontispiece: Jacob Burckhardt, courtesy of Corbis-Bettmann.
Used by permission.

Library of Congress Cataloging-in-Publication Data
Burckhardt, Jacob, 1818–1897.
[Historische Fragmente.   English]
Judgments on history and historians   /   Jacob Burckhardt;
translated by Harry Zohn; with a foreword by Alberto Coll.
p.   cm.
Originally published: Boston: Beacon Press, 1958. With new
foreword.
ISBN 0-86597-206-0 (alk. paper).—ISBN 0-86597-207-9 (pbk.:
alk. paper)
1. History—Philosophy.   2. World history.   3. Historiography.
I. Title.
D16.8.B813   1999
907'.2—dc21   98-17504

03 02 01 00 99 C 5 4 3 2 1
03 02 01 00 99 P 5 4 3 2 1

Liberty Fund, Inc.
8335 Allison Pointe Trail, Suite 300
Indianapolis, IN 46250-1687

Contents

Foreword

Readers should beware. This is a profoundly counter-cultural book, unabashedly and defiantly so. It takes on the prevailing truisms of our time across the entire political spectrum: the goodness of popular egalitarian democracy; the superiority of untrammelled capitalism and its consumerist, materialistic ethos; and the benefits of a welfare state that paternally provides for all. Jacob Burckhardt (1818–97) also strenuously challenged the notion, already widespread in his time and held even more tenaciously today, that the essence of history for the past four hundred years has been the march of progress and enlightenment.

In this book, composed of notes and manuscript fragments for lectures he delivered at the University of Basel between 1865 and 1885, Burckhardt carried on the debate against the numerous historians and commentators from Voltaire onward who insisted on judging the past against the standards of rationalism and liberalism that arose in the eighteenth and nineteenth centuries. While Burckhardt disagreed on many things with his former mentor Leopold von Ranke, he shared Ranke's view that "every generation is equidistant from God." An age may have a level of material prosperity or intellectual and artistic excellence lower than that of another, but it is not thereby inferior in its capacity for spiritual insight or nobility. Every historical epoch has its own intrinsic meaning and its own contribution to make to the collected intellectual and artistic treasures of humankind. The task of the historian, far from judging all things by virtue of their contribution to modernity, is to explore every corner of the past with an appreciative eye for the wonder and essential mystery behind the process of human creativity.

By taking this stand, Burckhardt emerged in most refreshing contrast with his contemporaries and many of his successors. For what he developed was nothing short of a psychology of historiography. The historian is to observe, contemplate, and enjoy the incredibly glorious richness of the human experience. He is to look for human greatness and creativity everywhere, even in periods that might seem alien and distant from him. His spirit ought to be one of enquiry, wonder, and empathy. Insofar as he allows himself to make moral judgments about the past, these judgments should be based not on contemporary verities but on more universal values. Thus, we may judge Tamerlane for his hideous massacres of innocent women and children, but it makes no sense to judge Charlemagne for his authoritarianism. Beyond all this, the historian is to search everywhere for the priceless achievements of the human spirit that transcend politics and economics—those great works of artistic and literary beauty and power, and those deeds of courage, nobility, and grandeur—which grace the history of civilization and inspire later generations.

Despite his injunction not to judge the past, Burckhardt did not hesitate to judge the present, with all of its smugness and self-confidence. Like Alexis de Tocqueville, he had deep misgivings about the advent of popular egalitarian democracy, which he believed would lead to ever higher levels of vulgarity, the simplification and corruption of culture and politics, and eventually the tyranny of demagogues. The main problem with popular democratic culture was its deification of equality as the ruling principle in all of life. It was one thing to argue that all men should be equal before the law, an idea Burckhardt did not find problematic, but quite another to argue that all men are equal, and even more pernicious to suggest that all beliefs, opinions, and ways of life are of equal worth, a *reductio ad absurdum* that Burckhardt believed would lead to the death of culture and the return of barbarism.

Burckhardt was equally harsh toward another idol of the nineteenth and twentieth centuries, namely, the spread of economic growth and development as the essence of "progress." Sometime during the seventeenth century, many people had come to believe that the chief end of life is to acquire material possessions and live with the greatest possible comfort and material ease. This belief, coupled with the growth of capitalism, industrialization, and ever more inventive technologies for the economic exploitation of the earth's resources, had created a culture of hectic acquisitiveness, materialism, and spiritual and aesthetic squalor. Burckhardt was appalled at the human, cultural, and environmental costs of this ever more voracious Behemoth. Late in the nineteenth century, he wondered what would have happened to the earth if capitalism, industrialization, and science had begun their joint work three or four centuries earlier. What would be left by now? he asked.

At a time when liberals everywhere were celebrating the aristocracy's decline, and Bismarck, with the support of the Reichstag, was busy organizing the first welfare state, Burckhardt noticed one central fact: the unrelenting growth since the sixteenth century of the power of the state. The new paternal state, despite its benevolent trappings, carried the potential for the unlimited exercise of power and despotism. With such barriers to state power as the Church and the aristocracy weakened by the advance of popular democracy, egalitarianism, and industrialization, it seemed to Burckhardt only a matter of time before state power would be put in the service of tyranny.

On the threshold of the twenty-first century, Burckhardt's observations appear as luminous and insightful as ever. Having barely escaped from the tyrannies of fascism and communism and the cataclysms of two world wars—all of which Burckhardt more or less predicted—many peoples are becoming as smug as Burckhardt's contemporaries. Millions see democracy, capitalism, consumerism, and technology as unlimited boons, and have no tolerance for anyone who might raise troublesome questions about these forces. Yet our triumphalism could use some tempering.

The mix of egalitarianism, consumerism, and the welfare state has produced widespread moral decay, political apathy, and an increasing dissonance between the requirements of a regime of ordered liberty and the capacity of that regime's citizens to fulfill those requirements. It is inarguable that Western societies are facing serious long-term problems. The exercise of liberty requires moral and intellectual virtues that oppose those habits fostered by the reigning economic, social, and cultural elites. The virtue most essential to liberty is self-control, yet the ruling principle behind egalitarianism, Hollywood-style hedonism, and unbridled materialism is the notion that one's appetites for pleasure and possessions should brook no limits.

For Burckhardt, another troubling aspect of modernity that has become even more destructive during the twentieth century is the Promethean quality of modern civilization. Long before the advent of nuclear and biological weapons, genetic engineering, and widespread environmental devastation, Burckhardt worried about where science, the primacy of economics, and the state's endless quest for power would take the West. In his own time, he despised the railroads, the ugly factories blighting Europe's beautiful countryside, and the rise of powerful nation-states armed with ever mightier arsenals of military technology. He saw these as elements in a relentless process as destructive of higher culture and the good life as the marriage of egalitarianism, consumerism, and the welfare state. At the dawn of the twenty-first century we have even stronger grounds for apprehension about where all this might end. Armed with Burckhardt's understanding of the dark side of human nature—itself a fruit of his intimate acquaintance with the tragic character of history—we reasonably can fear that the future will be more problematic than the optimists insist.

In spite of his scorn for democracy and much of modernity, Burckhardt was a philosopher of freedom on several grounds. First, he was a passionate believer in the human spirit and its ability to rise to great heights in the midst of the bleakest circumstances. No historian has affirmed the weight of human freedom against historical necessity more persistently than Burckhardt. The long-term trends and powerful impersonal forces all count, but so does the lonely genius—such as Luther or Michelangelo—striving to affirm his inner vision. History is full of broken trends that at one point seemed to stretch infinitely into the future but then moved in radically new and unexpected directions; many of these great historical surprises have occurred because of the force of human personality. In other words, there is freedom in the midst of necessity.

Secondly, Burckhardt affirmed that the highest form of freedom is inward—that is, the freedom to maintain one's soul and mind sufficiently detached from and independent of the ruling passions and conventional wisdom of the moment. Therefore, a society that aspires to be called free must defend those institutions, such as independent wealth and centers of economic and social power free from the state, that facilitate intellectual, artistic, and spiritual freedom. This view distinguished Burckhardt from the socialists, with their hankering after centralization, as well as from the liberal egalitarians, with their obsessive desire to destroy every vestige of privilege and inequality. Lastly, Burckhardt believed that a free society needs to guard against the demagogue—the "great man"—who in the name of the people would increase his own power and that of the state, and impose uniformity.

As uneasy as Burckhardt was with the forces shaping Western civilization in his lifetime, he was far from ready to renounce the West's heritage or be ashamed of it. He marvelled at the achievements of Western civilization, and particularly at the spiritual and artistic ones, which he believed were far more significant than the material and technological ones. Deeply aware of the multicultural richness of his own world, he believed it was incumbent on the heirs of Western civilization to know well their own particular cultural inheritance. There was no better place to start than the culture and heritage of classical Athens, where the idea of freedom first had flowered alongside some of the most sublime artistic and literary works in all of history. (It would have been better for all humankind, he noted, if Athens, not Sparta, had been victorious in the Peloponnesian War.) Burckhardt had one name for those not interested in their past: "barbarians." He was quick to judge Americans for their plutocratic ways, but he judged them even more harshly because he thought they did not believe they had much of value to gain from studying history. Indeed, in his opinion, Americans took pride in being "new," that is, in having no history.

Burckhardt found his ideal political community in the small city-states of Athens and Florence, where with varying degrees of success freedom had flourished together with high culture (literature, music, and the fine arts). The modern world, with its relentless march toward gargantuan cities in which human beings lead an alienated, lonely, stupefied existence anchored in triviality, vulgarity, and material satiety, frightened him. Yet he was too much of a skeptic to believe that there is a solution to this problem in the form of either a political ideology or a "great man" who could bring about a new renaissance. If there was a renaissance ahead, it would come about, Burckhardt surmised, as the unexpected fruit of the human spirit and the quiet work of a few individuals—"secular monks," he called them—who did not care about power but cherished the characteristics of the culture of "old Europe," foremost among these being the love of freedom and beauty. In the annals of Western historiography, few voices can match Burckhardt's in his affirmation of the grandeur of the human spirit or his insistence on the irreducible nature of freedom as an end in itself.

Alberto R. Coll

Translator's Preface

I consider it a privilege to be the translator of a work about which Walter Goetz, the editor of the *Propyläen-Weltgeschichte*, wrote: "It is impossible to imagine a more profound introduction to world history and its driving forces."

Jacob Burckhardt's *Historische Fragmente* were selected by Emil Dürr from Burckhardt's lecture notes for his history courses at the University of Basel during the period from 1865 to 1885. The *Fragmente*, which were first published in 1929 as Volume Seven of Burckhardt's Collected Works, may be regarded as a companion volume to his *Weltgeschicht-liche Betrachtungen* (published in English as *Force and Freedom*) [and in 1979 as *Reflections on History*, by Liberty Fund—publisher's note]. The present translation is based on the edition issued in 1942 by Benno Schwabe, Basel, and the Deutsche Verlagsanstalt, Stuttgart. It has been checked against the virtually unchanged new edition issued by the K. F. Koehler Verlag of Stuttgart at the end of 1957.

The very qualities that make Burckhardt's work so unique and attractive, even exasperatingly charming—the tone of improvisation; the compressed, elliptical style, by turns professorial and colloquial; the occasional contradictions and ambiguities; the abrupt shifts—also provide a real challenge to the translator. Burckhardt wrote in the rather austere Swiss German of the nineteenth century, and his language, moreover, seems to reflect his personal willfulness, his sharp criticism of his time. Within the limits of reasonably clear and idiomatic English I have tried to reproduce some of Burckhardt's stylistic peculiarities.

His emphases and question marks as well as other evidences of his erudite musings have been faithfully retained throughout; a few factual inaccuracies have been corrected. Since this edition is intended for the general reader interested in history as well as for the specialist, it was decided to omit most of the critical and bibliographical apparatus of the German edition, which consists in large part of specific information about Burckhardt's various manuscripts, variant readings, and passages later deleted by Burckhardt himself. Wherever possible, those footnotes of the German edition that were deemed essential have been incorporated into the text, but minutiae and bibliographical references to works not readily accessible today have generally been omitted in an effort to promote continuity and readability.

I should like to express my appreciation to Philip Rieff, Janet Finnie, John Rackliffe, Paul Alexander, and John Wight for their helpful interest in this work. The last-named kindly supplied the translations from the Greek and Latin. Katharine McCagg was good enough to compile the Index.

H. Z.

Judgments on History and Historians

I

Antiquity

1. Ancient History and Its Scope

A general introduction to history will be omitted here; the specific introduction to ancient history can be disposed of briefly. As regards the scope of our subject, this may be observed: Only the civilized nations, not the primitive ones, are part of history in a higher sense. Ample information has been preserved even about the latter (Herodotus). For the old ἱστορία [history in Herodotus' sense] is in itself ethnography and history in one. Primitive peoples, however, interest us only when civilized nations come into conflict with them, as in the cases of Cyrus with the Massagetae and Darius with the Scythians. The ethnographic is thus to be confined to its essentials. Of the civilized peoples, our discipline does not embrace those whose culture did not flow into European civilization, for instance Japan and China. Of India, too, only the very oldest period concerns us—first, because of the Aryan tribal type shared with the Zend peoples, and then because of the contact with the Assyrians, Persians, Macedonians, and others. Our subject is that past which is clearly connected with the present and with the future. Our guiding idea is the course of civilization, the succession of levels of culture in various peoples and within individual peoples themselves. Actually, one ought to stress especially those historical realities from which threads run to our own period and culture.

There are more of them than one would think. The continuum is magnificent. The peoples around the Mediterranean and over to the Gulf of Persia are really *one* animate being, active humanity par excel-

1

lence. In the Roman Empire, this being does attain a kind of unity. Here alone the postulates of the intellect are realized; here alone there prevails development with no absolute decline, but only a transition.

After renewed intermingling with the Germanic peoples, after another fifteen hundred or two thousand years, this active humanity strikes out anew, assimilates America for itself and is now about to open Asia thoroughly. How long will it be before all *passive* existences are subjected and penetrated by it? The non-Caucasian races offer resistance, give way, and die out. Egyptians, Babylonians, and Phoenicians have by now laid the foundations for this world-conquering power. Through slow development as well as by leaps and the arousing of opposition we are intellectually connected with them. It is a great good fortune to be part of this active humanity.

2. On the Intellectual Indispensability of Studying Ancient History

Among all the fields of learning in the world there prevails, like a fundamental chord that keeps sounding through, the history of the ancient world, i.e., of all those peoples whose lives have flowed into ours.

It would be idle to assume that after four centuries of humanism everything had been learned from the ancient world, all experiences and data had been utilized, and there were no longer anything to be gained there, so that one could content oneself with a knowledge of more modern times or, possibly, make a pitying or reluctant study of the Middle Ages and spend the time saved on more useful things.

We shall never be rid of antiquity as long as we do not become barbarians again. Barbarians and modern American men of culture live without consciousness of history.

In our problematical and wonderful existence we cling involuntarily to the knowledge of man as such, of mankind, empirical, as we meet it in life, and as it is revealed by history. The contemplation of Nature does not suffice us, does not console or instruct us enough.

And here we must not seal ourselves off from anything past, we must leave no gaps; only the *whole* speaks to us, in all centuries that have left us records.

Are the three great ages of the world perhaps like the three times of day in the riddle of the Sphinx? They are, rather, a continual metempsychosis of acting and suffering man through countless incarnations. A genuine inquiry will want to recognize *all* these mutations and abandon any partiality for specific ages (it is all right to have a predilection, for that is a matter of taste), and it will do this all the sooner the livelier the feeling for human inadequacy in general is. Once it is understood that there never were, nor ever will be, any happy, golden ages in a fanciful sense, one will remain free from the foolish overvaluation of some past, from senseless despair of the present or fatuous hope for the future, but one will recognize in the contemplation of historical ages one of the noblest undertakings. It is the story of the life and suffering of mankind viewed as a whole.

And yet antiquity has a great specific importance for us; our concept of the state derives from it; it is the birthplace of our religions and of the most permanent part of our civilization. Of its creations in form and writing a great deal is exemplary and unequaled. Our accounting with it in affinity as well as in contrast is infinite.

However, let us regard antiquity as merely the first act of the drama of man, to our eyes a tragedy with immeasurable exertion, guilt, and sorrow. And even though we are descended from peoples who were still slumbering in a state of childhood alongside the great civilized peoples of antiquity, yet we feel ourselves the true descendants of the latter, because their *soul* has passed over into us; their work, their mission, and their destiny live on in us.

3. The Limits of Civilization and Barbarism

We can no more begin our presentation of history with the earliest state formations than with the *transition from barbarism to civilization*. Here, also, the concepts are much too vague.

At what point, with what discovery, what accumulation of material comforts, does civilization begin? With the solar year? The alphabet? The loom? The chemical analysis of metals? Or with what else? And where does "barbarism" end? This is especially difficult in view of the ambiguous quality of the word in German where it is used in an intellectual and a moral sense. To some the Greeks are barbarians because they kept slaves and annihilated their political opponents. The Romans are considered barbarians if only because of their sacrifice of human lives in the circuses and amphitheaters. The Middle Ages again are barbaric for other reasons, because of religious persecution and the eradication of dissenters. In the final analysis, the use or non-use of this word becomes a matter of temperament. I consider it barbarism to keep birds in cages.

First one ought to eliminate those elements which have lived on from the infant days of mankind in petrified form in the most advanced civilization, perhaps for sacral or political reasons, such as individual human sacrifice. Then it might be asked whether such primitive peoples would not find some things in our civilization barbarism, i.e., running counter to their ethics.

And now we come to the real distinguishing feature which *essentially* separates barbarism from culture; the only reason it cannot serve us as a guiding rod or for the determination of the beginning is that the documentary evidence is inadequate. It is the question: Where does mere living in the present, such as the savage does, cease, and where does life in the past *and* the present, i.e., differentiating comparison, begin? When does the mere present, devoid of history, end?

A valuable possession of a people is its first heroic epic. In addition to daily life there at least exists an ideal past, such as Tacitus reports in his *De Germania: "Celebrant carminibus antiquis (quod unum apud illos memoriae et annalium genus est) Tuistonem deum terra editum et filium Mannum, originem gentis conditoresque."* [In their ancient songs—the only means they have of remembering historical events—they celebrate Tuisto, a god born of the earth, and his son Mannus as the origin and founders of their race.] This is the way a people with a great future acts.

To be sure, side by side with a very beautiful tribal legend like that of the Scythians utter barbarism can still live on and be preponderant, permanently drowning out the upright and noble features. It can do this in various ways: through excessive savagery (the annual communion of those who have killed enemies; the sauromatic virgins); through servitude to symbols, religious fears instilled early, and narrow views of the beyond (the killing of the court servants and an entire *equitatio* [funeral procession on horseback] at a king's grave); or through the impossibility of urban life and a sentencing to nomadism (the steppe, until people may move away from there). Purest barbarism is the behavior toward the soothsayers at the sickbed of a king (the king is ill because someone took a false oath at the royal hearth), and, finally, thralldom to nature magic.

Chronic, late wickedness which may be connected with advanced civilization may finally degenerate into pure barbarism with the decline of the people concerned.

At any rate, historically minded Egypt, with its records and comparisons, early moves into the first rank, as far as we can know anything. Even with an absolutely much lower culture, Egypt would take top place by virtue of its fondness for making written records.

4. Why Today's "Educated Man" Can No Longer Understand Antiquity

At our universities, the historians like to dump the Ancient History course in the lap of the philologists, and vice versa. Here and there it is treated like a poor old relation whom it would be a disgrace to let go to ruin entirely. But with the public at large antiquity is completely out of fashion, and the "culture" which is supported by this public even feels hatred for it. Various faults of antiquity serve as a pretext. The real reason is conceit about modern communication and transport and the inventions of our century; then, too, there is the inability to distinguish technical and material greatness from the intellectual and moral kinds; and finally, the prevalent views about refinement of manners, philanthropy, and the like.

But what makes it generally impossible for the present-day average "educated" man to find anything appealing in the ancient world is the total egoism of today's private person who wants to exist as an individual and asks of the community only the greatest possible security for himself and his property, for which he pays his taxes amid sighs, and who also likes to attach himself to the community in a specific sense as an "official."

On the other hand, the peoples of the ancient Orient, who lived tribally, impress us as races of which each individual is only a type, with the king as the highest type.

And even where the individual develops, especially since the Greeks, we still deal for a long time essentially with types, e.g., the heroes, the lawgivers. They are, to be sure, depicted as great individuals, and this is borne out by feeling and tradition; but at the same time they are all the more fully types and condensations of the characteristic and the general. And last, the complete individual in antiquity is, above all, πολίτης [part of the state] to a degree of which we now, in the present mode of connection between the individual and the state, have no idea. Whenever one breaks with the πόλις (*polis*) or when it is lost, it is a tragedy every time.

Finally, today's "educated" men are firmly resolved to make a bargain, with whatever power, for their existence at any given time. There is an enormous veneration of life and property. There is a mass abdication, and not just on the part of rulers! And there are numerous bargaining positions and concessions against the worst—and all this with great touchiness in matters of recognition and so-called honor.

With the ancients, on the contrary, it was all or nothing, with no fear of disaster. The fall of states, cities, and kings was considered glorious. That is something utterly alien to us.

5. The Historical Significance of Egypt

We must keep our view unaffected by the ease with which changes and new developments in state and culture now occur, and take a wide and high perspective. Then Egypt will appear in its unique greatness.

After thousands of years must have passed with a growing civilization of which, except at the Nile, no one had any inkling; after, possibly, even these advances had involved immeasurable sacrifices; after gods, heroes, and the dead had ruled for numberless dynasties, Egypt made a tremendous new stride under Menes and United Egypt was founded. And after that time there was here a state with a superior will, a nation, a way of life, a religion; while the Egyptians were *founding* and *recording*, in the rest of the world there can have been only primitive life or the first rudiments of a civilization. In addition, due to a providence most significant for us, there appeared the strongest impulse of the monumental, of recording and tradition. Gradually the other peoples, except for desert tribes, had to be affected by all this in some way. It is idle to argue about Egypt's priority. *Chronologically* it is assured, in all matters; its *influence* is obscured from our view, which does not make it any the less probable.

Even though the other peoples—the Babylonians, Phoenicians, Assyrians, Iranians, and others—may differ from the Egyptians in every single element of their civilizations, still they were most probably subjected to a *general* Egyptian impetus without which their development might have been delayed and perhaps not have occurred at all.

The period of the Old Empire offers us a complete government with numerous officials and priests; a very rich outward life, graded into numerous occupations; a monumental will to portray all this and lend it permanence; realistically alive, quite vigorous graphic arts (Beni-Hassan; the Scribe in the Louvre) and at the same time the greatest monumentality; but side by side with this, a true separation of the spiritual from the material, attached to the idea of life after death. Here belong the ideas of the tomb system (up to the royal graves, the pyramids) and embalming. Already at that time pre-existence and metempsychosis must have existed as fully developed doctrines; but the mere subordination of the transitory to the permanent, of the individual life on earth to a colossal community of the dead would be something of giant proportions.

Accordingly, even though life then was undoubtedly "a hard service, with many sacred customs," still there was no mere priestly tyranny and superstition. The Prisse Papyrus with the babbling beginnings of a code of ethics dates from as early as the fifth dynasty.

As the main feature of this epoch there stands out the will to feel and act as a united Egypt. Apart from the subjection of Ethiopia, the willingness to share glory is predominant.

6. The Phoenicians as the Earliest Creators of πόλεις (*Polis*)

Egypt and Old Babylon were great despotisms with sacred laws and universal obedience, Egypt, in addition, having a functioning caste system. Their outer life was spent in wars, marauding expeditions, the defection and subjugation of outlying countries.

The Phoenician cities were the first polities, constitutional states with city areas, *community* life, albeit under kings; some formed self-perpetuating aristocracies which not only had to be consulted, but must have had direct control of the most important matters. All of them later became republics. Their *constitution* balanced the claims of many. Did perhaps the patriarchal tribal constitution of the nomads serve as a model? This *polis* has the power of *multiplication;* while despotism can only deport, forcibly transplant peoples, and at best found military states, the *polis* creates genuine *colonies* and becomes a metropolis for many. The joint founding of Tripolis by Sidon, Tyre, and Arados is a voluntary action of higher intelligence.

To such a fatherland a real patriotism could at last attach itself, one that went beyond the dull Egyptian national arrogance and in the wide world outside was not a fish out of water, but bestirred itself all the more.

Whether the later Greek *polis* owes anything to the Phoenicians as models may remain quite uncertain. Ordinarily something like the *polis* does not come into being merely through imitation. Nevertheless, the Phoenician influence must have been inestimable. In any case, the Phoenicians are assured of chronological priority, and this fact redounds to their eternal glory.

To be sure, as early as Homeric times the Phoenicians were regarded by the Greeks only as land thieves, τρώχτης [greedy rascals]. Carthage, too, even before the contact with Rome appears in unpleasant political and military guise.

7. On Carthage

A little more respect for the tribe of Ham which furnished Egypt, Old Babylon, Phoenicia, and Carthage would not be amiss. The fact that it was accursed by the Jews did not make it fare any the worse in the world. A curse is, after all, only the product of violent hatred and utter impotence. The curse in *Genesis* IX, 25–27, was not fulfilled; Ham did not become a serf, but for thousands of years was a very great lord. We resent any demand that we base our historical standards on the hatreds of the Jews. If they make their patriarchs or their Jehovah curse in one way or another, or if they represent what happens to other peoples as the vengeance of Jehovah, it does not follow that we have to think about these peoples in any particular way.

It is very deplorable that instead of Justin's *Epitome*, XVIII and XIX, we no longer have all of Trogus Pompeius at least. It is the only halfway coherent and comprehensive piece of Carthaginian history from its founding until the fourth century B.C.

The fair number of Carthaginians who appear among the Greek philosophers in Diogenes Laertius are evidence of a pronounced talent in this field. Of their literature the Romans salvaged only the books about agriculture, much as Jiménez did with the Arab books.

8. Athens

Throughout the seventh century Athens does not seem to stand out especially from the other Greek communities. But from the sixth century on, these words gradually come to apply to it: *"Verum haec tantum alias inter caput extulit urbes, Quantum lenta solent inter viburna cupressi."* [But this city towers above others as much as the cypresses do above the swaying viburnums. Virgil, *Eclogues*, I, 24–25.]

From then on the inhabitants paid attention to the old peculiarities, to the regional myths almost wholly sundered from the Greek ones, to the old characteristic of no intermingling with absolute hospitality toward the persecuted. A unique development came about: in the political sphere, all transitions were accomplished without frightful peripeteia and reactions; Solonian legislation meant the complete victory of speculative thought and of gentle and fair customs; the tyranny of the Pisistradae was the most enlightened; the subsequent refinement of democracy from Clisthenes on was the calmest and most gradual.

All this demonstrates, first of all, consummate political aptitude. At the same time, the Athenians rise far above all other Hellenes onto the throne of education, art, and superior social graces.

The central location helped greatly to bring this about, but a more basic reason is the happy blend of rural and commercial life and the most favorable set of conditions ever encountered on earth. It was as if Nature had for centuries saved up all its resources to expend them at that time.

Through the complete, and also false, unleashing of all its powers, Athens wore itself out politically rather fast. But it had salvaged its cultural position and remained the intellectual capital of the Hellenes when the sites of athletic festivals and the Oracle of Delphi had lost their central significance. It saved itself materially as well and was able to finish its life decently under the Romans.

The great parallel to this is furnished by Florence and the Renaissance. *One* city desires most and accomplishes what a whole people wants and would like to accomplish, just as specific family traits may predominate most strongly in *one* son of a house.

It is hard for us to give a fair judgment between Athens and Sparta, since we owe an infinitude to Athens and nothing to Sparta, and because Sparta did not hold on to any venerable primitive piety in the face of rapid Athenian progress, but from the beginning maintained a depraved rule of force over subjugated fellow Hellenes. We do not know, however, whether *without* such an adversary Athens would not soon have degenerated in other ways, e.g., gone in for conquests of the type of the Sicilian campaign and other adventures.

9. Rome and Its Mission in World History

Rome, which had emerged from obscure Hellenic-Trojan-Italic beginnings, became the mistress of the Mediterranean and thus realized the historic moment of Italy.

The Orient with its attempts at world monarchies, Greece with its colonial world, Carthage with its location and its commerce, and the entire great barbaric West are fused into one Empire and one civilization; then this whole, close to collapse, is entrusted to a great new world movement, Christianity, under whose protective wing enough of it lives on to make possible a revival in the culture of the fourteenth to the sixteenth centuries.

Since then our horizon has been overshadowed by it. Rome is everywhere the conscious or tacit premise of our views and thought; if in the essential intellectual points we are now no longer part of a specific people and country but belong to Western civilization, this is a consequence of the fact that at one time the world was Roman, universal, and that this ancient common culture has passed over into ours.

That East and West belong together, that they constitute a humanity, the world owes to Rome and its Imperium.

The history of Rome is in the highest sense the second part of ancient history. The currents issuing from everywhere flowed together, not merely into serfdom, but into one transmissible civilization.

That is why we are concerned with the ῥωμαϊκὴ ἀρχαιολογία (antiquities of Rome—Dionysius of Halicarnassus) only to the extent necessary for an understanding of what was needful for the growth and development of Rome as mistress of the world; moreover, we shall gladly do without the true secret.

Among the individual peoples this is the mightiest; its individuality, to be sure, can be described and circumscribed like that of a person, but its remote causalities remain concealed. *Verum haec tantum alias inter caput extulit urbes, Quantum lenta solent inter viburna cupressi.*

After a semi-mythical, typical period of monarchy there begins a century and a half of struggle between two strata of the population in which a brand of politics and virtue is developed that differs from that in any Greek republic, and immediately after the end of this struggle Rome rises to the conquest of Italy as the property naturally due it. Its earlier political perseverance now reveals itself as greatness on a world scale, i.e., through a natural process Rome grows into all tasks of the management of power; it seems to have an innate talent for the proper handling of all matters concerning power, and it is equal to the greatest task. *"Tu regere imperio populos, Romane, memento, Haec tibi erunt artes, pacisque imponere morem, Parcere subjectis et debellare superbos."* [Remember, O Roman, to rule the peoples with power. These will be your arts: to impose the habit of peace, to spare the conquered and to cast down the proud. Anchises, Virgil, *Aeneid*, vi, 851–853.]

Rome shook the Gauls and the Etruscans, subdued the Samnites, and made its presence felt in lower Italy. Then the highest representative of the Diadochian war lords appears, Pyrrhus, and Rome is victorious and loses its fear of elephants.

Then Rome wages its first war with Carthage for hegemony over Sicily, in grand style and with the clear understanding that world dominion was at stake. Japhet and Ham test their strength and pay each other calls; Rome forces itself to become a naval power and gains victories at enormous cost.

From that point on, world history becomes σωματοειδές (systematic— Polybius). The inner weakness of Carthage, as contrasted with Rome's strength, is strikingly revealed in the war fought with mercenaries.

But a kindly fate lets worthy opponents for the Romans arise. Just after the Romans have subdued the Upper Italic Celts, it appears that one Carthaginian family (a branch of the Barcas—father, sons, and a brother-in-law) has been able to rid itself of any Hamitic acquisitive spirit and devote itself to the one goal of saving their homeland and destroying Rome. It is superior to anything else that we know about Ham and Shem. And as for Hannibal, in a certain sense he ranks above all Greeks, even Alexander. Rome could have reckoned with anything but such an adversary. And this adversary it overcame, confined Carthage to a strip of Africa, and surrounded it with the envious, like Massinissa.

After *that*, the Greeks and Diadochi are just a light morning snack; Philip comes closest to being a worthy opponent. But here Rome displays its initial veneration of Hellenism, considering itself the preserver and protector of the Greek tradition; the age-old Greek spirit stirs within the Romans. Rome Hellenizes itself, primarily under the leadership of Titus Quinctius Flamininus and the Scipios, who, for their part, had enforced Rome's political and military power in Greece.

However, with the enormous gains that were to be had from the Diadochi system, Rome grows brutish. It begins to take its percentage when it gives away whole empires, when whole flocks of kings and royal emissaries appear before the Senate, and when Egypt derives its internal peace from Roman protection.

There is a marked change in Rome after the destruction of Carthage and Corinth. Maltreatment of subjects, exploitation of the semi-freemen, and frequently wicked warmaking go hand in hand with growing ferment in Italy, even while Spain and the Gallic *provincia* are being acquired.

The City of Rome is demoralized by the optimates who have waxed rich in the provinces or want to do so. The Roman citizenry shrinks as compared to the world empire, even though nominally it is spread over all of Italy. Could all the agrarian laws in the world have helped? Or the wholesale addition of the Italici to the ruling people?

During the incipient civil wars military personalities become decisive—individually distinguished ones, but also wicked ones who stand out from the inadequate conduct of the war by the Senate, such as Marius in the war against Jugurtha and the Cimbri. The Italici are vanquished in the Social Wars. All popular excitement is now merely urban demagoguery, designed to exploit people for the benefit of the mighty. There is no hurry about the monarchy, however. Sulla's proscriptions restore the rule of the optimates; the dictator himself abdicates.

On the outside, power is preserved and extended from Spain to Asia, around the entire Mediterranean and the Black Sea, and victories are gained over Mithridates, Tigranes, and the pirates, while in Rome the republic cannot die and yet must be in dread of becoming at any moment the prey of an optimate, a democrat, or of the Catilinarians. The pseudo-rule of the Senate actually leans on a succession of strong men.

At length the First Triumvirate is formed.

It includes Caesar, the greatest of mortals. First he saves the Empire by conquering Gaul and securing it against the Germani, then he takes possession of it through his victories at Pharsalus, Thapsus, and Munda, and gives the tormented provinces a foretaste of government instead of mere desultory plundering by optimates.

The republicans find it a simple matter to remove him from the scene, but do not stop to consider that his veterans will still be mightier than themselves; then they console themselves with the dissension among his actual heirs, until the latter in the Second Triumvirate join in proscriptions and separate into East and West. Finally, after another terrible exhaustion of the available strength Augustus becomes sole ruler. Now it is realized that monarchy can no longer be swept away through mere attempts at assassination.

The optimates and their mentality are eradicated by the Augustan house. Lust for the principate quickly manifests itself; the transmission of power becomes extremely uncertain. The good governments of Vespasian and Trajan and up to Marcus Aurelius seem like extraordinary gifts of the gods.

But this is a great period in world history, independent of individuals, through the sway of practical realities. For, in the first and second centuries A.D., there occurred the most important consequences of the world empire: the uniform organization and administration of the provinces; the catching up on things neglected (Britannia, Dacia, Mesopotamia are conquered); the smooth adjustment of Greco-Roman culture and its extension to the westernmost regions. Only now is there full intellectual intercourse in the entire ancient world. And at the same time the religions are denationalized. While Rome Romanizes the Gallic gods, it is itself orientalized.

Then, with renewed unsteadiness of power and appalling individual governments, the deathly force begins to rise: Neo-Persians and Germani appear and make frightful incursions into the Empire. The multiplicity of imperators, such as the Thirty Tyrants, can be explained by local defense needs alone. But once more the Empire is saved and united by great generals (the Illyrians); the Illyrian triangle, now so passive, becomes the nucleus at that time. To assure the transmission of power, Diocletian tries his system of adoptions. This is overthrown by Constantine, who allies himself with the great new world religion.

Just as Rome had once made Hellenistic culture its own and thus enabled Hellenism to live on for all time (and on this depended all knowledge and understanding of the Orient), Christianity now took over the Greco-Roman heritage, to salvage it beyond the time of the Germanic invasion.

After a dreadful period of decline, Romanism lives on partly as the Byzantine state, partly as the Western church; gradually it gathers all heathen and Arian Germani into its fold, and from night springs the new day of the Middle Ages which finds its spiritual unity in Rome. *"His ego nec metas rerum nec tempora pono, imperium sine fine dedi"* [For them I set no limits in space or time, I have given them power without end—Virgil, *Aeneid*], says Jupiter to Venus.

What would we know of the ancient world if the Germani had taken by surprise a pagan Rome and therefore had established no other relationship with it but that of crudest possession?

Our intellect, however, no matter how independent of the past it may behave in science and technology, is ever renewed and consecrated by the consciousness of its connection with the mind of the remotest times and civilization. Indeed, it gets to know itself and value its lofty nature only through comparison with that which it, the *eternally unchanging*, has been in all times.

10. On the Roman Empire in Its First Two Centuries

The confluence of the ancient lands of Greek civilization with Italy, Africa, and the West into one world empire is no mere accretion of flotsam. Its significance does not lie in its size, but in the fact that it benefited so many peoples, stopped the wars among the nations, and let the ancient world come to about as favorable an end as was possible.

The Roman Empire as such is not responsible for the general heritage of antiquity, namely, the lack of human rights, the continuation of slavery (which, however, was no worse than in the golden age of Greece with its torture of slaves and its Attic mine slaves), the bankruptcy of the independent state (the Romans saved the Greeks from their internecine rage and destruction). As for the very impure world of the gods and religion in the process of decay, these are Greek, as are the speculative thought which respects nothing, and the disdain of all existence. Astraea, the goddess of justice, has already withdrawn to heaven in the writings of the Greek poet Aratus in the third century B.C., and Virgil's *"Iam redit et virgo"* [Now, too, the virgin returns] does not bring her back.

The complaints about evil humanity, e.g., in Pausanias, refer to the Antonine period, to be sure, but they do not prove conclusively that egoism was greater then than it had been previously.

To what extent is Artemidorus a source as to morality in general? And what about Lucian and Apuleius? Lucian, the last genuine enlightener and utter infidel, denier of *all* religion, bears witness to a general heartlessness, but is himself a poisonous personality of boundless self-praise.

Lucian's entire future life, with its ἰσοτιμία [equality of honor] where everything is of one color and no one is more beautiful than anyone else, is nothing but a shrill mockery, a void provided with a touch of life only to the extent that a few chosen ones may indulge in their mocking laughter and the celebrities of the ancient world may be maltreated. They are nothing but skeletons, so that a person's identity has to be ascertained every time (one is reminded of the medieval Dances of Death). Menippus is a mocking skeleton, Charon already a half-devil. The shades favored by Lucian, such as Micyllus, rejoice even during the crossing: γελασόμεθα οἰμώζοντας ὁρῶντες [We shall laugh when we see them grieving].

This future life, which was so miserable for almost everyone, was in contrast with the Christian hereafter and also with the striving of the pagans to catch up in some fashion with the Christian life to come through the mysteries of that time. In this connection one should not forget the small but distinguished band of Stoics under Marcus Aurelius that represented a veritable religion, complete with father confessors and casuists (regarding this a number of passages from Aulus Gellius can be cited). The virtuous among the Romans lived on a veritable diet of the soul.

To what extent is the general worthlessness of life also reflected in the evident readiness for death on the part of the Christians?

Lucian still bestows high praise on Epicurus as the liberator from all this-worldly and other-worldly superstition. But in the third century Epicureanism is extinguished.

The senescence can be admitted in a certain sense and degree.

How much might wickedness and wretchedness have differed from the wickedness and misery of all times and of mankind generally?

Gladiatorial combats and much else can sour us on the Romans in general, but so many things can make us dislike the Greeks of the so-called golden age!

In any case, the first and second centuries are to be viewed separately from the subsequent ones.

The character of the second century is determined by the Antonines.

It is really most remarkable that there were able to succeed to the throne of the Julian dynasty and of Domitian two great rulers and then two wholly virtuous ones, of whom Marcus Aurelius quite obviously seeks to tower above his enormous imperial office through his Stoic personality.

The influence of the Stoa makes itself felt among the jurists of the time and we get the beginnings of humane legislation; one direct consequence of this is that slaves are given some rights. But on the whole, "Roman law," for which Justinian's compilers were later given credit, is actually the work of the great emperors of the second century and the great jurists of the third.

To be sure, when Marcus Aurelius, who hated the amphitheater, sent the gladiators off to war against the Marcomanni, there was almost an uprising, as though the emperor wanted to force the people to philosophize.

He fought the war very conscientiously and efficiently, at least liberated all of Pannonia, then cleared the entire right bank of the Danube of barbarians and even penetrated far beyond the Danube. But for the revolt of Avidius Cassius he might have made Bohemia (the land of the Marcomanni) and Galicia (Sarmatia) into provinces.

The emperors since Nerva had found it easy to make wise adoptions if they were childless. Marcus Aurelius, who had his Commodus, observed the law of inheritance again and acted according to this expectation from his son's childhood on. As early as 176–177 he made him Imperator, Consul, Augustus. If afterwards he had wanted to disinherit him, considering the development of Commodus' character, it would have been too late. If, for example, he had let his son-in-law Pompeianus or Pertinax succeed him, the soldiers would probably have promoted Commodus notwithstanding.

In the third century there appear the instructive consequences of inheritability, pseudo-inheritability, and usurpation of the throne, until Diocletian introduces adoption as a complete system.

As the restorer of the Empire's unity, Septimius Severus is another Vespasian, but Caracalla, his campaign within his own Empire, and the emperor's dependence on the soldiers make everything uncertain again. Finally the Empire passes into the hands of the Syrian emperors, and even the best of these, Alexander Severus, is murdered in 235.

The Empire, which since the Augustans has been in charge of provincial officers, now comes under the control of petty officers and murderous soldiers. Prior to Commodus, the emperors who are murdered are monsters; after 235 the murdered are the efficient ones, those who want to maintain discipline. In addition, the barbarians now invade the Empire from all sides. A terrible period is the half-century from 235 to 284.

The greatest miracle and the justification of the Roman Empire is the fact that it could be reunited at all.

The Imperium contented itself chiefly with the maintenance of general obedience and of the taxes and boundaries; it was infinitely better than the predatory Senate government. Taxation was direct. The Empire had large tax and customs districts. The direct taxes were revised from time to time; the inland duties, a kind of indirect taxation, were high. The taxes were collected in grain, and goods were used to defray the wages of troops and officials. The rest was in large measure left to local life, the regional constitutions of the cities, *pagi*, and so on. The *polis*, the *municipium*, still existed, as did benevolence within it.

For the time being, outside of the governing power there was no spiritual or material magnet that could have alienated the people's loyalty.

Freedom of intellect and speech was almost unlimited. *Education* provided by the state, where it occurs, is, after all, not a tool of power. Private life was not controlled by the police. The Empire did not harass the people, but people did harass one another.

Of the cruel emperors of the Julian and Flavian dynasties (Domitian), only the raging wastrels were actually a menace to the entire Empire, because they had to resort to depredation on a grand scale and probably made use of a band of informers. But the Greek *polis*, too, had plundered its wealthy.

Absolutism was considered a natural thing in the Roman Empire and the principle of obedience was at no time in question. That is why the absolute state was able to act unabashedly and never, theoretically, in an underhanded manner. Obedience was not a matter of a doctrine that had to be maintained laboriously and systematically. The government did not need to defend conservatism, nor did it have to organize a bureaucracy as an army of loyalty, and least of all to make education the monopoly and basis of the bureaucracy with the aid of a system of examinations. A great many offices belonged only to the *municipium*.

In the whole Empire there was no political party with which the Imperium would have had to contend for power.

Here Mommsen's words apply: "Even today there is many a region of both East and West for which the imperial period marks the high point of good government, modest in itself, but never attained before or since. And if some day an angel of the Lord were to draw up a balance sheet as to whether the area ruled by Severus Antoninus is governed with greater understanding and humaneness today than it was then, whether morals and human happiness in general have progressed or regressed since then, it is very doubtful if the verdict would be in favor of the present."

The sole danger was from the military, especially from provincial armies, when they fought over installing an emperor.

The clamor of Greek democracies for "χοεῶν ἄφεσις" and "ἀναδασμὸς τῆς χώρας" ["freedom from want" and "a distribution of land"] was decidedly at an end, although it is threatened once more in Lucian.

But what never occurred was any attempt to restore the republic, except for a brief conspiracy after Caligula's death.

As regards economic conditions, we must not forget the great premise which is present in the anti-banausic thinking of early antiquity, especially that of the Greeks, the main reason for which was the presence of domestic, industrial, and agricultural slaves. After the third century one surmises at most a marked decrease of *domestic* slaves, because the tombstones of freedmen became far less frequent from that time on; at least the inscriptions cease. As want increased, perhaps it became more economical and more desirable to cut expenses and make shift with free servants rather than buy slaves for which there may have been no funds. Did a free domestic system begin at that time? This does not prove anything regarding the increase or decrease of *field* slaves. And the average condition of the *factory* slaves must be surmised rather than proved in any way. Their percentage was probably not great.

The only universal right of the slaves was that their masters could not kill them or take away the *peculium* [small property] they had saved. Otherwise a slave was a chattel and barely had a legal marriage, which his master did not respect in practice anyway. A distinction was made between a slave's death "after" or "in consequence of" ill-treatment; in the former case even the laws of Constantine the Great did not punish the master.

That free labor greatly predominated in the trades is shown by the existence of the *collegia* or guilds. They are to be differentiated clearly from the frequently prohibited and politically suspect sodalities whose purpose was merely social enjoyment, religious worship, and burial. The craftsmen can only have been free individual masters. Did they work more with slaves or with free men? In any case, they took part in the labor themselves. Where they did collective work, e.g., for armies, they probably shared the load and the profit. They also seem to have possessed joint funds. Later on there was compulsory membership in the *collegia;* whoever performed certain work had to belong to the appropriate *collegium*. The state reimbursed itself for the taxes through the *decuriones,* first of all, and then through these *collegia*. In an emergency the state made a squeezing machine out of each corporation. At the same time, both classes jointly bore the responsibility for municipal expenses, construction, supplies, and amusement.

In addition, the imperial factories (slave labor, because collective?) retained as a monopoly certain businesses, like armaments, purple garments, and mines; later this monopoly system was expanded still further. There, too, *collegia* are involved; these may be thought of as contractors. The *collegia* had common religious services and burying places; however, they appeared in complete form only in the larger cities.

Must not labor have been more highly esteemed than it was with the Greeks and early Romans?

Prosperity in general depended on whether the country in question had previously had a higher or a lower civilization.

Sybel complains of the absence of any large industry, an activity creating new value, in addition to the purely passive trade without exports. If things were really as bad as that, it is hard to understand how the Roman Empire was able to stand it.

As regards the cultivation of the soil, or rather, the alleged desolation and non-cultivation, we must differentiate among

(a) what happened through the fault of the Roman Empire;

(b) what had happened long ago, through the fault of the peoples themselves (Greece, as Dio Chrysostom, Pausanias, and Strabo found it, had been desolated only by Greeks); and

(c) what had been laid waste by enemy irruptions.

Latifundia and desolation were not yet necessary reciprocal concepts; at any rate, there were great differences in degree among the provinces. To be sure, the complaint about latifundia is justified for Italy. They originated through patrician occupation of the *ager publicus*, then spread throughout Italy and the provinces. But in themselves they would not necessarily be bound up with bad, not very profitable planting and with the maltreatment of *coloni* and slaves.

As reasons for the decline of agriculture Sybel cites the following: war service of the small farmers; failure of the medium ones because of their own wastefulness and the pressure of state taxes; the formation of a small number of colossal estates (latifundia) and the resultant unwholesome economic and social conditions for cultivation and yield, as well as the desolation and depopulation attendant upon them.

Aside from the fact that Sybel's reasons are very limited and insufficient and disregard the main causes of the decline of the Roman Empire, which do not become operative until the third century, it was Rome that put an end to collective property, the common pasture land of whole tribes, e.g., in the Celtic lands of the West, recognizing only definitely circumscribed property. Only after that did nomadic life probably give way to agriculture in many places. For Gaul it has been demonstrated clearly (Cellier) that the introduction and increase of the chief cultivated plants were due to the Romans.

However, every state of ownership has beside it an oppressed class which under certain circumstances makes an uproar. Even what now seems to us like a very imperfect, culture-impeding institution, such as collective property, the common pasture land of whole tribes, probably fitted in with the life of the time, and when, e.g., the Romans put a stop to such things, large segments of the population were made very un-happy. A shepherd does not become a farmer, as has been thought; he dies off.

Incidentally, apropos of latifundia, we have no right to shoot off our mouths, at a time when the whole farm-owning class is undermined by usurers, the bankrupt are in the majority, the Jews are in the saddle, and the peasants retreat to the cities.

Nor does it behoove us to consider the Roman Empire especially unhappy because of its lack of competitive factory industries with "free" workers.

And as far as the "desolation" is concerned, it should be noted that, e.g., the Hauran, east of the Upper Jordan, only now became a popu-lated country and remained so until Islam. By contrast, Dio Chrysostom described Thessalia as desolate, Arcadia as a wasteland, and Pausanias traveled through long, deserted stretches. In all these cases it was the fault of the Greeks themselves among whom since the time of Polybius intentional childlessness had come into practice. In Campania the marked decline in the cultivation of the soil appears to have occurred only later, and in North Africa, whose bread Rome ate, the very large number of bishoprics, 477, is proof of a large population. Britain's growth is evident also; there the Celtic language, now confined to Wales and Cornwall, had already given way to the Roman idiom prior to the Angles and the Saxons. In Gaul, both culture and population appear to have increased right up to the Antonines. This seems to be borne out by the long and vigorous life of the Gaulish language. The popu-lation of the *agri decumates* [land worked on tithes], arisen from the *levissimus quisque Gallorum* [every wisp of a Gaul] and the *inopia audax* [fierce want], appears to have been an overflow of the already Roman-ized Gallo-Romans. Trajan and Hadrian then drew the *limes* [boundary] around it.

All that Sybel adduces is thus very one-sided and insufficient to ex-plain the fall of the Roman Empire. The main causality, rather, is shown to be as follows: the internal disorganization of the Empire after Commodus, Caracalla, and Heliogabalus, along with the attendant imperial wars; further, after Marcus Aurelius, the new movements of the Germani on all borders and their great human resources—possibly a sudden increase; also, the Sassanids. As a counterforce and in part because of the inner disorganization of the Empire, the Thirty Tyrants appear to save the situation.

The restoration of the Empire by the Illyrian emperors had to be accompanied by force, even under the best of conditions, and the situation after that inevitably became a *permanent state of emergency*, even without famine and pestilence.

The Empire of the first and second centuries must therefore be regarded as distinct from that of the third. Would the abolition of agricultural slavery and the forcible establishment of arms-bearing free farmers have availed anything in the third century? Many such, but not nearly enough, were actually created through the settling of Germani. Instead, there was a most pernicious, unalterable financial system. But in an emergency it is difficult to change such a system.

At this point, a counterbalance should be drawn up. How much general and inevitable *human* misery was present and a contributing factor, as it is at any time? Misery is a relative concept and is equal to the degree of discontent within a given situation. One is not miserable until one realizes it and no longer wants to put up with things.

In the late third century the world empire had to reconstruct itself and remain together so that it could become Christian as a unit.

Let us have proper respect for the Roman Empire. No other dynasty of the world can boast of five rulers in succession like those from Nerva to Marcus Aurelius (mere hereditary dynasties cannot possibly achieve this), as well as a series of rescuers like that from Claudius the Goth to Diocletian.

II

The Middle Ages

11. On the Middle Ages

(I) [1882.] The term "Middle Ages" actually came into being as an homage to antiquity. It means "the middle period." The Italians of the fifteenth century were already aware of this. (Is *"medium aevum"* a translation of *"Mittelalter," "moyen âge"*?)

In this designation there was expressed the concept of a very expendable thousand years which may have existed for the chastisement of mankind; this gave it the reputation of barbarism, and its beginnings in fact had been an overcrowding of the world with barbarians. Hence the special ill-will of the Italians, who had lost their world dominion through the barbarians, although this had actually already happened under Constantine. It seemed to them that, basically, the more modern period could have started directly with the end of Roman history. Something like impatience was felt toward the Middle Ages.

This view was expressed first in the designation and in the meaning of the Renaissance, then, too, especially in the name of the modern "great power" (the atomization of power in the medieval state was deplored), and, finally, in the term "world civilization."

It was possible to misjudge the Middle Ages, to be sure, but in the long run one could not despise the period. The realization prevailed that our existence had its roots in it, even though modern culture was derived predominantly from antiquity. Gradually the specific qualities of the Middle Ages were appreciated in innumerable ways. Certain aspects even inspired veritable enthusiasm which, however, aroused hostility in completely modern-minded persons. On the whole, very strong and widespread prejudices against the Middle Ages have prevailed to this day, not to mention the more deeply entrenched ones. There is an optical illusion with regard to so-called golden ages in which great spiritual capacities come together in a society, as though "happiness" had a definite address or domicile at some *time* or in some *place.*

Above all, at our present moment in history, under the conditions of 1882, we have no business sitting in judgment on any past age—now when from every side there are complaints about, and threats against, our general situation as well as specific matters, and the nations are pitted one against the other, armed to the teeth.

Now that we are convinced that our knowledge of the Middle Ages belongs among our dearest possessions, that is, the great general knowledge about the continuation of the spirit which distinguishes us from the barbarians (including very modern ones), we had better omit any evaluation of the past according to our standards of happiness or unhappiness, since these are illusions.

Very peculiar is the interest of our time in all past things and its judgment of their relative intellectual value. Of course, our time is itself undergoing such great transformations that its judgments about the past vary greatly, too. This much, however, remains certain: today's European humanity has had at least a long youth in the shape of the Middle Ages.

The life of mankind is a unit whose fluctuations in time or place constitute an up and down, a weal or woe, only to our weak senses, but in reality follow a higher necessity. To trace the latter in detail remains a dubious and difficult task. Not everything that may now and then appear to an investigator as a decree of world history really deserves this title.

It is a universal human experience that the fringes of existence have always been miserable, because individuals as well as nations always push their existence to the limits of possibility; this is an existence just barely worth living.

There is something to be said for the survival of a people as such if at least it neither consumes itself, as the ancient Greeks did, nor is destroyed by other peoples. How many peoples disappeared in the great migrations of the Germanic tribes; as soon as they had no kings of their own, they lost themselves among the others. Are we to feel sorry for them at random? If they had existed longer, would they (and so many other peoples who had already gone down in early antiquity) have done great and good things or perhaps predominantly bad ones?

At any rate, the amount of unhappiness felt increases greatly in highly civilized, security-minded periods when conditions become completely insecure and violent, as, e.g., in the migrations of the Germanic tribes.

But we may properly feel a certain amount of pity and need not excuse ourselves with the barren argument that what fell did so for good reasons, or that after a fall there comes a resurgence. For by no means every destruction has been followed by rejuvenation (those involved and their relatives will have none of rejuvenation through decay), and the great destroyers of life remain an enigma to us. In the face of the ambition of an Attila, who did not have enough time, or of the accomplishments of Genghis Khan and especially Tamerlane, we remain perplexed, and can, at best, stutter that these men destroyed forces which, under certain circumstances, might also have become very harmful to mankind. The capital losses of mankind are enormous. And in particular the destruction of noble and universally admired works of poetry and art fills us with lasting sadness because we are convinced that they are irreplaceable, i.e., we know that never before has there been, nor ever again will there be, a union of precisely this naive strength with this beauty. (But let us close our eyes; experience teaches us that the human race has over the ages achieved very little of supreme excellence, and will do no better in the future; therefore, for the time being, we may well mourn when things of excellence are destroyed.)

Our only consolation—and a very uncertain one—is this: the survival of the greatest works of antiquity, now lost, would have stood in the way of the newer literature and art and made their natural appearance or at least their independence impossible.

As a rule, however, calling past times happy or pitying them is only partisanship in favor of *one* untenable thing against another such; and as it is, we are subject to the prejudices of our egoism (at best, to the predilections of our time) which approves of what seems akin to it and disapproves of what it finds incomprehensible or repugnant.

Thus, for instance, we have a powerful antipathy to Islam, with its arid religion, its art tyrannically kept poor, its forcibly restricted poetry, and its invariably tyrannical form of government. But as soon as the believers are given voice, we and our pity are sent packing. To this day, Islam gives its adherents enormously firm support, and they are proud of it and almost inaccessible to missionary efforts. But if one imagines history without Islam, one must also eliminate the at least temporary rejuvenation which, as an opponent, it brought to the Byzantine Empire and later, through the Crusades, to the West. (This great adversary quite materially kept the Byzantine Empire alive. That it finally did succumb to Islam was due to weakening from the West; remember 1204.) But the Mongols would have come nevertheless, and it is beyond all speculation in what condition they would have found a non-Islamic Near East and Europe.

However, just as dubious as pitying is felicitation. When it is directed toward victorious peoples, their happiness, the so-called victor's happiness, was tempered by the infinite misery of the vanquished, who were also human beings and possibly superior ones. Moreover, the joy of victory does not last long, if only because persisting in the same situation is not granted to peoples nor to individuals, and after some time there recommences, in one way or another, the struggle for existence which can grow to deadly proportions—and not by any means through arms only, but, as is the case today, through customs tariffs (because thereby one hits an activity based on free competition, namely, present-day industry, the current index of power and property).

Aside from that, one would have to be able to determine for all peoples and all periods how strong the active, the really free, segment was; for these people alone can have had an exalted feeling of their existence. But we do not even know the proportion of slaves in the Roman Empire, let alone the percentage of the half-free (the *litae*, etc.) and the unfree (*servi*) among the victorious Germani, nor do we know *how* these people felt about their lack of freedom.

Instead of any evaluation according to happiness and unhappiness, in place of any fruitless approval or disapproval, we shall confine ourselves to a consideration and understanding of the living forces, their succession, their interaction, their transmutation. To this end we need to be released from mere narration which may be given by handbooks. We have to *group* phenomena more according to their inner relations in which they form conditions, lasting states of affairs. The *history of civilization* comes into its own. Definitions of the concept vary; it will long have a subjective and dilettante appearance, as well as complicated and uncertain outlines, from the so-called antiquities to the so-called philosophy of history. Each individual will proceed according to his personal insight. However, one does not include in the history of civilization what one likes, but what one believes one should or must include.

The designation for what we have in mind is, at any rate, too narrow insofar as it leads us to assume that we are concerned only with the rise or decline of intellectual culture and the material exploitation of the earth; what we really aim at is an understanding of all the more significant and effective forces in general, and thus of the more or less constant conditions created by them.

The history of civilization overlaps with church history, the history of law, literary history, the history of communications, the history of morals, etc., according to its requirements, but it does not make any claim to being all these things itself. Its selection of data follows its inner principle. Its academic justification, recognized anyway, would, among other things, lie in the fact that it can compress the spiritually significant content of a period embracing many centuries into the brief scope of a lecture course more easily than can narrative presentation.

The relationship of the history of civilization to source studies is a very natural one. Sources are of interest to it as the monument and picture of a certain period and nation, not merely as the places where single events may be found; the historian of civilization reads with different eyes than does the historian. In fact, the history of civilization can be learned usefully only from sources instead of from handbooks.

(II) [1884.] As for the more recent enemies of the Middle Ages, they are the following:

First, those who consider Christianity in general as wrong and a misfortune; second, those who cannot bear the interweaving of great and strongly symbolizing folk imaginations with new religions (the imagination of Islam is half-tamed, that of the Christians is not); further, those who have no understanding for stabilizing elements, or those who are in a hurry to create a situation in which a man may do anything, but so may everybody else, and logically the most insolent fellow may do these things most of all—those who are in a hurry, then, for the unrestricted development of philosophy, the rapid victory of science, untrammeled communication with the remotest as well as the closest people, and the industrial exploitation of the world, from the surface of the earth on. Finally, count among these enemies *all* proponents of leveling sameness.

We may regard Renan as an adversary of the Middle Ages, with many qualifications; he repeatedly characterizes himself in his *Marcus Aurelius.* P. 588: *Le but suprême de l'humanité est la liberté des individus* [The highest goal of mankind is the liberty of the individual].—*L'homme ne doit appartenir qu'à lui-même* [A man must belong only to himself]; out of this, Voltaire, Rousseau, and the French Revolution made: *la foi nouvelle de l'humanité* [the new faith of mankind], p. 614.—"Christianity is robbery of the state," this especially on p. 590.—Religious peoples, e.g., Indians, are open to all conquerors, according to Renan. Only by drastically modifying Christianity in the Middle Ages were cities and states able to exist with it, he says. In Renan's view, there was no "fatherland" in the Middle Ages; people were Christians, Moslems, Buddhists.

Then, p. 603: "*La vie humaine est suspendue pour 1000 ans. La grande industrie devient impossible; par suite des fausses idées répandues sur l'usure, toute opération de banque, d'assurance, est frappée d'interdiction. Le juif seul peut manier l'argent; on le force à être riche*" [Human life is suspended for 1000 years. Large industry becomes impossible. Due to distorted ideas disseminated about usury, all banking and insurance operations are prohibited. Only Jews can handle money; they are forced to be rich], and then they are reproached with their wealth. Christianity "*coupa le capital par la racine*" [cut off capital at the root] by prohibiting the taking of interest; wealth became unproductive. "*La funeste terreur répandue sur toute la société du moyen-âge par le prétendu crime d'usure fut l'obstacle qui s'opposa, durant plus de dix siècles, au* progrès de la civilisation." [The deadly terror spread through the entire society of the Middle Ages by the alleged crime of usury was the obstacle which, for more than ten centuries, impeded the *progress of civilization*.] And a little before that: "*La* vie humaine *est suspendue pour 1000 ans.*" (At least now we know what it is that Renan calls "human life"!)

A further complaint of his is that work declined so much. According to him, the poor man had in Christianity "*le bonheur sans travail*" [happiness without toil] and hoped "*conquérir le ciel par la pauvreté*" [to win heaven through poverty].

Further, on p. 605 he says that "*le perfectionnement de la société humaine, ni l'augmentation de la somme de bonheur des individus . . .*" [the perfecting of human society or the increase of the amount of individual happiness . . .] had in no wise been the purpose of Christianity. (Here, "*bien-être*" [well-being] would have sufficed.)

Moreover, on p. 630: Concerning the Celtic, Italic, and other superstitions that infiltrated the Church: the world from the sixth to the tenth centuries was more pagan than ever; "*jusqu'aux progrès de l'instruction primaire de nos jours, nos paysans n'avaient pas abandonné un seul de leurs petits dieux gaulois. Le culte des saints a été le couvert sous lequel s'est rétabli le polythéisme."* [*until the progress of elementary education in our day,* our peasants had not abandoned a single one of their little Gaulish gods. The cult of saints has been the cover under which polytheism has re-established itself.]

Finally, on p. 632, about the third century: "*Des essais de christianisme unitaire, sans métaphysique ni mythologie, d'un christianisme peu distinct du* judaïsme *rationnel, comme fut la tentative de Zénobie et de Paul de Samosate, sont coupés par la base. Ces tentatives eussent produit un christianisme simple, continuation du judaïsme,* quelquechose d'analogue à ce que fut l'Islam. *Si elles avaient réussi, elles eussent prévenu sans doute le succès de Mahomet chez les Arabes et les Syriens.* Que de fanatisme on eût ainsi évité!" [Attempts at *unitarian* Christianity without metaphysics or mythology, a Christianity little different from *rational Judaism,** as was the attempt of Zenobia and Paul of Samosata, were nipped in the bud. These attempts could have produced a simple Christianity, a continuation of Judaism, *something analogous to what Islam was.* If they had succeeded, they would undoubtedly have forestalled Mohammed's success with the Arabs and the Syrians. *How much fanaticism would thus have been avoided!*] (But instead, fanaticism for Mammon would early have gained control, as it did with the Jews.)

Renan's religious wishes may answer for themselves.

But we will at least concede to the people of the Middle Ages that they were able to live without continual or continually threatening national wars, without forced mass industry with deadly competition, without credit and capitalism, without hatred of (albeit inevitable) poverty. If these people had mined hard coal, as is done now, where would *we* be?

The Middle Ages had greatness and sorrows of a kind very different from what Renan is capable of conceiving.

Greatness *can* appear at moments when mere calculation ceases and a way of thinking, a feeling, overwhelms everything. And at such mo-

*Burckhardt injects here: A good thing that Renan for once really lets it out! (Translator's note.)

ments it gives us, their posterity, the impression that it carried the feeling of happiness along with it.

(III) In contrast to the supposition that one has to make excuses for the Middle Ages, it is our task simply to describe the realities of past life, whatever it may be. The Middle Ages were the youth of today's world, and a *long* youth. Whatever to us is worth living for has its roots there. The Middle Ages are not responsible for our present decline! It was a time of natural *authority*. It is not its fault that we no longer have this nor can regain it, but are instead flooded by waves of *majority* from below.

The great impact of past times and forces lies not in their kinship with us, but in their naive quality, i.e., their being right as a matter of course. For example, the victory of orthodoxy over Germanic Arianism was not a matter of superior intellectuality, but of a temperament which *ipso facto* gained control over meager rival forms of the church.

The greatness of an epoch or a cause depends on the proportion of those capable of sacrifice, on whatever side it may be. In this respect the Middle Ages pass muster rather well. Devotion! And not a guarantee of regular pay!

Where does greatness begin? With devotion to a cause, whatever it may be, with complete extinction of personal vanity.

Greatness is not dependent on mental superiority, for this can be paired with a wretched character.

Greatness is the conjunction of a certain spirit with a certain will.

12. On Early Christianity

When, where, and by whom was the decision made to collect the three synoptic Gospels separately? It could only have happened at a time when their texts were already regarded as too sacred for anyone to dare to work them into *one* volume. In what communities did one previously have the gospels separately? Of the Apocrypha, the *Gospel of the Hebrews* had an especially wide dissemination; according to Eusebius, the Ebionites read it exclusively.

Islam immediately assumed a worldly position of power which at the same time took care not to permit any deviation from the faith. Christianity, on the other hand, set the imaginations of many in competitive motion at a time of great religious ferment, and for three centuries had to contend with heresies of all kinds, all sorts of secondary religions, magicians, Gnostics, and visionaries, who, in a body, were able to sweep many a community along, and it had to carry on this fight with no resources other than its own strength. People could be enraptured through the mere promise of the imminent Second Coming of Christ on Judgment Day, chiliasm, and the like, but notably through prophecy, as with the Montanists, and with sudden inspirations. Montanus regarded himself as the Paraclete.

With all this, however, one probably kept before him that the most outstanding men belonged to the right-thinking center, and especially the persecutions probably strengthened this center. If any authority ever came into being with enormous dedication, it is that of the church.

All Christendom at the time professes the faith; where there is any worldly-wise concealment, any participation in pagan rituals, etc., we are dealing with heretics, such as Basilides.

Bar Kochba's rebellion was, first and foremost, a bloody persecution of the Christians. A constant danger for the Christians was the pagans' belief, which became very strong in time, that calamities of all kinds stemmed from the diffusion, or toleration, of the Christians.

Miracles, including raising the dead, presented no problems to the Christians from the beginning, and in the community one actually thought that one saw charismata like prophecy and the healing of the sick continue, while all pagan miracles appeared as mere magic.

The mutual support of the Christians (until Constantine placed at their disposal the benefices of the state) may, practically speaking, have come quite close to the short-lived community of property of Apostolic times. Whoever became a Christian hardly remained rich. In Rome under Commodus there were a few conversions of wealthy people and aristocrats.

Upon martyrdom there follows immediately the worship of martyrs' bodies. At the persecutions of Lyon (Pothinus, Blandina, etc.) the persecutors burned the corpses and threw the ashes into the Rhône—not so much in order to prevent their worship as to prevent a resurrection.

Of the demonic, pagans and Christians held much the same views, but the pagans were here governed by a wild and colorful imagination, whereas the Christians harbored a rather uniform conviction.

Church literature was evidently very abundant from the beginning. Undoubtedly the collections of letters to colleagues and communities constituted a prime genre; then the refutations of heresies and apologetics directed against the pagans must be considered. Hebrew must have sunk into deep obscurity once there were no longer any real converted Jews. That Origen studied Hebrew is especially emphasized. By the third century there were already many scholarly theological works and commentaries.

After the persecution of Decius, on the occasion of the Novatian dispute, a *synod* of sixty bishops and numerous presbyters and deacons could already be held in Rome. They came from Italy, Africa, "and other places." Apropos of this, Eusebius also gives the statistics of the Roman community. The Antiochean synods concerning Paul of Samosata (after 270) were very large and well attended. Now the disputes over the treatment of the *lapsi* [backsliders] and the rebaptism of converted heretics increased, and in addition there was a continual dispute over the nature of Christ.

Christian influences made themselves felt at the imperial court under Commodus, Philip the Arab, Alexander Severus, and also under Valerian about whom Eusebius reports in his *Historia Ecclesiastica*, VII, 9: "In the beginning his entire court was full of pious people, indeed, had become a church of God, until Egyptian priests induced him to turn about completely and indulge in horrible secret sacrifices and perse-

cutions." Aurelian was an arbiter in Christian affairs and among other
things decided against Paul of Samosata.

13. Christianity as a Martyr Religion

Among all religions Christianity may be the one that has most
vividly retained its own advance in its memory through the cult of its
believers and martyrs. Buddhism venerates only relics of Buddha himself and has no specific memories of his individual propagators, because
none of their performances are worthy of him anyway. On the other
hand, Christianity, just as it takes seriously the salvation of the individual, also greatly apotheosizes its individual evangels and virtually transfers to their relics and graves a large part of its rituals and concept of
God. Where none are demonstrable, they are postulated and expected
to reveal themselves; this, to be sure, means a change to the second stage
in which *every* place *must* have its relics and there arises competition for,
and jealousy of, such possessions. This is the strongest localization of
the sacred, comparable in its way to that in Greek mythology.

In contrast to this is the paucity of Islam's shrines. In addition, these
are not special places of grace, but only of remembrance. (But what
about the graves of individual saintly marabouts, etc.?) Islam does not
spread the efficacy of Allah over places and persons.

It was highly important for the veneration of the various Christian
saints that one should know something about their legends. In Troyes,
St. Patroclus has a small shrine, with only one cleric (he is later called
lector). *Loci enim homines parvum exhibebant martyri famulatum, pro eo
quod historia* passionis *eius non haberetur in promptu; mos namque erat
hominum rusticorum, ut Sanctos Dei, quorum* agones *relegunt, attentius
venerentur. Quidam igitur de longinquo itinere veniens, libellum huius* cer-
taminis *detulit, lectori, quem in ipso loco servire diximus, prodidit ad legen-
dum.* [For the men of that place showed little interest in the martyr
because there was no account of his *martyrdom* available; for it was the

custom of the countrymen to worship more devoutly those of God's saints whose *martyrdom* they could read about. So a certain man who brought back from a far journey an account of the saint's *passion* gave it to the cleric who, as we have said, served at that place, to read.] The latter, highly pleased, immediately copied it and brought it to his bishop, but was severely punished as though he had thought it up himself. Yet soon afterwards a Frankish gentleman went to Italy and brought home from there the very same legend.

There is a superiority of martyrs over the other saints; the expressions for martyrdom are *passio, agon, certamen*. Christianity subsists here essentially on those who died professing it. It becomes entirely a religion of martyrs, in complete contrast to the religions of antiquity which made no fuss about their believers and had only a mythical view of their original propagators. (Dionysus and others; nevertheless, with Dionysus it comes closest to persecution, profession of faith, and martyrdom.) The persecutions of the emperors bring it about that Christianity immediately and everywhere has "classical soil" under its feet. A case in point is the enormous ineffectiveness of Diocletian's persecution in the face of a long-standing cult of martyrdom.

In reference to the "classical soil": In Arles, a falsely accused woman is sentenced to be drowned in the Rhône with a stone around her neck. In the water she invokes the greatest local saint, who once swam in the Rhône during a persecution: *"Sancte Genesi, gloriose martyr, qui has aquas natandi pulsu sanctificasti."* ["Saint Genesius, glorious martyr, who hast sanctified these waters by swimming in them."] She is saved, of course.

14. On Asceticism and Its Position

(I) Asceticism does not arise from justification by works (it does not become that until late), nor does it come into being as penance by proxy for others who in their lives on earth have no time to do penance (this, too, is a late concept), but it is the authentic expression of the genuine pessimism inherent in Christianity. Entirely consistent with this is celibacy—not by any means solely as a denial of sensuality, although this, too, plays a strong part in it (sensual enjoyment is a direct contradiction of Christianity which in this respect strongly sunders itself from the nature religions), but because the survival of mankind is not at all desirable. In the fourth and fifth centuries the will to extinction exists in the noblest minds quite independent of the external fate of the Empire. Side by side with this there lives a mob that in the midst of all the misery is fanatically devoted to circuses.

Only after the migrations of the Germanic tribes did the ascetically inclined *eo ipso* become priests or monks, and only then was the clergy as such obliged to constitute the ascetic caste, something that was often rather badly out of keeping with its real behavior. Christianity was to be put into consistent practice in at least one definite class. This explains the demand for celibacy which appeared repeatedly and finally prevailed. The clergy was to represent that perfection which a layman could not achieve; only in this way could the clergy be worthy of dispensing the means of salvation of the church. Only in return for such renunciation could the clergy demand that show of respect which was based on its being regarded by others as holy.

To be sure, penance by proxy and justification by works already appear here. In the meantime, the question of celibacy became involved with the entire gradually won position of power for the hierarchy, which had to possess the priests completely and safeguard church property from being squandered and used up by the priests' families.

How early was the *intercessory prayer* of an ascetic, the precursor of penance by proxy, considered valuable? How early were monasteries endowed for the sake of such prayers?

(II) Asceticism and its complete realization in the monastic life is the New Testament taken literally; the average Christian was no longer rising to its strict observance in his life on earth. Even by the second century the great Christian community had included also those of moderate virtue, the no longer quite saintly. Side by side with the century that had turned Christian there had earlier arisen fearful ascetic heresies like Montanism; later, however, orthodox Christianity peacefully detached itself as the monastic life and in this found its wholly justified representation. The monks are the consistent Christians, and the laymen salve their consciences with the thought that in addition to themselves such Christians exist and that perfection simply is not the business of the age. In the monasteries, too, charismata which are no longer possible or admissible on the outside may continue.

15. The Spread of Nicene Christianity

It may be asked how it could come about that Christianity, with the Nicene Creed, was allowed to enter into the fifth century as an enormous social power bringing men closer together, in both languages, and furthermore, through the Greeks who were the people to understand other peoples. Alexander and the Diadochi had brought close the Near East and brought about understanding between its civilizations and their own Hellenism. Rome, which gradually subjugated this Orient, had at the same time achieved a fusion of its mind with the Greek mind. This hardest of peoples could not resist Greek culture, its only enthusiasm. Under the emperors, a homogeneous Greco-Roman world had come into being. *This* was the world that became the scene and the object of the spread of Christianity. The homogeneity of Christendom from Britain and the pillars of Hercules to the Euphrates and the Tigris became the new substructure under the collapsing Empire. And now the peoples could come; in time they were all overpowered by Nicene Christianity. Without this, the Middle Ages would have been a den of murderers.

That is the way it had to happen so that the nations would not treat one another like wild animals. And all times to come will remember this.

16. The Church

Christianity as such was superior to paganism, classical and otherwise, with its unholy gods, its orientation to a no longer existent middle class, its exhausted poetry and literature, and its self-accusations concerning general wickedness and so on.

But the greatest miracle is that from Christianity an external form of power, the church, was able to take shape and that subsequently world churches, considered as orthodox, maintained themselves; further, that a recognized canon of sacred writings was able to come into being.

The inner characteristic of the Christian doctrine was, from the beginning, the highly personal relationship of the individual to the Christian realities and doctrines. Thus there necessarily resulted differing views, even within the earliest circle around the apostles, as evidenced by the existence of converted Jews and pagans. Many schisms arose even within the apostolic communities; this is revealed by the Pauline epistles. After the apostles had died off there was danger of there no longer being any sufficient authority. Then, too, there was the requirement of discipline, which certainly served to repel rather than attract. The *symbolum apostolicum* did not originate until post-apostolic times, possibly as the creed of the candidate for baptism.

On the other hand, the charitable love in the communities and the equality before God served as uniting forces, and, above all, the persecutions were the greatest promoters of concord; without them there might have been a lot of sects which paganism could have absorbed again.

But there was also an onrush on the part of Greek philosophy (even in the case of Paul), of Oriental theosophy and magic, in addition to asceticism which could be intensified at will. Other religions tried to gain influence; Simon Magus is a case in point. Several messiahs appeared, Bar Kochba and others.

Under circumstances such as these there took place the transposition of primitive Christianity into the world-view and culture of the late classical world, into pagan Christianity, and later the transference to the Germanic and Slavic worlds.

The impetus of Christianity is peculiar. It vociferously lays claim to crowding out all other religions completely. Then it makes sweeping progress as early as the first century; hence Tacitus' words *"Odium generis humani"* [an object of hatred to the human race] and the increasing hatred of the masses; until finally, under Constantine, the state has to yield by amalgamating this overwhelming power within its own, willy-nilly.

Christian doctrine had its perils, the heresies. We may leave out of consideration the entire dualistic Gnosticism with its eon theory as hardly able to form communities, despite its colorful variety and the manifold origin of its systems. We may likewise pass over the Judeo-Christian sects, the Ebionites and others (as late as the end of the second century there is the pseudo-Clementine study circle). Undoubtedly the Jews were too arrogant to bother much with this sort of thing; during persecutions of Christians they used to incite the pagans. Bar Kochba, too, murdered Christians.

The strongest pretensions to a church of its own were made by Manichaeism which treated Christianity as merely a varnish of pagan theosophy and ignored Judaism, betraying no Platonic influence, but offering Persian dualism with an admixture of Buddhistic ideas. The re-emergence of Manichaeism in the Middle Ages is evidence of its relative vitality. The Near East at that time was a veritable *vagina religionum* [womb of religions]; one should also bear in mind, for later, the situation under the Sassanids prior to Mohammed.

Finally there appeared around 150 Montanism with its ecstatic prophecies that proclaimed the beginning of the age of the Paraclete and produced a new outpouring of the spirit. Montanus regarded himself as the Paraclete (?). The sect was characterized by violent asceticism and fanaticism; it professed chiliasm. In somewhat toned-down form, Montanism had also an aftereffect on the East.

The schisms of Hippolytus, Felicissimus, Novatian, and Meletius are to be evaluated as mere deviations and disputes over practices of penitential discipline, coupled with personal quarrels.

More dangerous were the schisms over the Trinity, the Patripassians, a Paul of Samosata, etc.

In the face of all this, the church managed to remain united (the main document is Cyprian's *De unitate ecclesiae*); even to organize itself hierarchically; to hold synods, at first as required, later regularly; and to cultivate its universality with increasing determination. It not only sloughed off false doctrines and immorality, but also fought, as it had to, every deviation in external forms, constitution, and ritual. It achieved the complete sovereignty of the episcopate and the beginning of the Roman primateship. Irenaeus, III, 3, says: *"Ad hanc enim [scil. ecclesiam Romanam] a gloriosissimis duobus Apostolis Petro et Paulo fundatam propter potiorem principalitatem necesse est omnem* convenire *ecclesiam, h.e. eos qui sunt undique fideles, in qua semper ab his, qui sunt undique, conservata est ea quae est ab Apostolis traditio."* [Because of its pre-eminence, the whole church, that is, the faithful everywhere, has to *agree* with this [*i.e.,* the church of Rome], founded by the two most glorious apostles Peter and Paul. For within it there has always been preserved by Christians everywhere that tradition which stems from the Apostles.]

Without the last persecutions under Decius, Valerian, and others, the spirit of contradiction, of dialectics, and of ambition would most likely have split the church into sects, and paganism would then probably have overpowered them or at least stood its ground side by side with it. The life of the church was not attached to esoteric doctrinal interpretations and ambitious personalities, but on community feeling, the common feeling of being God's children, the brotherly helpfulness and beneficence. All this would have been dealt a mortal blow by a split-up into sects, and the specific power to conquer the pagans would thereby have vanished, regardless of the religious zeal of the individual sects.

When, under Diocletian, Christianity got ready to gain control of the Imperium, it was caught up in those dangerous schisms over the Trinity. Diocletian's persecutions did not, to be sure, remove these schisms, but they undoubtedly did marshal the spirit of unity which existed side by side with the schisms. And when Constantine had dealings with Christianity, he encountered a firm ecumenical organization as an established tradition. Without it he would probably not have shown Christianity any consideration.

If good sense had some say in matters of belief and opinion, most heresies would not have been promulgated, so that the church might remain powerful. However, the same force that made the church mighty also engendered the capacity for, and disposition toward, heresy—to be sure, with the help of much personal dogmatism. There is such a thing as a born sectarian.

17. Julian and the Prospect for a Restoration of Paganism

The fact that after Julian's death Arbogast and Eugenius virtually made this restoration their program, in which they could count on the pagans at least, proves that things were not yet decided by any means.

If one imagines Julian without the Persian War and with a reign of about ten years, he could have achieved a great deal.

Of course, it was impossible to organize paganism into a rival *church;* but the farm population and the people in many cities would have been available for great demonstrations. Presumably paganism would at least have established itself on a permanent basis, secure from any further abolition, and would then have maintained itself alongside Christianity for who knows how long as a religion inaccessible to any conversionary argument, especially through the possession of the benefice.

On the other hand, it is conceivable that in the face of such a situation the Christian theologians would have ceased their wrangling about the Trinity; the true forces would have become paramount again; the situation would have been comparable to the later one of the orthodox under the Arian Germanic princes.

Nevertheless, there would have been another great danger not present before or since: forsaken by the Imperium, the church could have been split asunder by countries as well as by sects, and it would subsequently have found it difficult to regain its unity. In Rome there would probably have been a real battle in which paganism would have carried the day and the diocese could easily have lost completely its beginning pristine preeminence.

18. Western European Arianism and the Jews

Renan moans in his *Marcus Aurelius* and is very sorry that in the third century the *"essais de christianisme unitaire,"* which would hardly have differed from the *"judaïsme rationnel,"* were defeated.

In the future, the Jews on several occasions stick with the Arians and fear nothing more than orthodoxy, as is attested by the Jews of Ravenna and elsewhere, by those of Arles (508) and of Naples, who, in 536, in the face of Belisarius' attack, promise to take care of the city's needs. The Jews in Visigothic Spain were evidently very numerous; here they took revenge by agreements with the Arabs who were ready for invasion.

The entire orthodox Middle Ages then kept the Jews down and persecuted them periodically, i.e., attempted to annihilate them. If, however, Western European Arianism had held its own, the Jews would in a century or two have become the masters of the entire property and would have made the Germanic and the Romanic peoples work for them even at that time. There would have been no Middle Ages, or they would have been quite different. If one judges according to desirability, one has this choice: either general dominion of the Jews from the seventh or eighth century, or the Middle Ages as they were.

19. The Breakup of the Western Empire

It is a general pathological fact that when a great organism comes to its end, a whole number of maladies and terrible accidents occur simultaneously or in rapid succession.

Whether accidental or not, there was the special circumstance that the Empire was represented not by strong emperors by adoption, choice, or usurpation, but by two legitimate weaklings whose leadership in decisive moments could or had to become a matter of competition, so that instead of vigorous harmony there was disharmony, created by subordinates. Added to this was the problematic nature of the army.

The bodies of troops seem to acquire individual wills of their own; Roman legions in Britain show mistrust of the central government and then revolt against it; invasion and Roman usurpation cross paths and the barbarian troops occasionally obey their own impulses more than the Empire's authority. The crises within the army assume the aspect of unpredictable elemental events.

To be added to all this is the pressure from the outside. The great barbarian world senses all at once that the day of its power has come (Radagaisus; the Germani in Gaul, 406). It need no longer be satisfied with mercenary pay, partial colonization, and so on; the dominant will of world history passes over to it. *Völkerwanderung* [the migration of the peoples] in a narrower sense means that parts of the Empire fall prey to Germanic peoples; the modes of this vary greatly.

As shortcomings of tradition these are to be emphasized: we lack a circumstantial Western historian, even an exact chronology that would be capable of determining months and weeks. However, the course of events is of necessity inwardly obscure, judged by the causalities, and unavoidably burdened with false motivations. Gigantic and inevitable destinies are, after all, conceived of as the faults of individuals. With the general suffering and misery there are fancies and fictions and, especially, recriminations, and the mania for accusation grips even those who could have known the truth. And so it is that the *nexus causalis* [causal connection], of which we are now and then informed, either was not present at all, or had an entirely different form.

In Claudian and Zosimus there is a garrulity which forcibly presses after the most secret intrigues and intentions. But in addition it is unfortunately true that at world-decisive moments base personal intrigues did play some part. Finally we must take into consideration the all-confusing sectarian hatred of the orthodox for Stilicho. In the Eastern as well as the Western Roman Empire, every defection of a province, every barbarian irruption is regarded as instigated by the competitor.

20. The Achievement of Clovis I

He passed from one stage of his power to another with complete assurance: 486–496–506. As lord over the largest part of Gaul he then did away with his Frankish fellow rulers, apparently with the full approval of the populations concerned. All his creations are shot through with crime. But one must not let every filthy wretch believe that when he is committing crimes, he is founding a state. At the time of his death Clovis is: (1) the leader of the entire Frankish nation in the narrower sense and of the Alamannic people, i.e., of contiguous Germanic populations; (2) lord over Romanic Gaul as a whole, with Paris as his *cathedra regni* [capital]. And all—the people, the ruler and the ruled—are or become Nicene-Orthodox. The addition of Burgundy had to be the next consequence.

As a *state*, the Frankish kingdom is still unwieldy and provisional. But it is a viable construction as compared to the artificial jerry-building of the conquering Arian peoples who think they can rule permanently over orthodox Romanic masses. In spite of everything the dynasty lasted for two centuries and a half, while among the Visigoths, the Lombards, the Anglo-Saxons, etc., dynasties could hardly be formed.

There were usurpations of the supreme power, but until Pepin no usurpation of the kingship. This state survived the most terrible blows and later brilliantly regenerated itself under Pepin's dynasty.

21. Mohammed as the Founder of a Religion, and Islam

A brilliant people, capable of self-denial, with boundless self-reliance of individuals and tribes, was to be summoned to a new faith and to world hegemony in the name of this faith.

There was a great variety of religions in Arabia; paganism glittered in every hue, and side by side with it there existed an old belief in Allah; Jewish tribes and Christians of diverse origin were living in the country; in front of them the Byzantines were engaged in a dispute among one another about the natures in Christ; the Sassanids had their dualistic religion; both empires were shaken to their foundations politically and militarily.

The specific thing that Mohammed encountered was the rite of the pilgrimage to the Kaaba toward which the entire existence of Mecca had been oriented from ancient times. He did not make it an object of loathing, did not try to create a rival sanctuary; the age-old Kaaba required only "purification"; the Black Stone was retained as a necessary mystery.

Since Mohammed could not evade the Kaaba and the pilgrimage (although they had per se no necessary connection with his faith), he had not only to incorporate them in his system, but to make them the center of his entire cult. For a while he has to flee from Mecca; then the enthusiasm of his entire following becomes all the more the desire for the Kaaba, and his decisive victory is then the capture of Mecca. That in the future all peoples would be infected with the longing for the Kaaba he can hardly have suspected. For the time being he *enjoined* all non-believers from the Kaaba and the pilgrimage.

With his scanty preaching alone he would have achieved only a modest and temporary success; but from the hegira on, he constantly procured new goals for his adherents: in addition to Mecca, which he promised them, the robbing of caravans and the conquests in Arabia together with the resulting booty. To this there immediately attaches as something natural the holy war against the outside as well. World empire is a simple corollary.

Mohammed is personally very fanatical; that is his basic strength. His fanaticism is that of a radical simplifier and to that extent is quite genuine. It is of the toughest variety, namely, doctrinaire passion, and his victory is one of the greatest victories of fanaticism and triviality. All idolatry, everything mythical, everything free in religion, all the multifarious ramifications of the hitherto existing faith, transport him into a real rage, and he hits upon a moment when large strata of his nation were evidently highly receptive to an extreme simplification of the religious; his genius lies in his divining this. And the peoples who were now attacked may also have been somewhat tired of their existing theology and mythology. From his youth on, Mohammed, with the aid of at least ten people, looks over the faiths of the Jews, Christians, and Parsis, and steals from them any scraps that he can use, shaping these elements according to his imagination. Thus everyone found in Mohammed's sermons some echo of his accustomed faith.

The very extraordinary thing is that with all this Mohammed achieved not merely lifetime success, the homage of Arabia, but founded a world religion that is viable to this day and has a tremendously high opinion of itself.

In this new religion, everything had to be within the common range of the Arabs, i.e., it had to be possible. Therefore Islam has the simplest catechism, and the main elements of this simplicity are as follows:

Oneness of God and his predicates.

Allah is neither procreated nor procreating.

Revelations by the prophets Adam, Noah, Moses, Christ, and Mohammed as the last of the prophets, but with intimations of a Mahdi.

The absolute decree; fatalism (Mohammed himself calls it "submission") which had a highly tonic effect on aspiring forces. In connection with untoward things one speaks of "Mektub."

Belief in angels (because Mohammed found devas, jinn, and peris).

Immortality and Last Judgment, Heaven and Hell ("Paradise lies under the shadow of swords").

Moral laws, all kinds of moral precepts, among them "No lying" (for Mohammed reserved lying for *himself*); part of this is the civil law of the Koran which is in force to this day.

Finally, prayer, fasting, pilgrimage.

Aside from any absolute value, it may be assumed that this religion and *Weltanschauung* corresponds in large measure to the universally human on a certain level of inner development. Genuine devotion, mysticism, and philosophy *can* and have been able to attach themselves to this religion. But the more profound elements in Islam come to it from forces outside it.

Islam trains its heads and hearts in such a manner that afterwards they produce only this form of state and culture and no other, whether or not Mohammed planned it that way.

This paltry religion (did it have a better moral effect than Arabian idolatry?) destroys over wide areas two far higher and deeper religions, Christianity and dualism, because they are undergoing crises. It holds sway from the Atlantic to deep into India and China, and makes advances among the Negroes to this day. Only few countries could be wrested away again from Islam, and this only with the utmost exertion. Where Christian governments rule over Islamitic populations today, they wisely leave them their faith; the Christian religion has no effect on it whatsoever.

Döllinger's prediction is idle when he says that Islam contains "seeds of transitoriness." This is his argument: "Of course, Islam contains seeds of transitoriness [and what about our Europe? Does it not also contain such seeds?*] if only because of the fact that it is a religion of set, rigid

*Burckhardt's interjection. (Translator's note.)

dogmas which encompass all areas of life and impede any development [alias "progress": does Islam *live because* it excludes progress?]* These dogmas, the product of a single people and a definite low level of culture, must prove inadequate and harmful upon their continuance and transfer to other nations, and finally must be shattered by the inner contradictions they arouse as well as by the requirements of life."

But as of now, this religion has lasted for a desperately long time, and the Islamic world at present *subsists* on this narrowness! For the Islamitic peoples, no matter how they fare, regard it as a vast misfortune for anyone not to belong to this religion and culture. This world religion has a high opinion of itself and considers the unbelievers unfortunate.

It is the general tendency of our minds to deduce *great causes* from *great effects,* thus, in this case, from Mohammed's achievement, *greatness of the originator.* At the very least, one wants to concede in Mohammed's case that he was no fraud, was serious about things, etc. However, it is possible to be in error sometime with this deduction regarding greatness and to mistake mere might for greatness. In this instance it is rather the *low qualities* of human nature that have received a powerful presentation. Islam is a triumph of triviality, and the great majority of mankind *is* trivial. (Present-day admirers of Mohammed pay themselves the compliment of mediocrity.) But triviality likes to be tyrannical and is fond of imposing its yoke upon nobler spirits. Islam wanted to deprive distinguished old nations of their myths, the Persians of their Book of Kings, and for 1200 years it has actually prohibited sculpture and painting to tremendously large populations.

Was Mohammed a soothsayer? A poet? A sorcerer? He is none of these, but rather a *prophet.*

The crisis of his life and his religion begins with the alliance with Arabs living outside of Mecca. His adherents begin to emigrate. In July of 622 his own hegira takes place.

*Burckhardt's interjection. (Translator's note.)

22. The Despotism of Islam

All religions are exclusive, but Islam is quite notably so, and immediately it developed into a state which seemed to be all of a piece with the religion. The Koran is its spiritual and secular book of law.

(1) Its statutes embrace all areas of life, as Döllinger states, and remain set and rigid; the very narrow Arab mind imposes this nature on many nationalities and thus remolds them for all time (a profound, extensive spiritual bondage!). This is the power of Islam in itself.

(2) At the same time, the form of the world empire as well as of the states gradually detaching themselves from it cannot be anything but a despotic monarchy. The very reason and excuse for existence, the holy war, and the possible world conquest do not brook any other form. But the tradition encountered is nothing but absolutism anyway (Byzantines, Sassanids, etc.). Then there quickly appears vulgar sultanism.

Only when genuine religious strife flares up does Islam again become honorable for a time. There once more appear rulers who live only for the cause, and the Moslem community again becomes the true master of the state (although it is never allowed to vote). Then the ruler is only the treasurer of the believers, as with Nureddin; and in the battles he seeks martyrdom.

But as soon as this stimulus is gone, ordinary despotism makes its appearance again. It tolerates and, under certain circumstances, desires material prosperity, but never and nowhere does it provide secure conditions for earning a living. Upon occasion it loves high intellectual culture, but on the other hand keeps it within definite bounds through religion. This despotism completely excludes modern Western "progress," in both senses of this concept: first, as a constitutional state; second, as unlimited growth of profitable enterprise and commerce, and through this it keeps its strength today, in contrast to the West. This way it escapes: (1) the transformation of the Western constitutional state into a mass democracy, (2) the transformation of the people into careerists and workers bent on pleasure. To be sure, it has learned to raise a loan, but any time it casts off the credit system again and goes into bankruptcy, this happens without most of the population even noticing it.

23. Islam and Its Effects

Through the sensuous delineation of a future life, Mohammed gives his own measure.

It is a low religion of slight inwardness, although it can combine with whatever asceticism and religious absorption it now and again *finds* among the nations.

Something very peculiar and rather unparalleled in the history of religion is the enormous degree to which pride is taken in this religion, the feeling of absolute superiority over all others, the utter inaccessibility to any influences; these characteristics grow into innate arrogance and boundless presumption in general. This is in keeping, *in praxi,* with the lack of any deeper culture and of clear judgment in matters of everyday living.

Further characteristics are consequences of the thoroughly despotic state form which passes over from the caliphates to all splinters thereof. Despite an occasionally very lively feeling for one's home region which attaches to localities and customs, there is an utter lack of patriotism, i.e., enthusiasm for the totality of a people or a state (there is not even a word for "patriotism"). This is an advantage; a Moslem simply is at home in the whole Islamitic world. That is why a call to arms is not issued in the name of a political home, but only in the name of the faith, ed-Din; the war preacher concerned knows that his listeners can be stirred up only through fanaticism, even though the real purpose of the war may have nothing to do with the faith.

Further consequences of despotism, at least in substance, are the following:

In all activities, tortuous paths are preferred to straight ones. Everything is spun fine and dragged out.

While openness and the citing of real reasons are considered pre-sumption, one's goal may be reached only through flattery and in-trigue.

Universal mutual mistrust.

A basic theme: egoism is directed less at honors and distinctions than at money and property.

Utter lack of gratitude to former benefactors.

In Islam, slavery has an important source, among others, in the harem system, which is inconceivable without eunuchs and black ser-vants. The blacks, however, are much better off here than on the former American plantations; the eunuch is the best and closest friend of his master, feared by the women who seek his favor; the black "house slaves" are treated like children of the house and are far above the rank of their Arab fellow house servants, the "chadams."

The strongest proof of real, extremely despotic power in Islam is the fact that it has been able to invalidate, in such large measure, the entire history (customs, religion, previous way of looking at things, earlier imagination) of the peoples converted to it. It accomplished this only by instilling into them a new religious arrogance which was stronger than everything and induced them to be *ashamed* of their past.

24. The Two Main Realities for the Papacy of the Eighth Century

(I) The multiplicity of Italy.

The dismemberment of Italy had been taking place since the Lom-bard invasion, as yet without the participation of the papacy. Now, however, this becomes the policy of the papacy, since it must want no one to be politically very powerful in Italy, while it will never itself be able to constitute the government of all Italy, as may have been the intent of the Donation of Constantine. It has a dread of too powerful Lombard kings and Italic national emperors. But it must desire to possess at least a state of its own. To be sure, its local position for the time being is such that it must wish it would never be defined exactly. But above all it must evade close dependence upon any state and especially the fate of the Byzantine church, though it cannot always do without the aid of one secular power or force or another. Thereby it becomes, under certain circumstances, the cause of outside intervention and of the continuing multiplicity, and therefore weakness, of Italy.

(II) The ecclesiastical unity of the West.

Europe searches for forms and forces for the totality of life, a higher unity. One such form was found in the Roman church, another in the emperorship of Charlemagne.

The unity of the West with all its corollaries was substantially dependent on the papacy; only ecclesiastical unity brought peoples closer together and was able to become a social bond of prime strength. The question now arises as to whether such unity could have been achieved without the papacy, or whether it could have been maintained without it. Would the Benedictine order, for example, alone have been able to save Christianity as the religion of unity?

25. Charlemagne

Our present view of the world empire and its desirability is determined by whether the *viri eruditi* [savants] of the individual peoples who once belonged to it regard the development of their nations since then as a good or a bad job; in this, the *desirability* of power is, as a rule, a principle taken for granted.

Any empire, i.e., any dominion over a whole circle of peoples, will, through inevitable leveling, curtail or destroy many individual national features that the individuals have hitherto cared much about (cf. especially Sybel, *Die deutsche Nation und das Kaiserreich*, p. 13).

Also, it will in general move as far away as possible from popular rule and incline toward a bureaucracy in which all energies of the masses are available for the aims of the government. In proportion to the size of such a state, its purposes appear the more tyrannical the more incomprehensible they become to the individual countries within the empire. In the case under discussion the Roman Empire was the best-known prototype. Even the ruling people which supplies the dynasty will hardly be in a better position.

But on this large scale, as on smaller ones, the real political purposes are traditionally replaced, in a greater or lesser degree, by dynastic, personal momentary interests.

Such empires cannot be imagined as really politically alive, with independent participation of the federated peoples in the general volition and action; a centralistic empire is more suitable for aged peoples that have passed their prime. As soon as political and individual-national life of any kind asserts itself again, no matter under what name, the empire goes to pieces. And whatever remnants of the empire do survive are then permanently inconvenienced by having to drag along the former obligations.

In recent times people have tried to tell Charlemagne that he had a legitimate and adequate task in the incorporation of the Saxons, the expansion of Germanic civilization plus classical culture, the spread of Christianity to the slave countries, and defense against the Normans, and that instead of these things he wrongfully strove for world dominion and waged world wars as a conqueror. This entire censure is actually directed only at his conquest of Italy and his relationship to the papacy.

However, by the thoroughgoing subjection of the Saxons he made a Germany possible for the first time. He annihilated the Avars; the Normans he knew only in their primary stage, but he was quite worried about them; no one will demand that he should have sought them out in their homeland in order to nip the danger in the bud. We simply must accept as a psychological phenomenon of the first order that one and the same individual force subdued the Saxons and at the same time renewed the Roman Empire. He who was able to do the one thing merely desired the other too.

But finally, the main complaint is Charlemagne's use of the aid of the Roman church to realize God's kingdom on earth and the consequent authorization to rule over all Christian countries and to conquer all non-Christian ones; a divine mission entitles the conqueror to employ any means. However, the papacy, which was invited by Charlemagne to co-rulership of the world, remained whole, whereas his empire went to pieces.

(And this might perhaps have been the dark supreme will of world history.)

For the time being, there remain certain the value of the memory of a great man, and, as the value of the Carolingian period, these facts: The peoples in question were powerful for about a hundred years; they were equipped for the future with a great common premise and memory, with their culture infinitely more homogeneous than it had previously been. After further intervals of barbarism, the peoples approached and understood one another again and again; a Western community feeling had come into being.

26. The Normans

After one would have thought the *Völkerwanderung* long since completed and while Europe believed it had only one deadly enemy, Islam, a Germanic tribe which had remained primitive and was possessed of extreme strength arose to plunder the European world whose culture was then in the ascendant. They are pirates, but no ordinary ones; their leaders want to win glory and glamor at home by taking booty. Moreover, their habitat, the North Sea, requires the utmost in boldness, strength, and sacrificial spirit. Enormous sacrifices of human life had to be expected, and this presupposes a greater wealth of vigorous manpower than Scandinavia was able to support. One can scarcely picture these predatory fellowships under their jarls as powerful and astonishing enough; breeding and elemental strength must have presented an appearance full of wonder and awe. Everything that they encountered must have seemed withered next to them.

They were destined to do the following things: to form the mightiest, most independent dukedom in France; to construct England through one last invasion in such a way that this invasion really had to remain the last—they founded the *definitive* England; from Normandy, to wrest lower Italy and Sicily away from the Arabs, Byzantines, and Lombards, and to fortify this region in such a way that Arabs and Greeks had to give up all claim to it; to found the Norman state of Antioch; finally, to establish a dominion over Russia which continued even under the Mongol yoke and finally was able to shake off the latter.

Everywhere the Normans create viable states capable of keeping willfulness and sacrilege in check and of pursuing great goals.

27. The Byzantine Empire and Its Mission

Its main test of strength came in its leadership in the contest against Islam. After huge initial losses (the entire East, Africa, Sicily) the Byzantine Empire stood its ground and kept advancing in Asia Minor, even as far as Mesopotamia. How would the multi-divided Europe, the dismembered Carolingian empire have fared without this state? There is something to be said for Nicephorus' mockery at the troops of Otto the Great.

It was impossible for the Byzantine Empire to come to sensible terms with the Western crusaders, to achieve a real collaboration. The Crusades did only harm in the East; they resuscitated the entire heroic fanaticism of Islam, which would not have awakened from the fight against the Eastern Empire alone; they took an ever worsening course and finally, in 1203–1204, the crusaders captured the Byzantine Empire itself, through an alliance with one of the local factions. The Latin Empire was wretched; only now did the opposition to Islam weaken fatally, and finally the Palaeologi actually succumbed to the Turks. And subsequently, at such a late stage of Islam, Europe had to tremble before the Turks for centuries, except where it had an alliance with them. However, as long as the Palaeologi had some strength left, they helped to protect Europe.

28. On the Iconoclastic Controversy

(I) The main instigators are generals, particularly generals who have become emperors, who come from heretic and Judaizing regions and proceed from a "fanaticism" which certainly had less *raison d'être* in the Byzantine Empire than the "fanaticism" of image-worship hitherto. It is a fanaticism of triviality similar to Mohammed's. In addition, Islam acquainted them with a state structure which, through the identity of rulership and religion, seemed a degree stronger than the Byzantine state where these still were different things. They were military men and had very big ideas about the compulsory force by which all adversaries could be destroyed; any non-military resistance or opposition made them furious and ready to do anything. Thus they waged an internal war at a time when the Empire would have needed the utmost harmony.

The external form of this struggle is one part of the church against the other, i.e., the patriarchs, bishops, metropolitans, etc., *appointed by each* against the others. The methods are partly those of Orthodoxy, namely, synods, church decrees, and so on, but also a bottomless brutality, in and by which one got to know the Empire as it looked when it was no longer restrained by any religious considerations.

Now one had to let destruction rage until generals, like those of Empress Irene, appeared, men who had realized what influence could be gained by siding with a horribly ill-treated majority of the people. And now partisanship flared up openly among victorious regiments and the iconoclastic bodyguard was overcome.

The second phase of the iconoclastic controversy, in the ninth century, was determined by the facts that in sections of the army the tradition still lived on and that Michael the Stammerer, a heretic general and a Judaizer to boot, ascended the throne and founded a dynasty. Leo the Armenian started in again, at first with religious indifference (cf. Leo, *Mittelalter*, p. 246); then Michael the Stammerer, just as indifferent in the beginning. The overall result was that the church was somewhat degraded, among other things in a main organ, the patriarchate. But image-worship and monasticism won a complete victory.

Islamistic optimists could draw up a counter-reckoning something like this: It was the greatest good fortune that the Byzantines were so disunited, through a church persecution, under such militarily efficient emperors! Otherwise they might have overpowered us.

In his *History of the Byzantines and the Ottoman Empire* (pp. 99 ff.), Hertzberg reveals that many present-day Greeks have taken a great fancy to Leo the Isaurian and give him enormous credit. Then he admits that we do not know *how comprehensive* Leo's church measures were meant to be, which among them were intended as permanent and which only "as fighting aids." Then comes the usual professorial opinion of the danger of brutish superstition, against which, he says, only an inspired religious reformer or gradual, patient counteraction could prevail. But Leo, according to Hertzberg, had had the alluring model of predecessors like Theodosius the Great who had done away with Arians and pagans alike. Whether Leo had also hoped to win Jews and Arabs is a moot point, he continues. On Leo's side were most generals, cultured laymen in Asia Minor (not in European Greece!), officials and higher classes, and part of the clergy (but what a part!). Against him were the masses and especially the women. Hertzberg admits the hopeless position of those opposing image-worship; one is more surprised at their great perseverance than at their final failure, he states. The controversy went much deeper than the disputes over the Trinity had once gone.

Or is it possible that under Leo the Isaurian the arrogant, appalling state began to regard itself as *lovable?* And perhaps to become *jealous* of anything that its subjects loved outside of it—the only thing they still had left?

(II) Among the few things which had hitherto made life bearable for the sorely afflicted Byzantines and in which the state so far did not interfere was image-worship. When the most image-loving pagan people had become Christian, a certain degree of the worship of the new religion was inevitably turned upon the images themselves; as it was, there were individual ἀχειροποίητα [images not made by human hands]. But it is nowhere demonstrable that magic or any other wicked superstitious practice was carried on with the images. In addition to the individually venerated images there was the colossal icon-world of the churches in fresco and mosaic. And when Islam abhorred all idolatry, people probably only became all the more fond of it; at least the Christians under Mohammedan rule were most zealously devoted to it at the time of the iconoclastic controversy.

Closely allied with the icon-world was monasticism, if only because the images very substantially emanated from the monasteries. At the same time, imagery was the visible expression of asceticism—poor, hard-working, widely spread in cities, mountains, islands. Images and monks, it should be noted, enjoyed an old dignity not contested by any emperor since Valens. Too, monkhood, through its asceticism and its origin, was an island of freedom outside the compulsory state, and also a main source of the episcopate. This could be inconvenient, e.g., when groups of monks helped to render the decision at synods, riots, etc., but this seems to have happened but rarely in the seventh century.

This image-cult and monasticism, like everything ecclesiastical, was the last thing people had left in the compulsory state, and this state ought to have spared it, since it reimbursed itself from the people in every other way.

Also, the iconoclastic controversy was not started by an emperor who might have wanted to augment the state's power once more by enslaving the church, its ceremonies, and the monkhood, but by a doctrinarian, Leo the Isaurian.

Presumably, there grew up inside him, indoctrinated and narrow as he was, a fanaticism of semi-education or enlightenment; the strength he derived from his military reputation. Possibly there had developed in him the lordly arrogance of the victorious state which begins to consider itself lovable and then, when some real cause for jealousy appears, as the only thing worth loving. This, basically, had been the position of the ancient *polis* which established worship for itself.

In this fashion one does not by any means become merely a dogmatic tyrant, but, above all, a dictatorial arbiter of *taste*. Such a man enrages the suffering people down to nerves and fibers which extend beyond religion.

In the course of the controversy, to be sure, there is formed an enlightened group (intellectuals, dissenters, profane people, politicians, etc.) which comes out in favor of icon-smashing. They are those who rejoice any and every time any religion suffers a deep affliction, and also military men and officials who regard as an impediment anything that does not want to be, nor can be, army or state.

29. On the Crusades

Ekkehard of Urach said the truest and most profound thing about them: *"Novitatem hanc iam senescenti et prope intereunti mundo pernecessariam."* [This novelty was essential for a senescent and almost moribund world.] The opponents of the cause he recognizes as Epicureans.

The ideal was: *"Regni sui caelestis ineuntes servitium"* [To enter the service of His heavenly kingdom]. It ennobles all of Western humanity that it desires something at once human and divine. Hitherto there had been only force and individual devotion; this time the power of all is placed in the service of a common holy aim. Europe realizes that something great must be accomplished jointly in the consciousness of full strength. People had a presentiment that they were regenerating, strengthening, and exalting themselves thereby. That common cause necessarily bestows a higher consciousness of existence, different from all strength and power employed hitherto. The difference between the Crusades and the conquests of Mohammed and the caliphs consisted in the fact that this time it was not a matter of the world, but of a venerated spot. Hope is not essentially directed at worldly possessions (because the defectiveness of the land must have been known from previous crusaders), but at the safeguarding of the most sacred relic. Thus their aim exalts the crusaders, while, after a short, holy, sacrificing war, the Mohammedans are debased by greed for more gain.

With the crusaders, the object is small, the volition great; with the Mohammedans, the object is the whole world, the volition is soon very low. The great things that happened through the crusaders could not be confiscated for base tyranny.

Once it had set that great volition in general motion, the papacy had accomplished what was perhaps its greatest mission. Only the papacy could have done this, and afterwards it was never able to do anything as great again. Innocent III, who in his sermons proclaimed the Albigensian Crusade with the knowledge that his bands were setting out chiefly to maraud and murder, looks small compared to Urban II at Clermont.

The Crusades completed the consciousness of a common Western life. The peoples who participated in them or completed similar tasks in a similar fashion, such as the Spaniards, have since then constituted the higher power in Europe.

There was no question of any precalculation of what actually happened; instead of that, people fed on dream pictures. The papacy, first to be informed about the great current, at least took the helm, for reasons suited to it and its previous nature and history. The Empire took its second European fall by *not* providing leadership. The world had postulated a great absolving central institution and forcibly given it ideal stature. This later became a crown-bestowing institution; now it commanded the European world to go East. Since that time we have been in the *West*.

30. The Sorrows and Sacrifices of the Crusades

The sorrows and sacrifices of the Crusades on the part of the Christians and the Mohammedans alike were not lost and in vain. In the West, the entire higher level and culture are, in some way, directly or indirectly, determined by the Crusades, the mighty struggle and the consequent spiritual enrichment. In Islam the spirit of the old religious war and its devotion flares up again brightly, in Syria and Mesopotamia as in Spain. The Seljuks had already made Islam honorable; in the fight against the Christians there awakens in it a moral greatness.

31. On the Evaluation of the Later Middle Ages

With some moderns this period has a bad reputation as a time of dissolution, universal wickedness, and egoism. But any epoch in which new forces make way for themselves against earlier constraint must give this impression.

These forces can never appear otherwise than in the guise of individual interests, therefore as selfishness and wickedness, since the old elements never give way willingly.

In the series of developments which have been the task of the Occident, this, too, has a quite necessary place. It is idle to ask whether one thing or another could have been done with more moderation. Only because people were as they were did they accomplish what they did.

Our moral criticism of past ages can easily be mistaken. It has a hard time detaching itself from the conflicts of our own day and transfers present-day desiderata to the past. Furthermore, it emanates from people who live quietly under the protection of an order guaranteed from the outside, necessary to the prevailing industrialism, and who have no conception of a violently agitated and hazardous life.

Finally, it views personalities too deliberately and according to set principles, and makes too little allowance for the pressure of the moment and daily self-protection.

This period is judged as one in which the ideals of the Middle Ages, church and chivalry, had gone to pieces or, rather, had been broken through on all sides. But it is a characteristic of ideals that they do not live forever (for their perpetuation they have poetry at their disposal), especially if they have such a meager life as did church and chivalry.

From beneath their ruins there already emerge the genuine new forces, even though still in confused form. The movement of life does not always take place through diametrical, great antitheses, but also breaks through disintegration. Life itself always remains visible.

The degree of embarrassment over issues into which narrow fanatics of the past and the present and philosophical construers of history get themselves is their business and affects us little.

III

History from 1450 to 1598

32. The Period from 1450 to 1598 and the Nineteenth Century's View of It

(I) [May 10, 1859.] The chief creation of more recent history is the Great Power, the life form of the most significant peoples. The balance among them is supposedly based on the number five (later the number six). But not only the small ones feel as insecure as ever with it; even the great ones themselves have never put down their arms in forty-four years of peace and have devoured in advance the money of future generations, in order to prevent one another's aggrandizement.

Internally, the state has centralized all power and all law; and the small states, too, have had to reshape themselves according to this model. Wherever the unhealthy, the oppressed, the resisting elements band together, the revolution is directed at the *entire* state, indeed, at all of existence. But we trust ourselves to be able to suppress this every time.

The virtues of this modern state, which lays claim to being a legal state, are as follows: equality before the law; the safeguarding of material interests through the elimination of any oppressive intermediate rule; tolerance through indifferentism and the bureaucratic mind (at least relatively speaking) and through the state's jealous guarding of its sole power; the refinement of private life and its pleasures; but primarily, freedom of thought and research, the objective evaluation of the world and of history.

To what extent is this favorable to the moral development of a man?

As a private individual he gains; as a citizen he declines, and he accustoms himself to appealing to some state omnipotence in any danger. The finest flower of genuine philanthropy can pair itself with utter political rootlessness.

Is the movement of Europe on the whole, therefore, a rising or a falling one? This can never be determined by mere calculation. The peoples are still unexhausted physically, and in the intellectual and moral sphere one *must*, in order to calculate correctly, *reckon with invisible forces, with miracles*. This applies here, too.

To describe this life of the modern peoples in the last three centuries is our assignment.

(II) [After 1869; 1872?] It is not long since the period from 1450 to 1598 was regarded in an essentially optimistic way and made the beginning of that "progress" in whose further expansion and development we thought we were living.

This, to be sure, was true only in general, for in particular cases one admitted that the despotism of the great states, the Counter Reformation, and other phenomena had exacted considerable sacrifices (one can certainly hear those who suffered if one wants to hear them).

But on the whole one continued to connect the supposed excellence or, at least, the great promise of the conditions under which people lived from about 1830 with the great innovations after 1450.

In view of the imminent crises of the declining nineteenth century, these pleasant arguments have fallen to the ground, and as to the desirability of the events and developments since 1450 in relation to us, we have reason to express ourselves more cautiously—indeed, to abandon entirely the concept of the desirability of past things.

But for all that, this period does not lose one iota of its great intellectual interest for us. For as long as our present Western culture can keep above water we shall be inwardly enriched by absorbing the colors and figures of the past and treating the intellectual conditions and transformations of earlier world epochs as a great furtherance of our own intellectual consciousness. Indeed, the ability to compare different periods of the past with one another and with the present is one of the main forces that separate us from the confused doings of the day and from barbarism, which makes no comparisons whatever. In this respect the period from 1450 to 1598 is undeniably one of the most brilliantly instructive.

But instead of an overestimation of that period's services to our present development, an objective appraisal is called for. Besides, we are not the ones who would be especially qualified for an absolute evaluation of past conditions, if only because we always have the criterion of material well-being before our eyes—that is, of continuing in it once it is attained. And yet the great forces, individual as well as collective, develop only in struggles, and these can be very terrible. That criterion, however, is intrinsically ridiculous, for greed and desires know no limit; one would always encounter a dissatisfied humanity.

On the other hand, our century is very well qualified to recognize the intellectual content of the past in the full richness of its shadings.

It must suffice us that the period in question has come down to us in great wealth of sources and in exceedingly vigorous and interesting colors and personalities.

We resist illusions—first of all, the illusion that humanity had been eager and longing, in the highest degree, to get out of the Middle Ages as a dark, unhappy situation. In a large view, the Middle Ages may have been a time of salutary delay. If it had exploited the earth's surface as we are doing, we would perhaps not be around at all. (Would that be a loss?) Let us assume that the period concerned was there, at least primarily, for its own sake rather than for ours.

Further, we resist the illusion that developments since then have, generally speaking, led to happiness. The self-deception of the years 1830 to 1848 actually came close to this delusion; but in view of the clouds which hang over the end of our century one will probably have to speak more carefully.

The earlier, very unclear and mixed concept of "progress" includes the following: extension of civil rights to larger segments of the population; moderation of the penal code; communication in the widest sense, including a global network of railroads and telegraphy; great dissemination of varied knowledge; movability of all values and properties; and other things.

The more recent study of the world, however, has substituted an entirely different conception for this progress (or put the same conception in a new light): the struggle for existence, beginning with plant and animal life and then basically penetrating human life. From this vantage point the concept of "happiness" must then be examined anew and perhaps entirely eliminated from historical investigation. In his *Philosophy of the Unconscious,* Eduard von Hartmann even calls the perspective, from the eudemonic point of view, of this continual struggle while the intellect is constantly rising a *horrible* one.

If Hartmann's arguments are applied to the "History Since 1450," this means the beginning of the subjugation of the inferior races of mankind, especially the red-skinned; according to him, this is to end with their complete eradication. (How will the victors thrive in this? The Spaniards in Mexico and Peru were intelligent devils.) A true philanthropist, he says, could only wish for the speeding up of these last throes. The faster the earth was occupied by the white race, the more quickly the struggle among the various divisions within it would have to break out and be carried on all the more fiercely because they are more evenly matched; but at the same time it would be all the more beneficial to the progressive development of the species. According to Hartmann, war is not by any means the only method of this struggle; industrial squeezing by a more highly developed people would do it, too. But with the earth having in this way become the prize of the most highly developed peoples, with the entire world population becoming more and more cultivated, the condition of the soil, the climate, and other differences would nevertheless create ever new seeds of development whose maturing again would only be possible through a joint struggle for existence. (In this process, human beings would gradually become veritable devils, and finally cripples to boot because of sheer development of the intellect.)

(III) [November 4, 1872.] In that period there were essentially spun the threads of that fabric into which we too are now woven. Any consideration of the past must tie on there at the latest. But all that was begun at that time has experienced great metastases.

The *system of Great Powers* and also the absolutism which once was the practice in smaller states, established in the spirit of the rulers, have today been transformed into a system of great nations. The will (passion as well as interest) of the peoples or of the classes that lead public opinion has replaced the will of the cabinet. Where dynasties are still in existence, they mainly serve to carry out the will of the people (confirmed: October, 1876).

Any single principality or single state within a nation is in direct danger, because even with the best of intentions it can no longer act for the entire nation.

And within and above the individual nations there looms as an obscure impulse universal democracy, sprung from the French Revolution with its belief in the goodness and equality of men. It arises with remarkable homogeneity; its basic feature is acknowledged by the sovereigns themselves in the form of universal suffrage which can be expanded into a general referendum on practically anything.

The main driving force of this activity is the great social question of property and *enjoyment*. There is only one method for the mighty to curb it or cut it off: the peoples must be urged to become conscious again of their old differences which were already getting quite smoothed out and to test their strength with one another. This can be done, because they still have conflicting interests through accumulated tradition and exploitation of the world, e.g., England and Russia, England and America, and others; because as yet the whole earth is not occupied by the most active nations which must yet fight one another for it; then, too, because in Europe there are still small things to be swallowed up which one begrudges the other; and finally, because in spite of all homogeneity of culture there live on very strong antipathies of race. But from great national wars there arises again and again centralized military and, depending on the circumstances, monarchic power (that is, it has been so up to now).

In this period there is an especially striking predominance of the oceanic (N.B. of *all* great oceans and no longer merely of the Atlantic) over the Mediterranean (which would have become a mere puddle if it did not, together with Egypt, have importance as a passageway and possibly as a battleground). Added to this is the weakness of Turkey, Greece, Austria, Italy, and Spain. But even of the oceanic nations, Spain and Portugal are deeply in the shade, as is Holland; they have their intestate heirs presumptive. The two great Anglo-Saxon nations with their immediate and colonial possessions are in the process of grandiosely exploiting the world through completely untrammeled activity. In spite of her slight coastline, Germany is forced into rivalry with them, in her merchant marine and her navy. The great destiny is based on the fact that an Anglo-Saxon colony like the Union [United States] has been able to achieve independence and remain united despite its enormous expanse. By virtue of its cast of thought it will in time brook no barriers on any ocean (unless internal barriers should be imposed on it. 1876).

The conflict between the Catholic church and its adversaries took quite a different form from what friend or foe could possibly have foreseen in the sixteenth century.

Protestantism came under the strongest influence of general culture. On the other hand, Catholicism as such remained stationary in the form which it assumed in the sixteenth century as the Counter Reformation. Those who do not want to go along with it and have surrendered to the modern spirit are abhorred and reciprocate with a vengeance. Catholicism has come to be in opposition to all such and to almost all Catholic governments and bureaucracies. At present it is highly remarkable as the only element of pure authority from above, something which no government is domestically any more. Its early connections with culture, worldly life, and science have largely been severed, its opposition to modern thought has sharply come to a head.

The subjectivity of the intellect, which in the sixteenth century was so vigorously astir in all new things and produced such strong personalities, has since remained legally untrammeled or has become so again after interruptions. There is nowadays no dearth of "permissions." It is a very different question, however, whether our time is favorable to primary, creative *geniuses;* whether it will impress any future generation with the same originality and profusion as did the period around 1500; whether the gathering of knowledge does not stand in the way of higher productivity; whether the acquisitive spirit and the general haste are not destroying the genuine great mood, in creative persons as well as in those who ought to appreciate; and whether present-day democracy does not bring secret mistrust and, under certain circumstances, open hatred upon the outstanding person in every form and direction. At any rate, with its program involving equality of enjoyment, democracy stands outside anything intellectual.

However, not only in democracy but in all classes and parties people desire, above all, material enjoyment. After that, of course, they would like, for the further amelioration of life, poets, artists, and probably even thinkers of genius, provided they keep nicely in their place.

(IV) [October 21, 1880.] The sixteenth century largely creates those great positions in the material and intellectual worlds which dominate the periods to come; it is a time of tremendous innovations. It possesses one particular advantage: it is possible here, if ever, to view history as history of the intellect and to master the debris of external facts—not only because in the movements concerned there was much idealistic, even metaphysical, drive, but because they are represented by original individuals, some of them of the highest order, in state and war, religion, art, and science. The intellect speaks to us concretely through mighty, expressive people. In particular the time around the turn of the fifteenth and sixteenth centuries altogether gives one the impression of freshness, spontaneous strength, and of a very extraordinary generation. In every activity Europe has available the most outstanding men—discoverers, conquistadors, military men, statesmen, founders of religions, scholars each of whom remodels his field, thinkers who occasionally encompass the entire horizon of the time in single words, utopians like More and Rabelais, finally poets and, especially, a group of artists of the first rank. But even people of the second and third rank participate in the general vigor to the extent that they, too, give naively whatever they have to contribute. In literature we begin to get those books that are still really read. In the second half of the sixteenth century, to be sure, there is no longer this multifarious wealth of great individuals, and those who are now powerful are no longer naive but reflective, or they serve a movement; but no matter which side they are on, they arouse the greatest participation through their tremendous strength. And we are intimately acquainted with their persons—Tasso and Camoëns, Shakespeare and Montaigne, St. Theresa and St. Carlo Borromeo, Coligny, William the Silent, Elizabeth of England, and Henry IV in his rise.

Apart from this individually concretized aspect of world history, the great movements as such are significant, the changes in state and society which carry with them a new era.

The concept of Western Christianity is dissolved. The West looks on almost inactively while, in the East, Christian civilization recedes before the Ottomans who crush the Mohammedan and Christian states that come into their orbit. The rise of their empire is to date the last great new formation in the Near East. The Mediterranean stagnates, Southern Europe is permanently and seriously threatened.

At the same time, however, the great compensation is gained: the setting out for distant seas by the Portuguese and the Spaniards. Europe crowds in upon old civilized states of East India and founds great colonial lands in America. While in Asia Minor Turkish city names proliferate, America is filled with Spanish and Latin names.

At home a shift in world power takes place, the transfer of the world accent to the Atlantic states with their Atlantic and generally oceanic interest.

The atmosphere of the Crusades has evaporated and their late-born representative, Don Sebastian, perishes. But to compensate for that, a new tinge appears in the air: worldly conquest and commercial profit. Of course, not until the following period does there develop the full modern exploitation of the world in connection with a new concept of labor in the European mother countries; it is the cycle of colonial raw material and domestic manufacture, with forced purchase in the colonies. For the time being, in the sixteenth century, all that the Spaniards wanted was to rule and to enjoy; they were in quest of an El Dorado; the possession of great American *empires* had strikingly little effect on internal, domestic Spanish life and its spirit. In the year 1580 Spain gained possession of Portugal along with its colonies. The French and English colonies were only in their infancy; but here, too, people sought a golden land for the costs of European politics and wars.

The medieval feudal state dissolved into the centralized modern state which at that time demanded primarily *power* (absolutism) and since then has behaved as a constitutional and equality state, as an institution of purposefulness and general welfare, with the resignation of the individual, and so on. A new concept of state power begins with the Italian tyrant state which is prefigured in France and now is put into practice in all states of Western Europe (N.B. including England), in Germany only in the smaller circles, while the whole falls apart all the more. The intermediary rulers are destroyed or reduced to mere honorary rights, the nobility are reduced to privileges; all indefinite and disputable duties are replaced by mandatory definite performances; even the most stubborn defiance is subdued. Finally, at the time of the Reformation the states which have become Protestant inherit the former political power of the church. But what did the rulers do with their power? They carried on experimental policies which soon became primarily policies of conquest or annexation (this had been the downfall of Charles the Bold). Such were the earliest joys of the *cabinet* and its doings.

The support and motive of such policies were *great national conflicts of interest*.

Would the nations have left one another in peace without the activities of the cabinets? We do not know today; arrogance and the clash of interests which, after all, are so very much intertwined, are unpredictable. Even the "happy ones" could not have borne their "happiness." And then there existed in several nations a palpable satanic arrogance.

Earlier oppositions continued to have an effect: France and England, Anjou and Aragon. Now that the major part of the middle duchy of Burgundy and all of the Spanish power had fallen to Hapsburg through inheritance, the inevitable struggle between Hapsburg and Valois ensued, and the next victim was Italy—certain parts of the land and the overlordship of the whole.

Italy and the great transformation of the European mind that emanated from it: the Renaissance. This everywhere broke through the knowledge, thinking, and viewing of the Middle Ages. The ancients and soon the moderns completely supplanted the Middle Ages as authorities, beginning with medieval scholastic theology. The entire intellectual horizon was newly oriented; in addition, there arose an art which soon overwhelmed or cut in halves the art of all of Europe. The time of Italy's greatest productivity coincides with periodic invasions; the so-called calm did not ensue until the rulership of Spain was decided.

In this Italy which was enmeshed and glorified by the Renaissance, but which at the same time had fallen prey to the Italian political spirit and let itself go in the most extreme way, the *papacy* dwelt as the possessor of an ecclesiastic state.

The papacy stands in a wholly irrational relationship to Italy and Europe, vis-à-vis nations that are already arguing and greedy dynasties. Oblivious of its earlier mission, the papacy had become something to be exploited and was for a considerable time in the hands of blas-phemers who had obtained possession of it because it had become too desirable and was poorly guarded, as in the days of the pornocracy. Now it faces the greatest danger of all:

The German Reformation. This produces, first of all, a tremendous in-tellectual change in Germany itself and then more or less shakes up all of Europe, partly in a religious sense, partly in a political or a financial one. The conflicts, far from remaining purely ecclesiastical, are colored and discolored, entangle or disentangle themselves, and a literature from a thousand pens records every shading. Added to this is the enor-mous effect of the press which is now for the first time active in a European sense. Knowledge of the most remote places and of the ear-liest antiquity coincided with the strongest religious ferment.

And now the interests of the contending churches interweave with the an-titheses of Hapsburg-Valois and of Occident-Ottomans. On one side of the scale of external destinies at that time there are the Protestants and Francis I and the Turks, on the other side there is Charles V. The popes become adversaries of Hapsburg which is fighting on the Catholic side, because it also wants to possess Italy. There are times when they wish for a Protestant victory. Especially striking was the alliance between the Catholic Henry II and the German Protestants against Charles V.

In the *Counter Reformation* the old church again gains a foothold in almost the entire Romanic world and in part of the Germanic, Celtic, and Slavic worlds. Supported by its own internal power and the exter-nal forces of the governments which had remained Catholic, it seeks to subjugate mankind again. It enters into an emergency alliance with Spain, which is at the same time fighting for world monarchy. In this situation the old church remembers and returns to its original mission, and it manages to a great extent to rejuvenate itself. The Reformation had produced a rescue as well as a menace.

All this flowed together in *the great crises of 1560 to 1593.* In them a new nation was born, *Holland.* At the same time there was also revealed the great European significance of *England,* of which Europe would have got a taste much sooner if it had not been for the ensuing Stuart strife. Only now does *Scandinavia* stand forth clearly.

The modes of life of this latter part of the sixteenth century are highly remarkable. There is a tremendous contrast to the beginning of this century; the world has become religious again or at least sectarian. The sixteenth century which had begun with such a brilliant cultural epoch had a frightful latter part. Great historical transformations are always bought dearly, often after one has already thought that one got them at a bargain price.

The Peace of Vervins, 1598, was inevitably only an intermission.

Let us once more stress the especial significance of the period 1450–1598.

In history in general there is among peoples of higher culture a wonderful juxtaposition and conglomerate of profuse mechanical forces, notably the massed might of the great state, on the one hand, and on the other, of the most delicate imponderables, like culture and religion, which in their highest manifestation depend on so few individuals and are able to carry away and shape entire nations. This is to be seen with especial clarity in the sixteenth century. The personal elements in their relation to the great mass destinies are here expressed with particular noteworthiness, precisely because the individuals concerned who stir this world are not all born princes and great men.

We reject the eudemonic, the so-called progressive, way of thinking. The fact that our present world situation is largely linked with the decisions of that period does not mean that as a totality it was especially happy or commendable, for then our century would also have to be considered as especially happy and commendable, which was actually the view particularly in the period from 1830 to 1848. The concept of the desirability of the past ought to be abandoned altogether, if only because the individual who speaks in this vein is not alone in the world. Actually, a historical judgment should always be such that it can be endorsed at least by all nations if not by all factions.

There is a widespread illusion that an innovation which came about once amidst the most terrible infractions of law and acts of violence is therefore justified, or that it was historically "necessary," because later there was based on it a situation that was somehow tenable and appeared to establish new legal conditions. Humanity simply added its healthy powers to the act of violence and adapted itself to it, like it or not.

ADDITIONAL NOTES

On the Dissolution of the Medieval Feudal State: Such copiously graded privileges and such indifferently performed duties.

On Experimental Policies: The more recently power has originated, the less can it remain stationary—first, because those who created it have become accustomed to rapid further movement and because they are and will remain innovators per se; secondly, because the forces aroused or subdued by them can be employed only through further acts of violence.

On the Papacy: As a state, it demanded, if it was not to be devoured, Italian politicians as rulers, i.e., people who also had the choice of being either anvil or hammer and then became hammers. In addition, however, it becomes the prey of covetous men and criminals.—Significance of the reign of Julius II.—What if Luther had encountered an Alexander VI in his path?

On the Reformation: It created states in which the clergy no longer constituted a political class and its heritage of power and property fell into the hands of the governments.

On the Counter Reformation: It is not merely resistance, but an inner remolding of the Catholic church under the influence of Protestantism.

On "Necessity" in History: There are, to be sure, historians who "hear the grass of necessity grow" (Hanslick).

The Dubiousness of the So-called Pragmatic View of History: In addition to demonstrable causalities, obscure forces come into play from all sides, and their *raison d'être* is established only after some time.

The Heightening of Consciousness in modern times is probably a sort of intellectual freedom, but at the same time a heightening of suffering. The consequences of reflective thought are postulates which can set whole masses in motion, but, even when fulfilled themselves, will only produce new postulates, i.e., renewed desperate and consuming struggles.

On the Progressive Way of Thinking: "This or that hallway would have to be the most beautiful if only because it leads to our room." What coldness and heartlessness there is in this attitude, the ignoring of the silenced moans of all the vanquished, who, as a rule, had wanted nothing else but *parta tueri* [to preserve what had come into being]. How *much* must perish so that *something* new may arise!

The Confusion of the Concepts "Concentration of Power" and "Improvement of General Conditions": The latter is highly questionable in the material sense, as compared with the period of 1500.

It is our task simply to observe and describe objectively the various forces as they appeared side by side or one after another.

33. England in the Late Middle Ages

Here there takes place around the turn of the century an increase in the royal power approaching complete absolutism and at the same time an approximation to the European great state. This happens through a destructive fight among all descendants of Edward III and all their adherents in which the noble families are eradicated as well—a bloodletting of the nobility comparable to that of the Romans in the civil wars, under the Augustans, and up to Domitian. Furthermore, this absolutism is made possible by a specific talent for despotism on the part of the new royal house of Tudor. Only England-Wales acts, and every time the entire country. Ireland is not consulted and Scotland stands hostilely aloof most of the time.

Even though the political development up to that time had come about by fits and starts, it could be considered a major step forward in the parliamentary sphere.

From the thirteenth century the House of Commons had had firm and assured possession of the power to tax, and since Edward I had acquiesced in this, it remained in a continual insolent relationship to the crown. It took terrible events to make it lose this position. For prudent kings, and especially for those successful in war, it had hitherto been an easy matter to keep on friendly terms with it.

But on occasion the House of Lords was turbulent, as was the royal family itself (the Plantagenets) with its ambitious and mutinous princes who bore titles and had intermediate rule of large areas; but this was not hereditary and did not lead to the formation of secondary dynasties.

Twice it happened that factions among the Lords, headed by princes, wanted to force upon the king a jointly ruling commission which would relieve him of the government (Edward II and the Duke of Lancaster, Richard II and Thomas of Gloucester, later Bolingbroke). In each case, first a prince and then the king concerned meets his doom. But Parliament remains strong.

During all this there prevails the general assumption that in England things were done *legally*, and this semblance of legality was then dragged on through the bloodiest times, with tragicomic effect. Even the most palpable outrage comes with parchment and seal in its hands.

Hitherto the regulator has been the ups and downs of success in the Anglo-French Wars, with the participation of Scotland and Flanders and the great battles of Crécy, Maupertius, and Agincourt. Finally, in 1420, the personal union between the crowns of England and France is introduced through the Treaty of Troyes.

But after 1429 things go downhill, and Henry V has been dead since 1422, God having grown tired of being kind to the English.

34. On Richard III

(I) When King Edward IV of the house of York died in April of 1483, his widow Elizabeth Rivers would definitely have had to turn over the regency for the minor Edward V to Richard of Gloucester, no matter what manner of man he may have been. But by the way she acted, one-sidedly giving away power and offices to her family, she had to bring ruin upon her house.

In Volume 5 of his *History of England,* Pauli thinks that with a calendar in his hand he can specify the day on which Gloucester was still loyal to his nephew before he started to strive for the crown himself. In vain!

Richard was no monster, but a terrorist. He did not commit a pointless crime; later he was fair to his victims. He acted in a spirit of "expediency."

Richard would perhaps have an entirely different accounting sheet for us than Pauli might lead us to suspect, and in June of 1483, when he had himself proclaimed king of England, he would have spoken thus:

"I know the forest fire which in this country simply consumes the tallest tree trunks. It will rage till it dies out. It is a matter of who will be the last to remain on the scene. When the Lancasters were in power, they persecuted one another to the death, and when we Yorks rose up, we did likewise. I for my part have always found the simplification of problems in wiping out those to whom a possible rival faction could attach itself, for it is high time that a strong kingship were preserved.

"That is why with my own hands I killed the Prince of Wales, Henry VI, and also, as they say, my piteous brother Clarence. But I have always seen eye to eye with my brother Edward because he knew how to reign. Now, when he has hardly breathed his last, along comes my double-dealing and yet so simple-minded sister-in-law and places her relatives in all offices, probably because I am supposed to be untrustworthy. Surely I could have been trusted; I would have been the most loyal guardian of Edward V, but they would have had to obey me completely. Of course, I had to snatch those Riverses and Greys away, and it is too bad one can no longer merely keep someone in prison in England. Then those so-called friends of my brother Edward IV block my path. Who are those gentlemen, anyway? As though I didn't know all about where they came from and how they got there. Nothing but intriguers! But I am a Plantagenet. Of course, one of them, Hastings, had to bleed, others had to sit in prison, and still others to come over to my side. Unfortunately all these affairs have so spoiled the situation that my brother's sons, if they grew up, would never forgive me; and even now, through their very existence, because they themselves could not as yet reign anyway, they are a constant cause for the splintering of our faction of York. Thus it is a necessity for me to seize the crown, and this logically involves the disappearance of my nephews. If this should make the hearts of many good Englishmen bleed, it is just because they do not understand the least thing about the actual realities of today's concrete English royalty. It may be that later I, too, shall perish; but my successor, whoever he may be, will justify me by giving the still extant offspring of our house, to which a faction might attach itself, a second going-over. The worst of it is that by killing my nephews I am doing that lurking Henry Richmond a huge favor, too. You good people don't know this Tudor yet, otherwise you would have more sympathy with me. You are shuddering. But how would things be without me? The so-called friends of my brother and my sister-in-law's relatives would now be giving battle to one another in the name of Edward V, and in the end there wouldn't be anyone left who was authorized and qualified to hold aloft the banner of England. At least I kill only those who are in my way. Govern yourselves accordingly."

(II) Richard is a Robespierre of royalty—at any rate, of his York branch. Just as Robespierre kills all republicans who do not subscribe to *his* conception of the republic, Richard destroys all those of the house of York and its followers to whom a split-off faction could attach itself, until he stands alone and goes down.

(III) With this crown, to be sure, the whole undiminished royal power passed from Richard to Henry VII. There was no legacy of disunion and conditionality attached to it, as was the case elsewhere after civil strife. The obscure will in Richard III had been not to let the crown fall into any powerless hands; this was now accomplished and he could die.

35. On the Wars of the Roses and on Scotland

It will never be calculable how strongly the mutual extirpation of the large and medium-sized noble houses affected England's development. It has since been predominantly a bourgeois one, despite all the aristocracy. The Tudors do not allow any more factionalism among the nobility to arise which could have swept the state to its side; only under Edward VI was such a start made once more.

In *Scotland* the succession was never disputed, but the royal power was. And the heads of the hydra—of the nobility—keep growing back again. The life process of the Scottish nobility, with the mysterious vitality of this caste which must have been very fertile, seems to have been such that people periodically killed one another off so that the active generation might always be a young one and one committed to further blood feuds, beginning with the Stuart dynasty itself, with whole retinues destroying one another.

All the first four Jameses died violent deaths and left under-age princes whose young years were accompanied by the wildest regencies. Although no weaklings, the kings later did not attain any decisive power. Lamentation and bitterness must have been their prevailing mood. The despairing government invites great men and has them seized at the royal banquet table and beheaded; at this the young king sheds tears in vain. The great figures are almost without exception nuances of one and the same boundless despotism and intractability throughout the fifteenth century. If one of them wants to assert himself, he can do so only as the chief of his clan, that is, at the head of a platoon of plunderers. Especially the people of the Dominus ab Insulis ["Lord of the Isles"] are always ready to break into the rest of Scotland. There are momentary abject humiliations of great individuals before the kings, kneeling barefoot in their shirts and invoking the sufferings of Christ, but with secret reservations. Now and then, in moments of strength, a king traverses the country and has thousands executed. From England there spread gluttony and guzzling.

In free moments, the crown laboriously organizes an administration and a government and becomes the support of what little culture exists—which even proved the undoing of James III. Trade and industry are periodically wrecked in the feuds.

Within the house of Stuart conspiracies crop up—Athol against James I, Albany against James III—in which outside vantage points are sought.

The retinue of mighty men are huge bands *equitum ejus ex ditione collectorum inter quos ingens latronum vis* [of horsemen collected by his power, among whom is a great force of thieves]; one either had to join a *dux latronum* [leader of thieves] or pay high protection.

Scotland's relations with England are little more than mutual devastation; the rest is intrigue. In addition, until about 1450 (?) there was in effect the military service of Scotsmen in France; Louis XI still had at least his Scottish guard.

James II personally killed William Douglas at Stirling in 1452. There ensued several years of feuding between the royal and the Douglas factions.

When a faction planned resistance to the king, it claimed that he was being corrupted by fawning courtiers.

The court was musical at least under James III. His opponents then killed off his retinue. The kings thought they were bothered by their adversaries' wicked witchcraft, among other things.

The Parliaments hardly figure in this bit of history. The cities are insignificant and weak. After all, whoever has power can wield it directly.

The history of Boethius, or rather, Ferrerius, closes with the catastrophe in which James III met his doom in 1488, after conspirators had seized hold of his son, the barely fourteen-year-old James IV, who, full of woe, was unable to save his father from the murderers' hands and full well realized his predicament.

This whole political situation continued in essence throughout the sixteenth century.

36. Burgundy

It is psychologically probable that Philip the Good's enormous luck in expanding beguiled his son, Charles the Bold, to pursue endless acquisitions. It is a legitimate question whether a self-contained great state *could* have developed out of the large, rich cluster of lands that extended from the Ems to the Somme, not including the two Burgundies. It is a legitimate question because, apart from any matters of power, a great cultural question is involved, and because such a considerable part of it has actually survived. If one imagines the Burgundian lands as having stayed together instead of having been torn asunder due to Charles's folly; if one thinks of them as the great Western European island of peace, prosperity, art, industry, undisturbed culture; if one also thinks of the possibility of a great colonial role, as was later played by Holland; and if one considers the many life forces which later come into play in the individual, separated parts, then one must conclude that these lands would in the sixteenth century presumably have been of paramount importance in the widest sense of the word. To be sure, they would have felt their oats, and from their very prosperity internal strife would have arisen.

At any rate, Burgundy did not have an easy time of it with Louis XI, but any other prince but Charles would have known how to manage.

37. Charles the Bold of Burgundy

With the exception of his very last period (when *Dieu lui avoit troublé le sens et l'entendement*) [God had dimmed his mind and his reason], Charles was not a madman, but only a terribly passionate man (it was *folie raisonnante*) in whom notable gifts and strength (for action as well as activity) were at every moment forced to do the bidding of a brutalized, absolutely obstinate will. And in practice this almost worked out the same as if he had actually been demented. A madman one could at least have locked up, but not him.

38. France and the Idea of Unification

To what extent and in whom was this idea really alive at that time? To what extent has it been recognized as desirable only by later developments and subsequently imputed to the fifteenth century?

Royalism in France, to the extent that it was a way of thinking, came into being through the regimes of Philip Augustus and Louis IX, and subsequently maintained itself primarily because the crown was the banner against England. After the great strife it came forward again in favor of Charles VII.

However, very large regions of France may have remained unaffected by it, and their rulers, the great crown vassals, were permanent opponents of royalty.

That royalty in general more nearly represented the interests of France was known to few, because as yet there was no France in the sense in question. A mere frame of mind would not have brought it into being, either. But probably everyone felt the burdensomeness of the crown.

The significance of Louis XI consisted in his laying, through harsh compulsion (which had already been started by Charles VII), that firm foundation on which later there could be established the habituation to royalty, the firm reliance on it, and the building up of the interests which were identical with it, as well as the safeguarding of business and intercourse by the police and the courts.

In this respect Louis XI represents modern France, much against the will and taste of the France of his time. But later Charles VIII and Louis XII had the newly formed royalism of interests and views to enjoy.

Royalism had existed even from the thirteenth century, as had an all-French way of thinking, but with the restriction of all sorts of internal intractability; it was *this* that was changing now.

Large regions still regarded it as a matter of honor to have a special intermediate ruler. As Comines reports, the Normans had always believed that such a large duchy *requiert bien un duc* [had great need of a duke].

With even more assurance the Dukes of Brittany and their country asserted their independence, *de facto* and on the basis of certain views of the rights of states.

Louis differed from the Italian tyrants in his great national power aims. He probably studied and admired those tyrants only in regard to *means* of power. According to Chastelain, p. 190,* he is supposed to have secretly sent for two Venetians to inform him about the Venetian regime.

The Italians' worry about Louis XI was an idle one, because they did not know how greatly he was overburdening himself with things to do at home.

39. Louis XI

Although only two battles, those at Montlhéry and Guinegate, were fought under his command, his courage was more than hussar's courage and analogous to the courage of Cardinal Richelieu. (After all, he could have become a Carthusian.) The psychic tensions which he endured in his reign do add up to a sort of greatness.

The France of later times fully sanctioned his kind of ambition and theoretically shares the blame for what he did, although his vulgar ways must be utterly repugnant to the national sentiment. At the very least, he was better than his adversaries; only there is something highly reprehensible in the way in which he handles them (from St. Pol on).

Through his extremely prosaic character he easily gives the impression of having foreseen and desired more than actually was the case.

He is deserving of the profoundest pity when, in front of his son at

*No further reference in original. (Translator's note.)

Amboise in 1482, he has to make the traitors and semi-traitors believe that they will all keep their jobs in case of his death.

The firmness of what he established is shown in the relatively easy suppression of the *guerre folle*. The general premise is already royalty and its power which soon becomes taken for granted.

It soon looks as though Louis of Orleans would have been glad to break away from a false position through his imprisonment. The way in which he governed as King Louis XII almost makes one think that he wanted to atone for something.

And so that all this might happen, Louis XI had to die at Plessis as his own prisoner.

He dominates French history not through splendor, but merely through what he has been to it.

40. The German Imperial Power Under Frederick III

The German nation had a memory—the Holy Roman Empire of the German Nation—as of an erstwhile world dominion which had assumed its mightiest form under Charlemagne, and under the Ottonians constituted at least a European primacy over Gaul, Italy, and the Slavs. But the tribal consciousness of the individual regions and then their inclination toward separate living always worked counter to the Empire, and since the Salians and the Hohenstaufens it had been possible for the individual princes to join the popes against the emperors. After the death of Henry VI, there was only a semblance of imperial power in Germany and it was not worth abolishing.

After the end of the Hohenstaufens royalty lived on in Germany only in very reduced form; its main value was the collecting of expired fiefs for the family. And a king had to hurry with this, for he was only an elective king, and every election was a new deal. But his power was little more than that of the territory concerned.

The nation which had been split into more or less viable pieces was divided into individual powers, parts that were contented, i.e., grasping, and parts discontented, i.e., threatened. In the latter, the old mighty Empire appeared as a dream image, the more glittering the more impossible it was, while the king, who was present in the flesh and had been crowned emperor on an Italian tour, was regarded as a caricature and all the more decisively deprived of the last vestiges of respect and obedience.

Friendship with the popes was a matter already fostered by the Luxemburgers, but completely inevitable in Frederick III's situation. And the Vienna Concordat only gained for him what Brandenburg, Cleves, and others also gained for themselves. Later others, too, found the emperor dispensable as a court of appeal and went to the pope for decisions on German affairs.

Much poison circulated about Frederick III is mere modern national liberalism. After four hundred years people trample on a man who was helpless in his time and chuckle over everything that in the remotest periods happened to the house of Austria in the way of sorrow and shame.

41. The Ottomans

The difference between them and most other Islamitic peoples and states is that the completely martial period which with the others marks the beginning of their power lasts centuries with them and is perpetuated by the institution of the fief and by the janizaries. In war the Turkish people learns to feel itself ever anew; in peacetime it tolerates an ordinary Islamitic despotism.

All this was in contrast to the West with its state structure of graduated power and bargaining over duties. In addition, there was in the West a multiplicity of centers, smallness of the individual powers, and these remained involved in their quarrels and wars of "succession." Under such circumstances, all that was possible was done against the Turks, especially if one takes the Franco-Turkish alliance into account.

In the vicinity almost everyone only meditated about the advantage to him if the Turks proved his neighbors' ruin. And yet there is no lack of vociferous prophets who continually proclaim the general danger. The Turks were very predictable; people knew rather exactly how things were in the lands trampled underfoot by them and that a transition of these countries to Western mores was permanently out of the question.

In addition to their martial predisposition the Turks possessed the thoroughgoing arrogance of an Islamitic community. And yet heresies never amounted to anything here, with one exception under Murad II, and Shiism came to be hated all the more as a Persian faith and was persecuted. The Ottoman world is orthodox and contains its church within itself, while the West went to pieces ecclesiastically and had its universal church outside of the states.

With the Ottomans, all "fanaticism" is immediately active as a political and military force in the service of the whole and does not go off at a tangent. Any war is a religious war. To Islam belongs *eo ipso* the world.

In government everything, including the greatest horrors, takes place in order to guarantee unity and the maintenance of power. It is only *one* man's turn—while in the West power and areas are still divided now and then, so that it may be the turn of several.

The West still knows and at least nominally honors hereditary claims. The Ottomans proceed only according to the naked right of conquest.

42. The Republic of Florence

The republic expanded from the thirteenth century on and, after 1406 including Pisa, created subject cities. These were governed by *commissione*. The constitutions of Florence, which one could die memorizing, succeeded one another in turn. The general things that one notices here are a supreme political consciousness as well as the par-

ticipation of a large proportion of the citizens in public life and in constitutional questions.

But it does not necessarily follow that these constitutions by themselves were the basis of Florentine *culture* or had even created it. It is,
on the contrary, something if they did not impede it, if they did not
make impossible that *society* which was to become the substratum, the
living soil of culture and art. It is a majority of tolerated forces that are
the carriers of it: the will and the understanding of the Medici, the
competitive zeal of other noblemen, a number of spiritual associations.
In addition, there is the general ambition of the Florentines for monumental activities and the definitely highest intellectual capacity (or at
least the one most diffused among the people) of all the Italians, in just
the same way that the Athenians were gifted beyond the rest of the
Greeks. Florence is the Italy of Italy, as Ἑλλάδος Ἑλλὰς Ἀθᾶναι [Athens
was the Greece of Greece].

Only in this way could a general disposition be formed: if this or that
were not beautiful, *non s'usaria a Firenze* [it would not be used in Flor-
ence]. And such a partiality can then survive even periods of decline
and keep up general standards.

43. On the War of 1494

(I) For the great states which have only recently become quite
powerful there now start years of indiscretion, of grand politics directed toward the outside.

It was as though France wanted to compensate for the austere prose
of Louis XI. Romanticism burgeons on every side. To the realist *par
préférence* it had to happen that his so well guarded son must become
a visionary (the daughter, Anne de Beaujeu, was a realist).

The other side of the French mind, the imaginative, comes brilliantly
to the fore. It was in this light that the Italians regarded Charles VIII.
To Savonarola he is the great, exalted head of the Guelphs; to Pisa he

is a liberator; to Naples a *sacra corona* [sacred crown]; to all a great new chance in that land of chances, Italy.

In his *History of France,* (4th ed., Vol. VII, p. 282), Henri Martin says in this connection: *"La portion remuante et guerrière de la population française garda, depuis la campagne de Naples, une aveugle fureur de conquêtes lointaines, une infatuation funeste de sa supériorité militaire . . ."* [The revolutionary and warlike element in the French population *retained,* after the campaign of Naples, a blind passion for remote conquests, a deadly infatuation with its military superiority . . .].

Basically, this campaign was pure folly. It would have been to the real French interest, at any rate, that Naples should belong to an Aragonese bastard line rather than to that Aragonese who already possessed Sicily. The greatest significance of these lands was to be the vanguard against Islam, a very difficult honorary privilege! The real France would not have had to give up Franche-Comté and Artois, but to acquire as much as possible of the rest of the Netherlands. On the other hand, Naples was at best a valueless possession for France, and Charles VIII would not have set out merely for the sake of Naples; could designs on Constantinople and Jerusalem have been the decisive factor?

The fascination of this period lies in the naive expression of egoism and enthusiasm. Out of a need for emotion, Florence goes through its republic and its Savonarola.

In the chronicles Comines and Guicciardini meet; and even Macchiavelli joins in (*Decennale,* I).

Could this whole swindle with Constantinople and Jerusalem have been only a mask—to lend a campaign of conquest the character of a crusade? Considering the Turkish menace at that time, a mere campaign of conquest against Naples was an enormous scandal; Alexander VI (in February of 1494?) reminds Charles that such a campaign could really not be undertaken *importuniori tempore* [at a less favorable time]; Ferrante might in utter despair throw himself into the arms of the Turks. Then, too, 30,000 men were quite insufficient for a crusade.

But the main consideration is one that is hardly ever brought up: through her invading zeal France incited the Spanish power, which was bent on increasing its might anyway, to apply itself likewise to further occupation of outside areas. The detachment of Roussillon and Cerdagne had not pacified a Ferdinand the Catholic by a long shot!

How safe is the Sicilian theory according to which Filippo Maria Visconti actually bequeathed his state to Alfonso the Great? According to this, not only Lodovico il Moro but the entire house of Sforza would have had to worry constantly about the house of Aragon-Naples. Was perhaps the marriage of young Giovanni Galeazzo intended to eliminate this worry? And the claim of the house of Orleans was cut off entirely.

(II) We are told, above all, that wars are necessary because the peoples stagnate in peacetime and the mightiest forces would no longer achieve representation.

To be sure, the victor does gain a heightened feeling of life. One does not speak about the vanquished and his misery; why was he not the stronger one?

In the case under discussion, Italy, which had been cast to the ground in an era or series of interventions, had no unity and lacked an organ of national resistance, to be sure; but it did have forces of the highest intellectual kind that were capable of creations for all peoples and all times, and the activity of these forces was certainly stunted in large measure through the misery of Italy. What the art of that time was prevented from achieving will probably never be recompensed by any future art of the white race.

For the time being, France comes along with crude enforcement of rights of succession—in the first place, Charles VIII with his Anjou parchments, in the second, Louis of Orleans (actually Rabaudanges) who already stands by with his Milanese claim based on his grandmother.

This arouses the Spanish beast. The scene is set for the Spanish-

French struggle for existence which always takes place partly on Italian soil and has as its object parts of Italy, until finally around 1555 the French are completely expelled from Italy.

And over this they have neglected the much closer and more important acquisition, the Low Countries. In 1493 Charles VIII sacrifices Artois and Franche-Comté in order to make sure of being able to start his Italian campaign, and subsequently France does *not* obtain the important French Flanders up to the mouth of the Scheldt where once French kings had won victories near Bouvines, Roosebeke, etc.

Who will then blame Philip II for promoting and exploiting in every way the disarray of France in the religious wars?

France appeared anew in Italy under Richelieu, under Louis XIV, at the time of the War of the Spanish Succession, then under Louis XV, the Directorate, Napoleon, etc., until finally, substantially through France's doing, there arise in Germany and Italy great national units with which France would probably not tangle lightly in the future.

It would be interesting to add up the sum total of that exalted feeling felt by the French *nation* (N.B. rather than its leaders); one would have to subtract from it not only the suffering of Italy, but also the humiliations of the French at their many retreats from Italy.

By all appearances it would be possible to close such an account today, for the invasions of Italy are probably definitely at an end.

But, finally, there would remain the counterquestion: what would the Italians have done to one another if Europe had left them in peace?

44. On the Power of the Papacy

It lays claim to refereeship between disputing nations and potentates; it commands (even though usually in vain) peace in the West so that it may unite against Islam; we know, for example, the commandment of Boniface VIII vis-à-vis the quarreling kings (England and France, Anjou and Aragon).

After the Avignon period and the schism, the papacy at least reasserts this claim: Eugenius IV decides the dispute between Castile and Portugal over the possession of the Canary Islands, just as Alexander VI later draws the meridian through the Atlantic Ocean between both. Nicholas V, too, issues bulls relating to the Portuguese discoveries.

To be sure, when Rome as an Italian territorial power was entangled with affairs of the whole world, the papacy could no longer maintain this claim; and yet Alexander VI (between Charles VIII and Ferrante) and even Leo X may have tried to do all they could. But alongside this there is Leo's naïveté when in 1513–1514 he desired Lower and Upper Italy for Giuliano and Lorenzo de Medici.

In addition, the papacy was the supreme resort in matters of faith and of ecclesiastical punishment and pardon.

Would the papacy have escaped the German Reformation even if it had behaved quite properly? Once the matter of payments to the pope really became a burning one?

A dangerous thing was the habituation to the spiritual weapons—excommunication, interdict, and so on. (Pius II included going around the alum pits of Tolfa among the deadly sins for which there was no indulgence!) Once conventional fear was overcome somewhere, it was not only at an end, but the adversaries hardened and fortified themselves through counter-curses, calling the pope anti-Christ, and the like.

45. Italy and the Rest of Europe

Outside of Italy, the nobility and the middle class were separated socially and remained so for a long time. The two had different cultures, almost; and each class was incapable by itself of supplying the basis for a complete culture. Especially in Germany the nobility became brutalized and ran wild; the bourgeoisie was pressed hard from many sides, to be sure, but was already in possession of more varied enjoyments of life. All the princely courts outside Italy were at that time incapable of being social centers of their nations, something that the pompous Burgundian court had already been. In France only Francis I was to form the social center. A few courts knew only display and wild enjoyment, others had to or wanted to economize.

Written culture outside of Italy was still substantially dominated by scholasticism which was not really research but rather support of what was already established through logical operations. Thus scholasticism and its school books predominate in the incunabula of the presses outside Italy. In place of the natural sciences, the pseudo-sciences, astrology and alchemy, flourished vigorously while in Italy they were already close to extinction.

So-called schools for poets were just being started; there were also here and there at Northern universities Italian and, soon, Italian-trained teachers of poetry, rhetoric, and jurisprudence, occasionally under strong protest from their colleagues. Cicero and Quintilian had to be maintained by force as subjects of instruction.

As regards emotional life, religious feeling was still very strong, varying with the countries; in addition, there were excellent small mystic communities and pious individuals. The lyric poetry of the French and Germans, to the extent that it was part of literature rather than continuing folk poetry, seems to us mannered and tedious; furthermore, there appears a wooden mockery, by turns more didactic and more cynical. Did tender feelings hide behind this? The only present value of this literature is in the field of cultural history.

In the field of art, possibly the most vivid aspect of art outside Italy is the fading of the Gothic into a sumptuous decorative style. In sculpture and painting the former ideality of the great Gothic period is past and a harmonic synthesis has not yet been achieved. Flemish realism has stopped halfway in the shaping of the human form and in the narrative, and this lack becomes paramount precisely in its concern with the individual. But side by side with the awkward and even barbaric there appear here and there beautiful, profound, and spirited heads. From the beginning of the sixteenth century there appear in the

North the great and still almost wholly independent advances.

Thus culture outside Italy is on the whole a disharmonious one, albeit one with great incomplete and latent forces.

Italy, however, is the country of a common culture which is at the same time one of inner *harmony*. The *form of intercourse* was a higher sociability independent of class differences, and its *content* was intellect.

Toward the end of the fifteenth century, that which to other Europeans was still conjecture and fantasy was already *knowledge* and a *free object* of thought to the Italians. Imagination was beautifully channeled into poetry and art.

The *scope* of the intellect, still a very close and narrow sphere among the other Europeans, is here enormously widened through the interest in an ideally conceived Greco-Roman *antiquity*, in a renaissance in a narrower sense, and in *nature* and human life; indeed, nature is expanded through a *universal urge* for knowledge, appreciation, and discovery that is no longer inhibited by the old scholastic system which still blanketed the rest of Europe.

And it is not only the intellect that recognizes the world and itself, but the *soul*, too, speaks to and about itself in a different way, and in so doing clothes or, rather, unclothes itself in beauty.

The despotism of most governments does little damage. There probably were other reasons why Naples (with Pontano, Sannazaro) and Sicily took but little part in the movement. Elsewhere there are enough tolerably independent positions, especially for frugal people. The tyrants themselves and even a few popes are at the head of the movement, e.g., Lodovico il Moro and others.

The republic of *Florence* is at the center as a focal point and exchange center of the first rank. Apart from the Florentine states as such, there takes place here a most complicated convergence of extremely dissimilar forces to produce a supreme, harmonious culture.

Its basis is, in addition to the favorable physical and economic conditions, the general conviction that everything could be done here and that one must possess the best. Without this conviction all the institutions in the world would have availed nothing. This was also expressed in the idea current in all Italy that if this or the other thing were not so excellent, *non s'usaria a Firenze*. There were the Medici, the many corporations and wealthy men who employed people and demanded works of art.

Thus scholars, poets, artists of high order were able to come together or grow up in Florence. One must add to this the Florentine colonies and individuals abroad as commissioners or creators. Even Boniface III called the Florentines the fifth element.

In literature, the Italian epic predominated from about 1450 as the main genre, just as lyric poetry had been the chief form of the fourteenth century. The drama ought to have become that of the sixteenth century. After Pulci the epic reaches for all tones and colors; it is high-heroic, semi-comic, topical, etc.

Italian humanism which was gradually filtering through was already making an impression upon Europe. Many Northerners studied in Italy and brought home the picture of a new science. Of poetry, however, they took home only the neo-Latin, and around 1500 nothing of Dante was known in the North, except perhaps *De Monarchia*, of Petrarch and Boccaccio only the Latin writings; Battista Mantovano was known, but neither Pulci nor Boiardo. Ariosto was only in his early period.

At the same time Italy's modern political forms, commercial institutions, and travelers took effect.

But what the conquerors had yet to *discover* was the *art* of the Italians, combined with the remnants of antiquity:

An architecture which for once expressed and sheltered a majestic and comfortable worldly life, which was no longer capable merely of giving form to churches and mere castles, but shaped palaces and villas as well, according to a uniform plan, with beautiful rooms and noble, grand forms. In harmony with this there was an art of *decoration* which was the exact opposite of the highly refined Northern type and was completely adapted to the new building style, having grown and flourished to endless expansion with it. Its general character was grandiose serenity.

Then there were *sculpture* and *painting,* which could already boast of the most magnificent work of Leonardo and the early works of Michelangelo, and then during the occupations and interventions continued to grow in a wonderful way at passably protected places (Luini in a sanctuary at Saronno!).

Medieval art had achieved the full majesty of intentions, Flemish art had attained the reality of individuals in small compass. With Leonardo, *this and still higher things* fused into a perfect truth, that is, majesty, a stirring life on earth which appeared as a guise and expression of a life spiritually moved in the highest sense. Everything in one piece: perfect loveliness of form and nobility of intention in Raphael; perfect appearance in life, air, and light in Correggio; festive, majestic existence in Titian; finally, the realization of pre-worldly, extra-worldly, and supra-worldly figures and occurrences in the later Michelangelo—not to mention the innumerable minor masters who still appear great. And all this with almost complete independence of classical art!

Thus there came about the uniquely fortuitous case in art history that the highest beauty and truth of sensuous appearance persistently was striven for and captured as a revelation of the highest spiritual life and that one was aware of it. Here we should remember Michelangelo's words: "True painting is noble and pious in itself, for the very wrestling for perfection lifts the soul to reverence by approaching God and becoming one with Him; of His perfections true painting is a copy, of His brush it is a shadow."

And during the invasions and occupations Machiavelli, Ariosto, and Guicciardini were writing.

46. Spain and Portugal

The grandees, to be sure, remain loyal to the crown after the deaths of Isabella (1504) and Ferdinand the Catholic (1516). But inner strife appears because the supreme power as such is in dispute, and finally the uprising of the *comuneros* turns against the Netherlands councilors of Charles V. But royalty remains in complete and sole control and, as soon as the division into parties had ended, achieves its highest apotheosis. The Inquisition crushes everything; the head of the Medina Sidonia bears its banner. Servitude does not seem to have been felt as such. The same nation which is cut off from whole large areas of thought and knowledge by an unheard-of preventive censorship remains fresh and creative in other areas and even develops quite late its best and most lasting elements. Not until the course of the sixteenth century are there added to the existing romance and lyric poetry the sacred and the profane drama (the latter again the tragic and the comic), the novella and the realistic novel (the beggar's novel). In art, which in the sixteenth century was still dependent on the outside, the true Spanish spirit achieves its flowering only in the seventeenth century when the nation was already dying.

In discovery and the founding of colonies, Columbus must work with the only powerful agent which sets people into motion; it is not even the promise of enjoyment, but the mere greed for gold; he must let the whole curse hold sway. Added to the unprecedented widening of the horizon is the worst surrender to Spanish sloth over money and power. In order to attain this, people undergo any danger and effort. Until Cortes the human element is greatly inferior to the *Portuguese* under Manuel the Great whose entire activity is devoted to outside journeys, but who, in between, also reaches the other European monarchs with exhortations to go on crusades. Here is a more active people that does not want merely to enjoy and to rule; from the smallest to the biggest it seems to be gripped by enthusiasm for the martial-commercial voyages, so that afterwards a great poet was able to focus this feeling. Furthermore, the leaders and viceroys appear to be nothing but loyal and united servants of the great idea which is personified in kings, and they had to suffer no infamies like Columbus, Balboa, and others.

They discovered no "New World," as did the Spaniards, although they obtained a share of it in Brazil; rather, they encountered an age-old and yet essentially unknown world. They found no mere savages and semi-civilized peoples, but a civilized world fraught with perils and warlike Moslems whom one keeps encountering as familiar, active enemies down to the farthest reaches of India. After Vasco da Gama one gateway to the Orient after another was burst open, and, after all, Portugal was at first still blameless in the war of the European peoples.

47. The Beginning of the Reformation: General Considerations

The transformation of the world through the Reformation was great in itself. First of all, the problem of "liberation" may be brought up.

Catholicism up to that time had exerted no substantial pressure, had not impeded any idea, not even atheistic blasphemy, and had allowed reformatory elements in particular to rise. But the church was subject to change (apart from dogma) in its hierarchic form of power and its property; for both *are* secular. (Still, someone who overthrows and steals power and property does remain a perpetrator of violence, even though sound forces may subsequently have associated themselves with the consequences of his actions.)

In Europe, church property was an open question for the universally needy secular class, and the church *state* was itself imperiled through the consequences of the activity of the popes.

The Reformation, as a religious innovation, diverges from all traditions of the Middle Ages. The Bible, which may be variously interpreted, remains the sole authority, and reformatory theology brought the difficulty of the doctrine of justification.

After 1520 Luther's goal was the complete eradication of Catholicism. He was execrated; his opponents were designated as "scorners" of the gospel, and tolerance was represented as blasphemy.

The reformers were fond of invoking the wrath of God.

No mercy was shown those who wanted to adhere to the old religion *optimo jure* [as having the best right]. (But anyone who is treated that way must be destroyed; if he is not, there exists an avenger.)

The most enormous spoliation of the institutions of a millennium took place. But a large part of Germany remained Catholic or became Catholic again, and in all the rest of Europe Catholicism stood its ground in the most important countries and considered as its duty the utmost resistance to the Reformation and absolute self-preservation.

On account of that, with the Thirty Years' War Germany paid as dearly for the Reformation as is at all conceivable. On the whole, things went very badly, and all desperate hatred has to date not been able to change this. The "others" are still around and are Christians, too.

Upon the Catholic "human statutes" there follow the Protestant ones. The reformers and "freedom":

Today they are chiefly regarded as battering-rams—not on account of what they taught, but because they did their best to destroy Catholicism. Little notice is taken of their doctrines, and at bottom they are held in low esteem. Protestantism is regarded as liberal, something it became only after it was no longer Protestantism—and the state dictated it anyway.

The reformers bewailed "spiritual freedom." Every one of them conceived of his dogmatism as a condition of the soul's salvation. They bitterly complain of being despised—here one suddenly does not even believe Luther himself. They shudder because with their innovation all of ethics has got out on the high seas (God as the Creator of Evil, and the like), while folk fancy and greed, now based on the Bible or even only on the spirit, rise to ever new evolutions (Anabaptists).

Yet the force which carried the Reformation materially was the general defection from good works, from alms, tithes, indulgences, fasting—in short, the general lack of discipline. The reformed not merely rejected asceticism, but went to quite the other extreme.

The Reformation is the faith of all those who would like not to have to do something any more. With Calvin this later changed.

The worst and socially most dangerous elements were soon in the foreground. They brought about a general break with all historical traditions. In addition, there were active among them those carried away by the spirit of rhetoric.

Even when the storm of the Peasants' War was over, the general licentiousness in action and thought remained and spread to the areas of governments which had remained Catholic. In 1532 Tiepolo was afraid that in consequence of internal strife the victors or the emigrating vanquished might hurl themselves at the neighboring countries.

On the intellectually more advanced there was an inner pressure. The absence of any mood of exaltation becomes characteristic. Higher education did not advance, as is thought, but retrogressed for decades. The humanists became silent.

German art declined, through icon-smashing, through the atrophy of its higher tasks—it had been deprived of its myth—through the participation of the most important artists themselves in the Reformation.

48. On Luther

The initial element in him was not speculative thought, but terribly powerful basic feelings, such as occur now and then in deep natures of the old, advanced races. Such men sense the profound vanity of everything earthly and, according to predisposition, period, place, and race, feel it as an apostasy of all living creatures from God.

In accordance with the temporal (Germanic and monastic) covering which gave the external form to his spirit, Luther perceived it as sin. However, he did not content himself with the remedy for sin customary in his environment, namely, penance, and its superficial buying off, the indulgence, did not suffice him at all.

Luther's personality is described by Kessler [*Sabbata*, I, 122] who saw him in 1522: "He was rather corpulent by nature. His carriage was erect and such that he bent forward less than backward, with his face turned toward heaven. He had dark eyes set deep under his dark brows; his eyes twinkled and flashed like stars, so that one could not well bear their glance." (Cranach has nowhere managed to give us an idea of this.)

The decisive thing about Luther was the fact that in addition to indulgences he also abhorred good works in the widest sense. But these will always have on their side natural feelings which he *likewise* trampled underfoot along with all follies of Catholic practice.

For a Christian it is natural (but for that very reason not theologically correct?) to want to atone for his failings, to impose suffering upon himself, to give away a part of his possessions and enjoyments. Only optimists are blind to this. Real Christianity even imposes upon itself permanent penance in the form of asceticism, and Luther hated the latter most of all once he had said good-by to it.

The reformers then were quick to realize what had been lost with the *ecclesiastic* practice of alms and drew up programs of public charity.

But they would have succumbed to their own impotence unless princely and municipal governments had for good reasons safeguarded a firm ecclesiastic organism. The governments then had to take the benefice, too, under *their* care in large measure, even though they entrusted the clergy with it in part.

49. On the German Reformation: Its Causes and Spiritual Consequences

It is a pretension of modern Catholics that a corporation which has taken to itself as much of the secular as the medieval hierarchy had done still ought not to succumb to the laws governing all secular things, but should enjoy the privilege of eternal immutability in the midst of universal change. But earthly property and power *are* transitory. And yet the hierarchy had grown and constantly changed. It had attained full growth in about the way that a religion of immortality under the supervision of priests had had to mature. This religion could not and would not pretend to be Biblical any longer; hence the grudge against the Bible in the vernaculars, as it is expressed, e.g., in Jiménez' principle that the three languages in which the "I.N.R.I." was written were sufficient. This attitude might have been affected by the memory of the Lollards who, after all, lived on here and there into the sixteenth century.

Now there were merely the alternatives: Would the church be shaken by the gradual defection of the subjectively cultured, modern, profane, personally examining people, or by a sudden great religious crisis—the latter in conjunction with the financial factor?

How long would it have taken without the indulgence industry of Leo X?

A counterquestion: What would the course have been without Luther? Undoubtedly there would soon have been changes of some sort in church property throughout all of Europe and particularly in the church state, but a large part of the dogma and the hierarchy would have remained, alongside of which the personal development of the individual could hardly have been suppressed.

The spiritual result, apart from the religious elements, was as follows. In any event, infinitely more individuals were spiritually awakened and matured than had previously been the case. And through religion's becoming more inward, the psychic element was developed more and in much wider circles. (?) But inevitably an equal amount of native, primitive strength was lost in favor of this common possession. This is why there was a predominantly weak literature and poetry after the Reformation. Added to this was a feeling of oppression under the princes, and, above all, under the new dogma (justification through faith) which, burdensome per se and not designed for everyone, was a more oppressive burden than Catholicism had been previously, as it really was, with its thousand accommodations and its highly liberal practices whenever one wanted them.

Both churches, Catholic as well as Protestant (*Protestantism reawakens Catholicism*) became oppressively dogmatic and demanded that men should all become one-sided again, after many-sidedness and freedom had characterized the beginning of the sixteenth century. The Protestant countries later become places of "spiritual freedom," not because they were Protestant, but to the extent that they no longer were zealously so.

Later compensation for what was lost is imponderable; it is impossible to judge how desirable delay may have been.

It should also be considered how the Reformation, and at the same time the Counter Reformation on the Catholic side, regulated the Renaissance and took it into their service.

In a letter to Goethe dated September 17, 1800, in which he comments on K. L. Woltmann's *History of the Reformation,* Schiller calls the history of the age of the Reformation "subject matter which by its nature tends toward a petty, miserable detail and moves along at an infinitely lagging pace." What matters is "to organize [this material] into great, fruitful masses and to abstract its spirit with a few big strokes."

50. On the Reformation: Protestantism and Tradition— The Intolerance of the New Doctrine

The appeal to the Bible alone was rejected by the Catholics with very eloquent reasons. Glapion, for example, said that the Bible was a book comparable to soft wax which everyone could pull and stretch at will. He offered to prove by individual passages from the Bible much stranger things yet than Luther did. One ought to pay attention to the oldest usage of the church, he said. In order to establish and maintain an *edifying* view of the course of the Reformation, one would have to suppress the psychological experience of all times and all men. In point of fact, it was easy to demonstrate the total separation from the earlier life form of the church, from tradition, as something unfair and foolish. Christian truth, he said, consists of both things, the Bible *and* tradition, the spirit *and* the vessel which it had created for itself in the earlier times of full religious strength.

Later, when it had become old enough, Protestantism gradually was able to form and establish a tradition of its own. Two generations sufficed to manifest here, too, what henceforth was considered as self-evident; the accustoming of the masses took place relatively fast.

But when its theology began to burden itself with "scholarship," Protestantism became sick from it and showed a tendency to shift to rationalism.

In the sixteenth century, however, mutual execration stepped between the old and the new. (Often people mistook their own rage for the wrath of God.) Anyone who was to tolerate a minority of different faith might think that he was incurring the wrath of God over himself and his country. After all, the minorities were not merely "unbelievers," but "scorners."

Sebastian Franck says about the evangelical territorial churches: "Everyone believes so as to oblige the authorities and has to worship the regional God. If a prince dies and another regulator of the faith appears, God's word soon changes as well." From a very early time (1520), Luther had issued the most vehement calls to destruction against Catholicism and demanded complete abolition and eradication of everything old. The Catholics immediately had a life-or-death struggle, a fight for self-preservation, on their hands. As early as 1520 the pope was, to Luther, the anti-Christ who is darkly alluded to in 2 *Thessalonians*, II, 3. The Hussites had already applied the term "anti-Christ" to the pope.

Soon the ecclesiastic power of the Protestant state brought on the persecution and destruction, or expulsion, of the Catholics *ipso facto*— a terrible hardship for those who wanted to adhere to their accustomed faith *optimo jure*.

The doctrine of justification through faith in Luther's version now has been abandoned by all prominent Protestant theologians. In 1531 Melanchthon wrote to a friend: "Believe me, the controversy over the justness of the faith is obscure and difficult."

Germany paid about as dearly for the Reformation as is imaginable. Whatever elements were able to save themselves from the terrible exclusiveness and militancy of the new movement never recognized this new force and felt themselves entitled to any reaction. Hence the Counter Reformation and the Thirty Years' War. The memories of reformatory compulsion were still alive in the grandchildren when the reaction came.

The assumption of control over the church is one of the greatest steps toward omnipotence that the state has ever been able to take. In the Catholic areas this step was taken indirectly through the appointment and taxation of the clerics; with the Protestants it was done quite directly and openly. And to what extent is this state qualified to rule over souls?

51. On the Reformation: The Establishment of So-Called Spiritual Freedom

Today's rejoicing that the Reformation established so-called spiritual freedom, to the effect that the reformers were the battering-rams against *any* authority in favor of *any* lack of restraint, was actually even then the attitude of many, but to the disgust and lament of the reformers themselves, who regarded their particular dogmatism as the *sine qua non* for all salvation of the soul.

Subsequently the governments helped them to establish well-defined creeds, but not until after they had made sure of the church property and in order to maintain it. It was the governments, municipal as well as princely, that carried through and maintained the firm creeds, for the reformers by themselves would most certainly have succumbed to their disunity.

The people, however, where they participated, in the beginning greatly enjoyed the general lack of discipline.

Apart from that esteem of the reformers as battering-rams against the greatest and thus, by implication, any authority, few people would want to know of them today. Not even the pious strictly believe in their systems of faith any longer.

What if someone had been able to lift the curtain of the future for the people and show them how a hundred years later they would have to pay again for what had been won so very easily?

Forces like those of the Reformation always delude themselves into thinking, in the exultation of the moment, that they are alone in the world. Afterwards they are surprised and abandon themselves to outbursts of execration when the old elements not only have remained in significant numbers, but have grown to great, new strength, because they derive from the innermost core of mankind.

At one time, however, people did not have the slightest scruples about immediately destroying the old faith through interdiction, persecution, exile, etc., to the extent of each government's power. This was an abomination; it brought about the despair of millions and could not be justified on any legal grounds. Then, too, the *religions* occasionally do it differently. The Christendom of the fourth century took a long time before it proceeded to persecute paganism—not until it was completely harmless—because it was acting according to religious impulses. On the other hand, *confiscators* have to act immediately with cruel exclusiveness. To be sure, the properties and endowments of the pagan temples had been a trifle compared with the loot that the governments of the Reformation had before them. Hence the horrible compulsion to Protestant sermons and Holy Communion. Otherwise the booty would have been in danger.

The reformers, to be sure, assisted this as much as they could with their doctrine that the wrath of God was incurred by a country that still tolerated idolatry. But without the consideration of safeguarding the confiscated items their clamor would not have been heeded.

From the very beginning, in Germany there was danger and self-sacrifice only for those who adhered to the old church. Hutten's *"iacta est alea"* [the die is cast] is ridiculous. It was different in France where the adherents of the new faith exposed themselves to mortal danger.

52. On the Reformation: The Masses, Their Motives and Consequences—Luther

A large proportion of the population certainly was quick to join. It was pleasant to skip confession and penance immediately, to break fast, to be rid of vows and indulgences, and, as was thought, not to be paying tithes any longer (of these the peasants were nowhere relieved). The Reformation must have had an enormous attraction for all *those who enjoy not having to do something any longer.*

Bonnivard stresses this throughout his *Advis et Devis des difformes réformateurz*. The large majority of the people, he says, conceived of the Reformation as the *opposite of asceticism:* (*"Ce monde est faict à dos d'asne"* [This world is made like a donkey's back]; if a bag hangs too far to the left and you try to center it, it falls to the right). How different was the effect of Christianity on people in its beginning: repentance, surrender of property at the feet of the apostles—and now, by contrast, *"nos évangelistes de taverne"!* The worst elements of the population rose to the top. In the time of transition, brutal acts of violence against priests and the like occurred. Where was the preaching of the gospel followed by an improvement of life, except *"en la val d'Engroigne* (Waldensians) *et nostre ville de Genève"?* And even there this happened only late and with an effort, for initially *"peu de gentz de bien"* [few people of means] took part, but rather *"les plus desbordez"* [the most downtrodden] in the city and within a radius of ten hours, with maltreatment of the priests and monks, plundering, and the like. This was done only out of hatred of the church, not out of love of the gospel; otherwise they would have started their reform with themselves. (The Reformation made its great strides not through its positive teachings, but as a negation of something that had existed up to that time; without this negation the masses would not have been won over.)

On the whole, the reformers may have felt very queer in the midst of lustful masses of people, greedy governments, wretched colleagues (quickly advanced clerics of all kinds), and vis-à-vis one another: the Anabaptists, i.e., the forward-pressing essential spirit of the Reformation, a continual admonition from out of the dark. The frightful imprecations against the papacy probably were made in part because they wanted to cut off forcibly the secretly tempting way back. How gladly Melanchthon would have remained in some sort of a relationship with the old church!

The Reformation stirred up in people the most diverse spirits: a break with *all* historical things; because people broke with so much history, there was, for many, no limit. Furthermore, there were remnants of all kinds of traditional heresies which had only been forced back into obscurity.

According to Lang's conscious or unconscious view, the *Reformverein* [Reform Union] actually ought to have followed immediately upon the Reformation. But without immediate, dogmatically very firm and one-sided churches, everything would have broken up into tumult, baptizing, appeal to the spirit, and so on, into general disunity (not "enlightenment," but baptizing would have dominated the scene for the moment), and the reaction (which later set in strongly enough) would then have gained control easily and completely.

To be sure, the religious fanatics now and then make an optimistic start at collecting themselves into a people of God with strict discipline, as did the Hussites once, but there is far too little harmony, and the attempt of Münster came much too late.

Through the problems of justification, good works, predestination, and the like, *all of ethics got out into the high seas.* The idea emerged that God was the creator of evil, too (Hans Denk and also some individual reformers, e.g., Zwingli, were logical enough to attach to this the eventual salvation of the wicked, even of the fallen angels).

Many were probably drawn into all this confusion only by their mere inborn *fondness for talking*. They are those who would be equally inspired to talk by the opposite.

Who are we anyway to demand of Luther and the other reformers that they should have carried out *our* programs?! This particular Luther existed and no other; accept him the way he was.

There are complaints about Luther's "obstinacy"—but without the pig-headedness, so entirely incapable of capitulation, of this one man everything might perhaps have reverted to the *status quo*.

Luther's doctrine of justification, an innovation vis-à-vis the entire church up to that time, is currently actually abandoned by all Protestant theologians, even orthodox ones. In fact, it is explained in a way that the reformers and their authentic successors would damn as Papist or Arminian.

53. On the Reformation: Governments—Confiscation of Property and Dogmatism—Church and State

The territorial *"churches"* which arose at that time were essentially only districts for the seizure of property and for confiscation; within them the new clergy established itself somehow in as wretched a fashion as is conceivable.

With its sermons, when they could be given, this clergy would only have produced ever new evolutions, i.e., a rapid disintegration through ever new dogmatic disputes; and the people, continually confused by this, would have reverted to Catholicism all the more easily. Luther complained bitterly about the impotence of the sermons and the religious spirit in general.

With its own strength the new church would not nearly have sufficed to create an Archimedean point, a banner to rally round; it would have declined into nothing but sects.

But the *governments* were interested in church *property* and an increase in *power*, and with their *"quos ego" they* had to create state churches which the people, and, note, their clergy as well, were not allowed to leave any more, while the nobles were granted varied participation in the looting. The governments did not care about the *dogmas*, but they did want a strictly defined *dogma* as a political and police barrier around their subjects. *They* had to be much more merciless toward Catholic remnants than were the reformers. (Albert of Brandenburg, Gustavus Vasa, etc., prohibited Catholicism on pain of death, and this was most certainly not due to religious fanaticism.)

The governments aimed, first of all, at stunning the great masses who in the intoxication of their initial undisciplined behavior staggered into their arms anyway, and also at making the opposition defenseless for decades until it should be thoroughly habituated.

The *governments* were in a hurry about a definite faith. The clergy would have continued disputing, and every individual would have been right by himself.

Münzerism, the Baptist movement, etc., with their claims on state and society were in a direct and fearful competition with the governments even more than with Protestant dogma.

The governments needed a firm dogma to safeguard their confiscations. Without this desire of theirs, Protestantism would have split up into small sects or factions.

Firm orthodoxy was tantamount to holding on to stolen goods.

Catholicism had been extremely tolerant in living and letting live, and had left the convictions of the people alone. The great totality was able to stand a lot.

In Protestantism, on the other hand, the clergy cannot tolerate or ignore anything, and the governments see in every deviation a threat to their enormous confiscations.

Highly significant is the large number of eminent men who after initial sympathy turned away from the new movement: Pirkheimer,

Wicelius, and others. Even Reuchlin, although he was sentenced in Rome as late as 1520, adhered to the old faith and was completely averse to Luther's undertaking.

Those who suffered inwardly and yet were outwardly prudent sympathized with the moderation of the *reversionists* who worked toward a council.

Thus Paul Lang wrote around 1520: "What I have said about Luther thus far, I did not say *assertive* [as fact], but only *admirative* [as admiration], and have never sworn by any magisterial words, but since I, like many others, am waiting till it shall be decided by an ecumenical, universal, and general council what shall be believed, I shall always accept instruction from those who are truly wise, and meanwhile submit all my writings to the judgment of the church of Rome."

Afterwards only Calvinism appears quite spontaneously and autonomously. It wants to dominate the states, above all to impose its religious will upon them, and in Scotland, e.g., it treats state and world *en bagatelle*. It at least seeks to approximate an organism which stands above the individual states, and has achieved a *Synodus Dordracena*.

Luther, on the other hand, never organized his church, but immediately left its form and fortunes to the individual secular governments. He *teaches*, but the governments act. For from the beginning they stood on the sidelines and confiscated the church properties in which they were more interested than in all justification and salvation. Of course, Luther probably did not foresee what later happened and had to happen. For the time being, the princes and municipal governments were only supposed to set up the gospel and the new church, not to become the highest authorities of faith and supreme judges over religion, doctrine, and church.

But he was no longer able to combat this rapidly adopted practice, because without the governments the Reformation after 1525 would probably have retrogressed among the people. At any rate, the clergy of the new faith were derided and abandoned by the people when the state did not assist them. In his quiet moments, however, Luther may often have been haunted by the thought that the governments offered little guarantee as to their *future* right thinking. On the other hand, his mind was quite at rest as far as the (enormous) increase in the governments' power was concerned, and he congratulated himself on having contributed to it. For the present he thought that the princes would follow the advice of their theologians, but a prince chose his father-confessor himself and appointed or removed entire faculties of theology.

In this connection we are reminded again of Döllinger who writes as follows: "The church was completely integrated into the state and regarded as a wheel in the great machine of state. He who wielded absolute power over the noblest and otherwise most inviolable things, namely, religion and conscience, necessarily could gain control gradually of every other area of life in state and nation as soon as he cared to reach for it. Accordingly, with the setting up of the consistories as the sovereign authorities governing church interests there began the development of bureaucracy, of the omnipotence of prince and state, of administrative centralization."

If there is anything that characterizes the modern state, it is the hatred and worry it feels when it has to tolerate a religion which has connections beyond its borders and belongs to a totality that the state does not control. Nevertheless, until the eighteenth century the state pretended at least to *have* the religion whose church it had admitted to its officialdom. Since then things have changed.

It had at first been an advantage of the state that it made one batter out of Lutheran orthodoxy, possession of the church properties, and political omnipotence. But if one of these three had to be the first to go, it certainly turned out to be Lutheran orthodoxy.

The enormous power of the state over the church in the sixteenth century suddenly was there in fact; no one was in a position to set any limits for it. Practice had to supply them in time.

Protestantism originated as a state church, and when the state becomes indifferent, it is in a dubious position.

It is the greatest step toward omnipotence which the state has taken in past times. Then there followed on the Catholic side Louis XIV. The subsequent completion of state omnipotence through the theories of the Revolution could not have taken place so easily without this preceding Caesaropapism.

The *brachium saeculare* [secular arm], which the Catholic church had once called upon for individual action, has control over the Protestant church a priori.

The church surely did not want it that way in the beginning. But when in the heat of battle it wiped the sweat off its brow for the first time, it had to realize that it was in the hands of the state, if only through the marriage of the clergy.

54. The Origin of the Territorial Churches

While Calvinism was creating, in Geneva, Scotland, and elsewhere, a dominion of religion over the state and a possibility of ecumenical action, such as the Synod of Dordrecht, while Zwingli in Zurich became the outright head of state and only later sects placed themselves *outside* the state, Luther could not or would not organize a church in Germany. He taught, wrote, and preached.

According to unchanging laws of psychology, the princes and city governments, given the way they were constituted, could not be made edifying. Despite the new dogma their morality, such as it was, remained primarily greedy for confiscation. They now created just as many individual territorial churches as there were confiscation districts; in this they often had to share with the nobility which had hitherto lived on benefices, and all these units at the same time became dogmatic districts. The people and the clergy were no longer allowed outside, so that the confiscation would not become dubious again, something that was to be feared with every deviation.

Hence the absolute intolerance toward the Catholics, and note that it was not out of fanaticism, although this was in keeping with the reformers. This is also true of Zwingli the politician, even more than of Zwingli the reformer. In addition, the princes and municipal governments endowed (miserably enough) the new church.

If one imagines the reformers without the governments, they would have caused fragmentation through dogmatic dispute which would have confused the people or made them backslide. They were incapable of attaining by themselves an Archimedean point, of raising a banner round which all might join in security.

The governments, however, were interested in stunning and habituating the masses, in decades of defenselessness. *They* were in a hurry to have a settled creed, and they forced the agreement of the clerics who would otherwise have continued quarreling. *Their* competitors, even more than the clergy's, were Münzerism, the Baptist movement, and similar movements. This explains the even assurance with which they proceeded. The only things which kept the German Reformation alive were the confiscation and the interests attached to it; only they produced the endurance of those political forces which maintained the cause. Thus, without Luther's wanting it, the *governments* became the supreme authorities of faith. He had no assurance as to the future and eternal orthodoxy of the governments and their estates, but only the hope that they would follow the advice of their theologians.

In sum: The clergy, forsaken by the people, dependent because of their marriages, had to accommodate themselves to an organization which they could not have replaced by one of their own. Catholicism, on the other hand, salvaged its organization. The territorial churches constitute the most enormous step toward state omnipotence, toward Caesaropapism. Soon there occurred a tightening of the reins, even though the consequences did not fully develop for centuries.

In England, too, there now occurred a tremendous increase in royal power. In Sweden this was actually made possible only by the Reformation.

The theory prevalent in modern times claims absolute and universal power of the state as a major aim of all existence. But power usually does not make men better and scarcely ever happier, because of their inner insatiability.

However, for the German princes, this particular increment of power (a hitherto jointly ruling class had dropped away and they had inherited its property) was a most powerful means of asserting their liberty vis-à-vis the emperor and the Empire. What if in the fifteenth century the great French vassals had possessed something like that against Louis XI? And thus Myconius is able to write Calvin from Basel in 1542 about the "pestilential dogma of the laymen: *Senatus ecclesia est*" [the civil government is the church].

The Lutheran governments would have protested against joint synods and all common institutions and would have prevented such things by force as an interference with their rule. No Lutheran catholicity came into being, while Calvinism had the makings of one.

In this context there belongs the extremely revealing letter from Luther to the Elector John, dated November 22, 1526.

55. On the Reformation After 1526: The Inevitable Caesaropapism

Myconius wrote to Calvin from Basel in 1542 a letter of the following content: The laymen are presenting a dogma *"valde turbulentum et pestilens"* [very confusing and pestilential], namely *"Senatus ecclesia est"*; they have appropriated to themselves the right to excommunicate. All the former papal power they now claim for the magistracy, asserting that Moses as a secular ruler had given orders to Aaron and that David and the other pious kings had commanded the Levites. Why should it not be the same in the new covenant? Calvin flies into a rage, e.g., when the council of Bern presumes to give the final decision on the faith. But in the early part of the Reformation the governments had simply been given free rein, without anyone protesting.

The people did not have any higher regard for the married priests than for those living in concubinage, and this was one reason for the contempt of the clergy that was bemoaned by the reformers.

There arose no Protestant catholicity. Even Calvinism, whose individual countries later did have a much closer religious connection with one another, achieved the *Synodus Dordracena* only one single time. Lutheranism, on the other hand, displays nothing but territorial churches, some of them quite minute. It lacked the means and the will to form itself into a big community, having become far too much a matter of the individual governments. But these would undoubtedly have prohibited big synods and similar organizations as an interference with their rule. The Caesaropapism of the individual governments is the enemy of everything universal.

Since that time, it has been impossible for Protestantism as a religion to establish *from within itself* an authority with universal validity.

56. On the Coming of the Reformation: The Reformation and the Fate of Art

At this point we must bid farewell to German art which at that very time seemed to be in the most glorious ferment before the consummation it was destined for. The fact that all the famous artists, starting with Dürer, were for the Reformation was probably in part due to their hatred of a high clergy which spent its enormous endowments on anything rather than the commissioning of altar works.

The Reformation deprived art not only of its main subjects, but also of true naïveté, which probably would have maintained itself merely because of the penetration of the Renaissance. It was as though one had suddenly prohibited the Greeks in the highest early flowering of their art from depicting their myths and left them only portraits, historical subjects, and genre painting (cf. Islam's prohibition of painting). The still unbroken strength of the Germans would have succeeded entirely in assimilating the Renaissance and blending it with the great Italian art; there would have been no half-style as in the Netherlands. In addition, in many regions there was outright destruction of paintings.

Since only very few were able to participate seriously and inwardly in the suddenly demanded sublime emphasis on ethics in religion and, at the same time, there was a general and very sharp split into parties, a feeling of inward pressure and a timid reserve became characteristic for those intellectuals on whose support art ordinarily depended. If people had no more sensible arguments against paintings, as, e.g., Zwingli and Leo Jud at the Zurich main dispute of 1523, they said that the admissibility of paintings could not be demonstrated from the Bible and *that* was why they had to go.

A decisive factor was that even in the areas which had nominally remained Catholic, Protestantism for many decades actually dominated the minds of men, at least of the non-peasants. Whether it went deep is a matter of indifference. Church art came to a standstill there, too, so that later, with the Counter Reformation, Italian art immediately gained predominance.

The change in people is very strikingly revealed through portraits. At the beginning of the sixteenth century there prevails in paintings and sepulchral sculptures the utmost openness and strength; from 1530 on everything appears dammed up and anxious.

That, basically, artistic feeling and joy in the beautification of life had not ceased is shown by the architecture and ornamentation of the German Renaissance.

Come to think of it, aside from some boasting about Dürer, whom probably everyone would have liked to do his portrait, German humanism had even before the Reformation been rather hostile to art, or at least completely aloof from it, as were the philosophers in antiquity. In reference to the luxurious tomb of Thomas à Becket and the marble splendor of the Certosa di Pavia, Erasmus preaches the most insipid "charity," saying that the money ought to have been given to the poor and that flowers were sufficient adornment for a saint's grave. (The poor of the time would soon have consumed the money concerned, and we would not possess the Certosa, etc.) Then Erasmus polemicizes against the artistic embellishment of noble graves in the churches generally.

57. On the Situation of the Catholic Church: The Direct Effect of the Reformation

Through his writings of 1520–1521 Luther had already placed an abyss between himself and the church. He no longer demanded reform of its head and limbs, but the destruction of its entire organism, the abolition of the ritual and of several sacraments; only the sermons were to remain.

This rage of the reformers against the old church was there before the church was able to exert the slightest repression; it is not the effect of persecution, but rather, in part, of self-stifling. Actually, in the lands where the Reformation was victorious, there immediately set in the most colossal spoliation.

Catholic princes, clergy, and peoples knew from the very outset that they faced complete suppression as soon as their adversaries were strong enough; all writings of the reformers demanded the eradication of the old church. Thus there was to be expected, on the Catholic side, a fight for self-preservation which would be just as unrestrained in its methods. As for the Protestants, in their lucid moments they must have foreseen such a future resistance, if they still knew the Catholic church at all. Hence their theory of the destruction of the Catholics later was supported by the conclusion that the Catholics for their part would take the most extreme reprisals once they regained power.

The accomplishment of a thousand years, the vessel of a religion, the correlate of a thoroughly formed popular custom had been stolen from them and destroyed. And in Germany this had not even happened in tragic battle, but with a sudden appeal to general undisciplined action, beside which the positive new "faith" meant little.

This explains the fearful determination to absolute repression from the start, by any means at all, in *the countries not yet overrun*, especially France.

From the beginning, the purposes of the confiscating governments were served only by a complete dogmatic defection from the church. Any compromise between the new and the old would somehow have made their loot uncertain again.

It is a ridiculous assumption that power which otherwise, in all of world history, makes men neither particularly good nor particularly happy, should have accomplished this miracle with the German governments of the sixteenth century just because they were Protestant. And to these rulers the old believers had to submit in mute surrender, because for the time being the rulers had on their side the taste of the masses for no discipline.

But for the Catholic church it was high time for the Lutheran Reformation to come. Without it the church would of itself no longer have been capable of an inner transformation, not even with the most incisive insights of its more serious minds. Even the saintliest pope, if we imagine him surrounded by saintly cardinals and curials, would have availed no more against the general situation (entanglement with all worldliness and all superstition) than did an Adrian VI. Only the most terrible danger brought about *in all countries* the rise of those religious forces that were capable of starting a Counter Reformation.

Protestantism, however, has since then consistently and at times vociferously betrayed the anxiety that, if things were at all allowed to take their natural course, Catholicism would regain the upper hand—and not by force, but for psychological reasons.

58. On Zwingli's Later Period

The Reformation brought on a time in which people felt much closer to their *coreligionists* than to their compatriots.

Even before that, headlong political action and unscrupulous methods had become general practices.

Added to this was the opinion of Zwingli and many contemporaries that through the toleration of a situation not in keeping with their metaphysical concepts the *wrath of God* was incurred on the whole country. (Was this opinion genuine with Zwingli? It might have been his own wrath.)

In this there was a basic difference from Luther, who might have been saying generally, "The world will not exist *that* long!" and who took no responsibility for what the mighty of this world were doing, admitting the wrath of God as a *permanent* scourge. Zwingli, on the contrary, considered himself religiously and politically responsible for the whole situation (or had talked his way into it).

Our assumption of high treason through *foreign partial alliances* in that period is an erroneous one. The contemporaries on both sides did not feel that way.

It was impossible in that period to operate with *numbers of people;* Zwingli "believed" that the poor people in the five cantons of the Catholic interior of Switzerland were suppressed only by the powerful.

In Bern the government certainly made the decisions in the main, for the enormous mass of country folk would surely have remained Catholic and the highlands dared an insurrection because of that. Were things very different even in the common prefectures? At least in the Thurgau and in other places where later they let compulsion cease, after the second battle of Kappel, Catholicism appeared again, partly of itself.

And when it was a question of *war,* Zwingli looked its conditions straight in the face and proposed the methods then in universal use, as early as in the Memorial of 1526, much like an imperial field commander.

His *political* machinations, too, were essentially determined by the goal.

He was an optimist and wanted to establish *new conditions* for all times. His clear intellect told him, even without specific historical knowledge, that every single founder of power who achieved something thought the same way.

What proved to be his undoing was his imagination, which to the last deluded him into thinking that he could sweep *Bern* along. He had particular hopes of this because after 1528 Bern was seriously estranged from the five cantons through the participation of Unterwalden in the revolution of the highlands. But here he faced a wall. Bern wanted primarily to secure its inherited exercise of power under all circumstances, and it cared more deeply for this than for all theology. Politically it acted entirely in its interest for a long time, as it was accustomed to doing. In the wake of the Zwinglian revolution it would have lost its primacy.

It was a good thing that Switzerland at least took care of its own disputes without the intervention of nearby foreign aid on both sides.

It was naive of Zwingli to discountenance very sharply any more masses in the canton of Zurich, but to demand of the five cantons in their own areas tolerance for the "Word of God." This shows that the statesman was carried away by the metaphysician.

59. Charles V and Francis I

Both started their reigns with a legacy of fearsome programs; one (Charles) reaches rock bottom financially, the other (Francis) gets into trouble through enormous indiscretions of his own or of others.

Both confronted frequently unpaid soldiers who are capable of reaching for the first security that presents itself, including the commander-in-chief. (Even the unpaid Swiss of Charles VIII were ready, after the battle of Foronuovo, to seize him and send him off to Switzerland.) War aims and politics were constantly subject to the disturbances resulting from this.

Charles was visibly impelled toward world monarchy in the sense that his very scattered and in many places vulnerable power forced him to keep committing hostile acts against the potential or actual center of the small powers, France. The smaller nations were in part actually threatened, in part they believed themselves to be continually threatened. Francis was a center and Charles a periphery.

Charles and Francis had to give themselves the appearance of wanting to protect the church and yet secretly they were full of thoughts of secularization which were somewhat dispelled only by enormous partial concessions on the part of the clergy and the pope.

The modern state in their hands is constantly insolvent and has its reason of state for every robbery.

France's further national development is now determined by the opposition to Hapsburg Spain, as previously by the opposition to England. This is later interrupted only by the brief period of the Ligue. The enormous inner coherence and the omnipotence of royalty as a banner is increased in the process.

60. On Charles V

(I) His power was at bottom an unhappy and chimerical one, apart from the facts that his financial means were entirely inadequate in relation to the extent and dispersal of his territories, and that the muttering Netherlands could not eternally foot the bill for everyone.

His generally assumed striving for universal monarchy or, at any rate, for supreme command over the entire Occident had a highly irritating effect. His adversaries felt entitled to the most unnatural alliances and to attacks at will.

France he was never able to satisfy or pacify, even though in 1540 he may have dedicated himself to this idea and had the policies of Constable Montmorency in his favor.

For a time he had seriously thought of making great sacrifices, was about to give Milan or the Netherlands to a French prince and make him his son-in-law. But Francis was still hoping to get Milan or something else *without* Charles's good will. If they had reached an understanding, they would have crushed the Reformation and would also have been able to subdue the Turks. At the same time they would have finished off all republics. (All this was roughly Montmorency's program also.)

Instead of this, Francis again took up with the Turks.

Charles, however, had only become more active and belligerent as his health declined, as though he wanted to use the presumptive last years of his strength for decisive blows, so as to be able to close the account.

He let himself be carried away to fight the Schmalkaldic war partly due to his urgent desire to finish the job, partly because of his deep repugnance for the Reformation, which was in such strong ferment in the Netherlands as well. But his alliance with Duke Maurice, who was allowed to trade upon his Protestantism, was a vital defect in the whole undertaking. For Maurice the temptation once more to make deals against Charles with Protestantism in the face of the hated interregnum was entirely too strong, and the alliance with France was too easy for a man like Maurice. The Turks were also on the march again.

Charles later may have stuck too obstinately to the siege of Metz. And yet he acted here in an entirely imperial manner and would have put his opponents to shame if they could have been put to shame.

At the very end, after the alternating of the two lines in the Empire had failed (did Charles give it up quite officially?), he again resorted to the idea of a division. A second son of Philip, expected by the Catholic Mary, was to receive an Anglo-Burgundian empire.

His abdication at Brussels was the most pathos-filled scene of his life. He felt and showed more emotion than at any other moment.

(What would have happened if the house of Hapsburg had in 1519 put Ferdinand instead of Charles on the imperial throne and then nevertheless waged a joint war against Islam? One thing would have been prevented by this: France's sticking together with the German Protestants.)

At Charles's abdication at Brussels, when he said that his times of greatest happiness had been marred by so many disagreeable things that he had never felt complete contentment, the hall was still draped in mourning for Juana; there were no funds for special decorations. For the same reason Charles had to wait four months for passage to Spain.

When Charles abdicated, the lands of the house of Savoy and the Lorraine bishoprics were in French hands; Charles, to be sure, kept Milan and Naples.

(II) Charles's greatest vindication always lies in his leadership against Islam. In his conscience he was always able to feel like the shield of Christendom and to refer back to this. The relationship was an actuality for him when he was king of Spain, and even more so when he was the emperor. Even if he did not get around to this task directly until about 1530, his wars before that date must be recognized as preparatory work. Of course, for the war against the Turks, the forces of the entire Occident gathered in one hand were scarcely sufficient.

Charles's tendency to rule over the church is reminiscent of Maximilian I's two-time designs on the papacy.

The two other great tasks were the ecclesiastical problem and the fight against the house of Valois and its allies.

Italians such as Contarini emphasize his seriousness, his brand of devotion to duty, his inclination toward melancholia, and his good memory for insults.

At Worms in 1521 he told the princes very clearly that in addition to his many other crowns he had also desired the imperial one—not out of self-interest, but for the sake of the Empire itself which was only a shadow and which he wanted to bring to the top again, devoting his body and soul to it. This alone may have sounded suspicious to those who had let themselves be bought to elect him.

Marino Giustiniani in 1540 discussed Charles's chances if he himself were to embrace the Reformation. Instead of that, his permanent desire was a reform of the Catholic clergy, in the Spanish rather than the German sense, which was certainly a heritage of Ferdinand and Isabella and their reform.

Characteristic of his personality is the answer he gave when his councilors held before him the example of Caesar concerning the complete exploitation of victories: "The ancients had only one goal before their eyes, honor. We Christians have two, honor and the salvation of the soul."

(III) To sum up: In the end, through Charles V, Spain did become and remain *the* great power. And the Spaniards themselves, no matter how they might fare, considered themselves the only great power. It took the greatest effort to beat Spain to the ground long after Charles V.

61. On Henry VIII

A mixture rare among princes: Henry VIII is at once a lout and a devil.

Yet in the face of terrible special forces which could break forth again out of the dark it can be highly desirable for the general welfare that one person wield the rod. And such a person then can behave as he pleases, circumstances permitting.

62. Gustavus Vasa

Gustavus Vasa, unlike Henry VIII, did not inherit a paternal, well-mastered empire and a treasury.

He was simply on hand when the Swedes needed a leader in order to throw off the Danes. And when the pressure of the moment determined that such a man should most appropriately appear as a king, he knew how to act. It was very useful to him that Christian II was expelled by the Danes, which meant that he was spared a war with Denmark, and that Frederick I of Denmark recognized the identity of his interests with those of Gustavus. It was not necessary to wage war for the three crowns.

One conclusion a posteriori about his very extraordinary personality is permissible. Above all, he did everything himself and had no Wolsey and no Thomas Cromwell.

Suddenly he *is* all of Sweden. And then Sweden suddenly has a will and experiences her military and political day in world history, although the question remains whether, on the whole, this was to her fortune. But what Sweden has done since that time quite obviously goes back to Gustavus Vasa, without whom it would be unthinkable.

He must have been the prototype of a Swede, so that his nation was able to recognize itself in him.

His dreadful side is displayed only in connection with expediency and is not entangled with murderous matrimonial matters, as with Henry VIII.

63. The Community of the Elect

Luther had developed his doctrine according to the Bible as he understood it and had in his creed effaced everything papist. To be a Lutheran meant to be severed from the Roman Catholic church. The governments which attached themselves to his doctrine completely rooted out the papist elements in their areas. Their people then gradually became subject to a new ecclesiastical organism. We know the laments of Luther and all Lutheran reformers about their behavior otherwise: that the stopping of good works had brought about a total brutalization. But Luther considered his responsibility as fulfilled when the people remained removed from any papist influence; the rest he left to God—and he was not the governor of the electorate of Saxony. Next to the pulpit there come the secular authorities and not a controlling presbytery. Compulsion is confined chiefly to a person's no longer being allowed to be a Catholic.

But he knew quite well that in addition to all this there still existed a doctrine of election by divine grace, of predestination, based chiefly on *Romans,* IX, and Luther went into this question in his *De servo arbitrio.*

But Luther at least did not concern himself more closely with the doctrine of the small number of the elect, their general proportion, which gives the doctrine of predestination its full fearfulness.

The Anabaptists had wanted to constitute a people of the elect, but their appeal to the spirit was anarchic and their goals, where they were able to organize, were in the beginning crassly materialistic; their decline was inevitable. Nevertheless, Hans Denk had taught the eventual blessedness even of the damned, including devils, which was consistent with the vision of a world empire. It uses ἀποκατάστασις ἁπάντων [the redemption of everybody] as final decoration.

The effect of the Reformation on Europe was, in the first decades, German, Lutheran. Its distinguishing doctrine was that of justification by faith, its distinguishing outward feature the complete abolition of good works. As for its form, wherever it could, it submitted to the state as a territorial church.

The first Protestants in France, England, Italy, and Spain were, or were called, Lutherans. The propaganda of Zwinglianism outside of Switzerland died out with the battle of Kappel. Denmark and Sweden became strictly Lutheran states.

However, toward the end of the 1540's a new spirit becomes discernible in the Western countries: Calvinism. It becomes the Reformation of those countries that had an antipathy toward the Germans. Its characteristic doctrine was that of predestination, its distinguishing form the community which, if possible, was to be a community of the elect. Wherever it is able to do so it controls the state or at least does its best to impose its point of view upon it. Through their elders the communities supervise private life.

Subsequently this doctrine proves capable, to a much greater degree than the Lutheran, of forming communities in countries where the governments maintain Catholicism by force. Moreover, a doctrine of the "few elect" is necessarily missionary, something that Lutheranism never was.

It fights in France and is victorious in Scotland and Holland. In England it is met halfway by an old Lollard religion with its own doctrine of the small number of the elect. Furthermore, the Reformation takes this new direction after 1547, not as a free one, but with the imposition of a rigidly organized state church with royal supremacy against which the absolute spirit of predestination later has to stand its ground as a sect (later the Puritans).

64. On Calvin

(I) Here the dogma is not the sole decisive factor, but rather, in substance, the dominion of religion over the state.

Where the state rules, as in every Lutheran country and, on the Calvinist side, in suprematist England—and in the Bern region—the people bear this without any particular inward involvement, and, conversely, because they do this, the state is able to rule.

Lutheranism is extremely weak, even with the greatest numerical diffusion, as soon as it has to proceed without the government, merely with superintendents, synods, and the like. A case in point is the German-Austrian lands; here the needful desperation must have been wholly lacking at the time of the Counter Reformation (with the exception of Upper Austria at the time of the Peasants' War of 1626). Here Protestantism had on its side the powerful nobility; independently it lived only in a segment of the urban population.

One hardly notices the people who are becoming Lutheran cooperating with their North German governments in any way except by breaking fast and other things, generally negative ones.

Calvinists, on the other hand, are able to establish communities and a church in areas under Catholic rule, from below, through the inward impetus of the doctrine of the elect which carries with it the necessary desperation and a scornful mortal hatred of Catholicism.

From this a *Presbyterian* organization results naturally. In countries where the government does not cooperate or still is Catholic the community cannot possibly consist *only* of preachers and listeners; only where the preacher is assured of a stock of select laymen does it come into being and really exist.

If, in addition, the Calvinist *dogma* encounters a highly congenial national spirit, as in Scotland and with the English Puritans, there arises a complete dominion, even over the state and the life of the citizenry. On the other hand, the zeal for predestination of the masses in Holland in 1618 has always been suspect to me. The Scots remain pessimistic and poor; the Dutch want to become rich and are oriented toward the world, acquisition, and possession. (Hm? Calvinism, with its certainty of unique chosenness is, at bottom, even more comfortable and consolatory than Lutheranism.) To what extent can present-day North America be given as an example? Frantic money-making is hardly compatible with a belief in the small number of the elect from eternity.

Here, too, the activity against Catholicism from the very beginning is even more filled with execration and scorn than it is with Luther. The Catholic church is from the very first threatened with complete destruction because its substance is regarded as idolatry. Thus the Catholic defense is adjusted to this.

A dubious aspect of the presbyterial organization was the fact that it was far from making the church popular. It led to distressing tyranny and provoked opposition. These moral courts were always held only in small towns and villages where everyone knew everyone else. Selected lay elders who sit in judgment on their fellow citizens are, on the one hand, subject to the temptation to give rein to personal advantage, revenge, and malevolence, and, on the other hand, are prone to the corruption that attaches to any system of informers and to general hatred and suspicion which finds *them* suspect, too. What one will put up with from a clergyman who is outside of daily life one will not tolerate from one's equals.

(II) Calvin's goal is to "build a community standing under the discipline of God's word and the Holy Spirit," unlike Luther, who left it to the power of the gospel to penetrate into the masses of the people.

Farel had already started with a reform of morals in Geneva. But only Calvin, from 1537 on, successfully insisted on its being carried out, and upon his return in 1541 he organized Geneva into a community in his spirit, with a Presbyterian organization and with discipline.

The relationship of the community to predestination was as follows: Since the small number of the elect from eternity cannot be ascertained and only God knows His chosen, this church is not to be confused with the visible church community, which contains those who profess externally, as well as true members of the invisible church, as long as sermons and sacraments are handled properly. This is also the reason why one should not detach oneself from the visible church.

Now Calvin arranges his visible church according to this mixture of *few* elect and *many* hypocrites. He will at least outwardly tolerate no resistance against the purity of the appearance. The godless must be kept in bounds, i.e., become dissemblers. (He does not want to win them over, nor to create faith in general, because, after all, the believers have been elected from eternity; only secondarily is the church discipline also a friendly means of punishment for fallen elect.) For this he enlisted in large measure the aid of the secular powers which, to be sure, he had inspired. His highest ecclesiastical authority, the Consistory, which at the same time administered the church discipline, had three-fifths secular members and a syndic as president. Another part of this system was the continual visiting of families and individuals.

That is why finally everything was suspect to Calvin, and the slightest gleam of resistance, not just of the ecclesiastical but also of the political and personal kinds, was unbearable to him. He spent far too much time on those who he knew or suspected were not for him. In the end he knew that he was hated by the great majority. All actual or supposed opposition he had to take personally.

It is a psychological fact that at any time there are a certain number of people who persistently concern themselves with the *petit nombre des élus* [small number of the elect]. That is a necessary consequence and development of the stricter New Testament doctrine of the beyond. These people are recognizable among the English Lollards of the fourteenth century (Knyghton). They will at any time readily renounce the earthly comforts of other people. Their view is necessarily also a wide one, since in their vicinity there might be too few *élus*. Thus Calvin, too, desired to attach the *élus* of all nations to himself. Geneva was his workshop and no more; for example, it could not be passed off as a besieged fortress. He knew that his emissaries incurred the greatest danger of destruction. It was a misfortune for France that its chances for reformation came entirely into Calvin's hands.

Opposed to Luther, he agrees with Zwingli in that he, too, must completely dominate a small republic as a proving ground of ecclesiastical and political life. Even later, Calvinism is complete only where it can enforce its kind of policing through a mass of people (Presbyterians and others) or through full disposition over the secular arm—e.g., in Scotland and for a time in Holland, also in England at the time of the Commonwealth. But dogmatic Calvinists are bad ones! Yet everywhere there begins a quiet inner defection as soon as the life and business of the world put individuals in an optimistic mood.

(III) It has been necessary to erect whole bastions of palliation around Calvin's behavior in Geneva (the downfall of Servetus and other things). In fact and truth, the real Geneva had the greatest possible antipathy toward him. The deep humiliation of the fact that people had had to put up with him nevertheless could best be masked through subsequent idealization.

The tyranny of one single individual who makes his subjectivity the universal law and not only enslaves or expels all other convictions,

including very good *Protestant* ones, but also every day insults everyone in the most innocent matters of taste, has never been carried farther.

Geneva endured him, the greatest pessimist, the stranger. Afterwards
she herself produced the man who, despite his plaintiveness, was the
world's greatest optimist: J. J. Rousseau, the preacher of the goodness
of human nature, which is the view currently held by the masses all
over the world.

(IV) *Calvin's effect upon the West.* First, he had an influence on France
through his writings, his correspondence, and his emissaries. The latter
he often sent to certain destruction (?), and on this one can have one's
special opinion just as in the case of Mazzini. In great matters he found
the stage already occupied by the Renaissance and profane blasphemy
(cf. Calvin's revealing work *De Scandalis,* 1550). The subsequent movement against the court and government of Henry II found Calvinism
present and made *partial* use of it.

Without the participation of the French nobility after 1555, which
happened for anything but dogmatic reasons, his work would have
been in vain.

However, in England, starting with Edward VI, the local Protestantism clearly had a Calvinistic complexion (a transformation of the Lollard one?).

Scotland knew only Calvinism from the outset.

In the Netherlands, where as late as the 1530's the more extreme
defection was Anabaptism, the Reformation was Lutheran; Calvinism
comes to the fore in the 1550's and becomes the active faction.

65. On Protestantism in France

Royalty did not need it economically, because it had already
made the church property indirectly subservient to it through the concordat and its consequences. Anyway, in a confiscation it would have
had to share with the nobles to a considerable extent.

Hence the government, which in France has of old had such great scope, did not give the signal for undisciplined behavior and depredation, in contrast with Germany.

Besides, there was this great difference between the behavior of the French and the German city populations: In France, the burghers and proletarians nowhere waxed enthusiastic about the stopping of good works, the breaking of the fast, and other things, although part of the nobility did. This aspect of Protestantism was not for a moment popular with the masses, even though in France the clergy was probably mocked no less than it was in Germany.

Added to this there was the firm resolve of all authorities under Francis I to prevent the penetration of Lutheranism by every possible means. One absolute, namely Luther's view of the Catholic church, was confronted with an equally strong absolute.

When Calvin's doctrine appeared, it did, to be sure, prove capable of driving a small minority, which was small even under the Huguenots, to the utmost resistance. But the nation as a whole was completely antipathetic toward it, because it demanded a dominion even over the innermost parts of man, and a Frenchman can stand this sort of thing less than anyone else.

Calvinism, however, demanded not merely tolerance, i.e., its little place in the sun—far from it—but destruction of idolatry. Anne du Bourg spoke in the *séance royale* of *"turpitude romaine."*

66. German Culture Around 1555

The Reformation had an extremely strong effect even on the areas which stayed rather aloof from it.

There had not been much to spoil in poetry as far as is discernible in literature before 1517. And now there at least was the Protestant church hymn, and the language had been refined by Luther. But earlier there had been Catholic church hymns as well. Moreover, in all of literature in general, the *intercourse,* the *cohesion of all German lands* was extraordinarily heightened; everything, including poetry, was now much less provincial than before.

The great sacrifice had to be made by sculpture and painting. With the fall of Catholicism both had lost nine-tenths of their occupation at a high point of their development, even before they had been able to take the step from achieved truth to life to perfect beauty. Now they were reduced to portraits, allegories, medallions, coats of arms, and the like. They were also too weak to achieve a live inward transformation of the Italian influence. No longer fructified by the best Italian art, they vacillate between affectation and unlovely realism, no longer capable of expressing with their own means the highest idealism of the nation.

Only secular architecture was in a better state now. It displays an original transformation of the Italian Renaissance, an application to ideas which are still basically medieval, similar to what was done in France (Heidelberg, Offenbach, Mainz, Stuttgart, Bamberg, and other cities; after 1600, the castle at Munich, Aschaffenburg, and other things).

Beside the theological squabbles within Protestantism, which were now raging insufferably, science, which was mainly in secular hands, manifested itself as one of the highest fruits of the intellect which had been awakened by the Reformation even more than by the Renaissance.

There appeared a great and important interest in philology, with personalities like Joachim Camerarius, Hieronymus Wolf, and others, at whose disposal the Basel editions and publishers placed themselves. The study of Roman law was represented by, e.g., Gregor Haloander, medicine was advanced by Paracelsus and Vesalius, natural history by Conrad Gessner, and astronomy by Copernicus (1473–1543). In historical research and presentation there are Sleidan and the Magdeburg Centuriators in Germany, and in Switzerland, Tschudi, Stumpf, Anselm, and Pantaleon of Basel as translators and authors of historical works. In cosmography there are active such men as Sebastian Münster and Gerhard Mercator.

67. On Camoëns' *Lusiads*

Camoëns was a great poet, full of passion for his cause, and was *entitled* to give form to the heroic story of Portugal.

His cast of thought and enthusiasm are such and so suffuse the *Lusiads* from beginning to end that the colorful and curiously composed work seems all of a piece. And Camoëns wrote at a time when the whole strength that he apotheosizes was still alive.

The entire epic is evenly permeated with the glory of Portugal and with patriotism, as a force still alive, not merely in retrospect, as with Italian epics about Scipio and the like. On the whole, everything has a purpose, something that had long since been impossible in Italy.

It must be of great value to Portuguese families to be named in Camoëns. In Vasco da Gama's expedition he comprises *all* of Portuguese history, previous and subsequent, in three great episodes: first, the kings before the lord of Melinde; then, the picture gallery of the heroes and generals on the boat; and finally, in the speech of Thetis, the discoverers, the viceroys, and others. It is an encyclopedia of glory, possessing which a real Portuguese can do without all the other literature of his country. Every poetic and universally human feature that is salvageable has been preserved in the *Lusiads*.

It is a unique thing in literary history that here, in a historical rather than a semi-mythical period, there speaks a man who, in his person, is entirely a kindred spirit to his heroes and has had the amplest share in their battles, privations, and victories. Camoëns is accustomed to dealing blows to Mohammedans and Malabar Indians, probably fighting one against ten. No dust from the road whirls in his poem, but the salt of the sea; it is life on shipboard, sinewy, severely simple, fine-blooded, replete with martial fervor to the point of extreme fanaticism. It, too, is austere. Nothing but the roaring of the sea and the clangor of arms is audible.

He repeatedly voices profound complaints about his nation's harsh, austere insensitivity to poetry; it is still wholly caught up in acting and acquiring and is not yet ready to listen. And yet he expressed its feeling clearly and completely at a time which still tolerated true feeling. And only today, when people talk much more about poetry, would he be completely lost; the cities would either ignore him or seize upon his palpable imperfections and finish him off.

Camoëns still satisfied the best of his times and of his nation. There is no longer any satisfying the best of *our* times!

Os Lusiades, the Lusitanians! It is the whole glory of the nation, but simply more or less loosely tied onto one central point, the voyage of Vasco da Gama.

To portray each of da Gama's colleagues individually would have been not only superfluous but impossible, since every time the same Portuguese hero would have emerged. The composition of the epic as a whole is completely *sui generis.*

Camoëns utilizes the old world of the gods, to be sure, without having any ideas of whom he is dealing with.

About the Spaniards he is almost completely silent.

Further, he expresses his thought not only in the actions and speeches of his heroes, but also directly, and these passages are among the most powerful. The erstwhile lyric poet becomes a Jeremiah and prophet against the mighty, the courtiers, fawners, epicureans, even against wicked priests. At the end he addresses a very earnest exhortation to Don Sebastian to seek for the tremendously brave and devoted nation more liberal laws and better ministers. He offers himself to Alexander as an adviser on the expedition to Africa.

Camoëns is not a poet for an entire civilized world, as was Homer. The culture of all later times does depend on Greek, but not on Portuguese, culture. Also, he is not for all moods, but national, narrow, obtrusive! But he was of inestimable value to a nation sentenced to early, undeserved bondage.

A national drama was not granted to this nation. But before the Spanish conquest Camoëns compressed all the stirring moments of its great history into his *Lusiads*.

Perhaps the epic had an invisible and yet substantial share in the uprising against the Spaniards in 1640.

68. On the Counter Reformation

Its originators and further propagators had the best consciences in the world, such as one can have only when one puts an end to an enormous wrong, an unparalleled spoliation. Moreover, they were at least as confident of their Christianity as were their adversaries. Their task was not by any means merely a cancellation, but primarily the prevention of further collapse. They entered in the middle of such a process and pitted themselves against it. What must have substantially sustained the leaders among them was the vision before their inner eye of a church that was renewed, purified, and oriented toward religious forces. In personal dedication they were fully equal to their opponents. The only thing lacking was for the papacy to come substantially under their guidance, indeed, into their hands.

German and Swiss Protestantism had from the outset indulged in those things that one can permit oneself in the certainty of being the stronger forever. Now it was to be revealed that this was by no means such an absolute thing.

That reform within the church which Luther had made impossible after 1520 now actually came about, but under the auspices of the papacy itself. The transformation of the world that had emanated from Germany necessitated an *inner* restoration of the church which then received the help, albeit selfish, of powerful states. Meanwhile there broke out world wars in which the two religions became the mainspring and the battle cry. And now the old church could in many countries be saved completely again and develop its new style.

69. St. Ignatius Loyola

He was born in Guipúzcoa and was thus a Castilian, something not without value for his career. As an officer he was extraordinarily ambitious; he swept the others along in maintaining the defense of Pamplona.

It certainly made some difference that he possessed, on the one hand, the bearing and habit of power of an officer and, on the other, the general background of a man of culture and station. In his conduct toward people of all kinds, even powerful ones, he was then not subject to the sudden changes and unpredictable behavior which commonly appear in a man who has risen from the bottom, from peasant or urban stock.

How much did he associate with the court of the *reyes católicos* [Catholic kings]? He gives us no evidence of this later.

His further career is hard to unify psychologically and presupposes a highly extraordinary, certainly iron personality. He had to complete his pilgrim's life of contemplation and penance. With the vast majority of men there would then have remained only a mendicant or a hermit. What kept him on top must have been, apart from an iron constitution, the joys of mysticism.

To make up for that, he was spared the doctrinal toil of the reformers, the disputes about nuances of faith and exegesis. In a highly desultory fashion he caught up on his studies as an obligation, because he had to become a priest at any price.

His danger was an impulse toward preaching and pastoral pursuits before he was entitled to them. But the inquisitors, who examined him about five times in Spain and France, must each time have quickly convinced themselves of his complete orthodoxy.

His power lay in the fact that he was able early to gather around him companions of subsequent significance, make them completely submissive to himself, and inspire them. He swept along Contarini and Caraffa.

It is a very extraordinary thing that he did not found an order of penance, such as the Trappist order, but an entirely practical one, apparently with extreme intellectual effort, though directed by visions. Here there emerges the old officer. Instead of choir service there resulted a widely varied outside activity.

But in addition he harbored a firm belief in a periodic spiritual regimen or diet: *exercitia spiritualia* [spiritual discipline]. Anyone who underwent it then thought like St. Ignatius. It was no cramming in of a certain mass of knowledge for an examination, because such knowledge one might later throw away with disgust.

For the time being, this order was confirmed at a moment when one wanted to let all existing orders perish as degenerate.

It was utterly impossible to establish a competing institution within Protestantism, whereas the Jesuits were able to induce precisely their most gifted pupils to remain in the order, because they felt happiest there.

70. The Jesuits

Any mere examination of the institutions and the discipline of the order, as based on the *constitutiones* and the *exercitia spiritualia* increases our understanding only moderately. Institutions were not lacking in the other orders, either; but the Jesuits *lived* by them in the decisive periods. Other orders, too, had in stock asseverations and precepts, especially as to obedience.

All very powerful orders are centralistic in effect and are parallels and props of the papal system—for instance, in the thirteenth century the mendicant orders, a veritable undoing for bishops and priests. The Jesuits then made a special cult of the papacy.

Around the middle of the sixteenth century the dangerous situation of the universal church definitely demanded a stronger, more constant activity from the center and a greater availability of ecclesiastical resources in all countries. The Jesuits and the Council of Trent achieved this.

A half-unconscious total will, stronger than the intentions and cal-

culations of Ignatius, his colleagues, and the popes, drove the phenomenon to the fore.

When St. Ignatius (his physiognomy was uncanny!) arrived in Venice
in 1537 with companions and good recommendations to the Spanish
Embassy, he hoped for the friendship of Contarini and Caraffa. But the
latter took him for a swindler and would have nothing to do with him.
Contarini, on the other hand, was soon bewitched by him and became
his protector. In October of 1538 he set out for Rome, with Contarini's
recommendation to the pope himself. After strong resistance Ignatius
prevailed. On September 27, 1540, Paul III sanctioned the founding of
the order.

Strong influences from Ignatius' military past might have shaped the
idea of absolute subordination that is characteristic of his discipline. St.
Pachomius and St. Martin of Tours had also been officers.

The decisive thing about Jesuitism is that *it established close contact between the Spanish reform and its way of thinking and the Roman papacy.*
Henceforth we are concerned with the universal church. Nevertheless,
Charles V and Philip II might still have been of the opinion that they
knew how to guard the interests of religion and church better than the
popes.

The Jesuits are the strongest idealizers of papal power, the infallible
teaching office, the universal episcopate, and papal world dominion.

To what extent did Ignatius himself realize the significance of his
foundation?

71. The Jesuits and the Papacy

A founder who combined a fanatic's devotion to the church
with a mind of military obedience and a few, mostly Spanish, colleagues whom one at first encounters mainly as theologians (Salmerón,
Lainez): these were the beginnings.

Except in Portugal under John III, the dissemination of the order did not even take place very rapidly, and not without resistance even in Spain.

However, the order unfolds a great, intensive life. It gains a disproportionately large number of members who can be put to a variety of practical uses and quickly becomes the driving element of the church.

This church it recognizes substantially in the papacy, and therefore it raises the papal theory to the highest point. In this way it also gains an influence over the papacy, as the mendicant orders did once, and like them has a centralistic influence. In times of struggle it becomes indispensable through the absolute homogeneity of will and the availability and uniformity of its membership.

At such times mere fanaticism does not suffice if it is bound up with fatuous self-will and passion; there must be disciplined fanaticism. The danger lay in the possibility that some day the order would regard as its purpose itself, its own existence and power, instead of the church.

The resistance which the Jesuits encountered at the University of Paris for a time at first probably derived somewhat from Gallicanism as well as from the fear that they might monopolize the legacies, but mainly *"d'aspirer à ruiner l'enseignement salarié de l'Université par leur renseignement* gratuit . . ."* [aim at ruining the paid teaching of the University by their *free* teaching]. However, their Collège de Clermont, Rue St. Jacques, which opened in 1564, maintained itself, but without being attached to the University.

Regarding the power of the Jesuits: It is not so hard for firmly united, clever, and courageous men to do great things in the world. Ten such men affect 100,000, because the great mass of the people have only acquisition, enjoyment, vanity, and the like in their heads, while those ten men always work together.

72. The Third Council of Trent (1562–1563)

(I) It may have been clear to only a few people, perhaps especially to Pius IV (he kept the council from screaming for a long time) and the real church politicians, how enormously important and urgent the goal was, namely, to create a harmonious formula for the reconquest of the world and put an end to the provisional situation behind which all enemies could hide. The seeming efforts to invite Protestant governments as well were not serious.

The major difficulty resulted from the facts that Paul IV had embittered all Catholic governments through his manners and that the papacy had to fight with their greedy special desires as well as their actual problems.

France was at the same time going through its first religious war, and its government, which had been pushed so far to the left even in 1560–1561, at the moment desired great concessions, especially in ritual, in order to impress its Huguenots, too. At the same time it had to maintain its sham glory that everybody at Trent had to dance to its tune; hence the behavior of the pompous Cardinal Guise. Bavaria and Ferdinand I were in a real predicament because Protestantism had penetrated, and Ferdinand was still soured because of Paul IV. Philip II, however, assumed a darkly threatening mien in order to blackmail the worried papacy into further confiscations of church property, a crusade bull, and other things. But then the Spanish bishops propounded the theory, about which the king, too, might possibly have had misgivings, that the episcopate derived directly from Christ and was a divine institution. Finally, there was in reserve the always irritating question as to whether the council was not higher than the pope. And the concrete Pius IV could die *durante concilio* [while the council was going on]!

But the big difference between the third Council of Trent and the first and second was that in the meantime the spirit of the Catholic reform had rapidly become stronger and no longer trembled before the vellеities of a council, but dared to win *through* the council. The atrocious talk about the curia and the clergy had exhausted itself in the first and second councils; now people were no longer afraid of it.

(II) The result had thus been achieved through an understanding between the papacy and the great Catholic courts which had recognized the homogeneity of the papal power and their own as well as the partial identity of their interests, and, begrudging the council any embarrassing initiative independent of themselves, desired its shortening (could Philip II alone have wished for its prolongation?).

The most important thing was that now orthodox dynasties as well as the curia and the inquisition had a definite *coercive formula* by which the world could be bound. Only now were they able to pass from the long defensive to a *regular offensive.*

Church discipline was renewed; the power of excommunication was strengthened; seminaries were established and subjected to every strictness; the parishes were regulated. Regular diocesan and provincial synods were at least desired, as was the visitation of churches. Definite norms were set up for sacraments and sermons. The participation of monks in ecclesiastical life was regulated. The bishops were disciplined and had to sign and swear to a special document regarding the observation of the Tridentine Decrees and complete obedience to the pope. Then the bishops' own authority to punish was defined. In addition to the bishop's oath, *every* cleric now had to make a *professio fidei Tridentina* [Tridentine profession of faith].

The papal theory had hardly been touched at the council, and papal power had been expanded rather than limited. The authorization to *interpret* the Tridentine Decrees for all eternity became exceedingly important. The abuses lucrative for Rome had only been affected slightly, and the appeals and dispensations curtailed somewhat. On the other hand, the annates and the pope's rights over the bishops remained unchanged.

And now there also came into being a new church architecture and a corresponding church style; for the entire ceremonial service had been retained.

Catholicism has since then been "stationary," but certainly to its benefit; for now it was also secured against sinking still deeper into dull superstition and brutalization of the holiness of good works, the doctrine of indulgences, and so on. As for indulgences, trading in them at least was prohibited. To be sure, instead of scholasticism there soon appeared casuistry.

Lutheranism was also stationary, and Calvinism became so. All the religions of the time prohibited their own further development, their "progress." Toward the outside, stationary Catholicism began to live all the more through its forces of the Counter Reformation, which were now tremendously disciplined and applied to definite purposes.

The effect of the Reformation upon the Catholic church had been a beneficial one. With the strict sifting of the doctrine at Trent (henceforth there are no more marginal doctrines and waverings) and the complete crystallization there takes place a rejuvenation in other ways as well.

The permission of the *lay chalice* had been left at the papacy's discretion. In 1564 Emperor Ferdinand and Albrecht of Bavaria actually requested this permission from the pope, but no longer needed to make it an actuality. The Counter Reformation was marching rapidly.

73. The Popes of the Counter Reformation

The terrible popes after Paul IV were indispensable for the curia primarily because without true terrorism it would have mocked at any reforms, as, for instance, vis-à-vis Adrian VI. As long as it could hope to get a mild pope through poisoning wine and other methods, nothing could be done.

74. On the German Counter Reformation

The wry faces with which German seminaries and Benedictines greeted the Jesuits in the beginning were unjustified. For without the effectiveness of the Jesuits they might have succumbed, one after the other, to the Protestants and to secularization.

75. France in the Year 1562

The Catholics, too, were a popular party here, just like the Huguenots.

The great and sudden danger was that the state power, upon which everything depends in France more than anywhere else, had not been strong enough to prevent the arising of two popular *masses* where two distinguished *parties* already existed. Despite all her desire to keep above both, Catherine de Medici was forced actually to veer about between the two.

However, for the military heads of both masses the chances were rather uneven. The Huguenots must have known that in general they would be the weaker by far, while for the Guises the civil war, i.e., the beginning of the *voies de fait* [assault and battery] was the most convenient means of stopping at any time mere deliberations which ended with concessions, to take control, and in the decisive moments to pull the royal house after them.

The only question was to what extent the dissolution of the normal state power and its administration would spread.

Added to this were the unabashed foreign alliances and the foreign recruiting of both parties.

There are nations, religions, and parties which endure minorities and some which do not. Of the French the latter is true, no matter what is concerned.

76. After St. Bartholomew's Night

The refugees and pamphleteers recognized only a religious intention of the action and devised an agreement with the pope and Spain for the eradication of Protestantism as a whole.

However, the action had been aimed at the Huguenots, who were allied with the *politiques,* as a *political* party, especially at Coligny, not as Protestant, but as party head. If the intent had been merely religious, Navarre and Condé would not have been spared.

Regarding the murders in the provinces, it may be remarked that they did not occur at all in precisely those provinces administered by the Guises and their followers—in Picardy, Champagne, Brittany, Dauphiné, Auvergne, Languedoc, Provence. Nothing happened anywhere in the open country.

Where murders were committed, this was because people in the cities concerned had feared armed uprisings and raids by Huguenots with which religious wars had always started. Especially in Lyon people were worried about this. Following the news of the defeat of Mons, a list of the Protestant citizens and their servants was made in Lyon, and those who were not citizens were ordered to leave the city. Governor Mandelot was completely loyal to the king. After the decision of Mons the governors of the most important towns, almost all fortified ones, were commanded to provide for their safety.

To be sure, here, too, the fanatical rabble interfered and continued even after the king had ordered a stop; thus it was in Meaux, Orleans, Bourges, and Lyon. In Rouen and Toulouse the persecution did not break out until the middle of September. In the entire country there were maybe 20,000 casualties. The number of communities decreased little; as late as 1576 there were 2000.

Only if one does not lose sight of the essentially political character of the massacre of St. Bartholomew does one comprehend the following: that the French government did not join with Philip II; that it did not pass into the hands of the Guises whom Charles continued to hate; that Charles IX in the Declarations of August 26 and 28, in which he takes the responsibility for everything, declares that the Edict of St. Germain remains in force. But the Huguenot ritual practices were curtailed, "for the protection of the Protestants themselves from mob excesses," as was explained for the benefit of foreign countries. The Montmorencys remained in the royal council. Philip and Alba for the time being were pacified by the court's complete dissociation from Coligny's Netherlands activities; but the desire for Flanders continued, with only its fulfillment postponed. Geneva, in its concern over Savoy and Spain, was hastily assured of French protection, and soon negotiations with Orange were being carried on again. The project of a marriage between Elizabeth of England and François d'Alençon, the brother of Charles IX, continued on its course. Where is it that one reads about Elizabeth receiving the French envoy in mourning? She was the first to congratulate Charles IX on the averted danger!

In Poland the French court constantly leaned on the Protestant faction in order to accomplish the election of the Anjou. To frustrate this became a major assignment of the refugee Huguenot writers, especially in Geneva: Hotman, Donneau. They painted the conduct of the royal house and the Guises in the most horrible colors.

That the king took everything upon himself and asserted categorically that the Guises and others had acted on his orders was a formal French practice, on account of the prevalent idea that nothing could happen except by royal order. He fabricated a four-year premeditation on top of that.

Later, when the Huguenots had gained the upper hand again and the court had turned against the Guises (1576), Charles's share was decreased again and the action itself disavowed. Later still, under the Bourbons, the Valois were treated with consideration and left out of the picture, and the murder plan was laid at the door of the Guises.

The main sorrow in the period of 1572, however, did not pertain to the number of casualties or the perfidy of the proceedings, but to the frustration of the great seizure of power by the party which had been about to seize the crown, take Belgium, and push Catholicism back over the Alps and the Pyrenees. This frustration was *la grande trahison* [the great betrayal].

Instead of this, the court continued with the policies of Henry II: repression of Protestantism at home and Protestant alliances abroad.

The court thought it had by no means committed a "crime" that would have to be palliated, neither Charles nor Anjou nor Catherine de Medici nor the Guises and the fanatical citizens of Paris. No one denied his participation, except the court later, and then for political rather than moral reasons.

77. Murder as an Expedient

It stands to reason that in the absence of any legal recourse one judges one's own cause and that a government or an individual undertakes the destruction of an adversary.

The next nuance would be that one could arrest one's opponent, but not judge him without dangerous currents of feeling, uprisings, and other consequences, and that as a rule one would be too late to thwart plots and the like. Here applies the saying: *Salus reipublicae suprema lex esto* [the safety of the state shall be the supreme law].

Not only princes indulged in murder, especially after the latter part of the Middle Ages, but also cities, such as Augsburg and others; secret agents were kept for this sort of thing. In the sixteenth century Ferdinand I had Martinucci killed, and Philip II Escovedo. In addition, the supposed secret executions "on the black velvet" should be mentioned.

The second side of this is the scholarly and at times also popular view that *tyrannicide* is permissible, even commendable.

On this they all agree: "gentle" Melanchthon and even Luther. The former desires it against Henry VIII, after the execution of Thomas Cromwell. Later the Jesuits represented a corresponding view.

Religious zeal unfailingly produces this phenomenon and its commendation on both sides. In 1563, when their cause was extremely hard pressed, the Huguenot preachers saw their only salvation in the murdering of François de Guise and publicly praised Poltrot as a tool of God. Later it happened likewise on the Catholic side with Jacques Clément, the murderer of King Henry III.

78. The Special Character of the French Court

It consists in the king's always being surrounded by factions which divide favors and offices among themselves, or get everything into their hands, if possible.

The parties at the court of Philip II, such as those of Alba and of Ruy

Gomez in their contrast, are of a quite different kind, and the country need not find out about it. The Tudors, including Elizabeth, completely dominate their court, according to their own changing caprices. Here only the minority of Edward VI made a difference.

At the French court the women are powerful, and not the queens. Catherine de Medici becomes something only as a regent. Around the court there is general and continual gossip, a general attentiveness to the chances for favor or disfavor. It was the subsequent misfortune of the royal house that the crown got into a "false position," like anyone who is to represent right or fairness, i.e., the permanent interests of the nation among raging factions. In the face of passions, the representative of right has always been in such a position.

On the course and the *result of the French religious wars* depended the religious fate of the entire West. France determined the continuation, or restoration, of Catholicism in Belgium, Switzerland, and Germany, even its safeguarding in Italy and Spain, at least indirectly. Things would have happened differently everywhere if France had become Huguenot.

But in that case things could have turned out rather strikingly! The Huguenot king would have got into the hands of a fanatical Huguenot preacher faction and been forced to act toward all of Europe as an intervening and conquering Calvinist caliph—a Calvinist Louis XIV. For all around people would have had cause (N.B. toward Lutherans as well) *"de venger Dieu et sa sainte église"* [to avenge God and His holy church], and the preachers had within themselves the never-extinguished passion against everything that was different from the way they were. However, the French nation could, as always, have been appeased only by constant successes on the outside.

79. On the Conversion of Henry IV

Once Henry IV had, through Henry III's death, become king not only of the Huguenots but also of the Catholic royalists, his conversion had to come as well; he was being crowded.

He was, above all, a king and a Frenchman; the rest had to follow. After 1560 the Huguenots were an armed political party like any other.

The possibility of a Gallican patriarchy was a mere dream at that time; Henry IV was no Henry Tudor and did not live on an island; the Tridentine Counter Reformation with its positive zeal was already flooding 'round all religious relationships.

Added to this was the general exhaustion, including that of the Huguenots. Gabrielle d'Estrées was converted, too, and after the end of 1591 Henry's own mind must have been made up. His *ministres courtisans* [courtier ministers] must intentionally defend the Huguenot faith only weakly in disputations. Even Duplessis-Mornay let himself be involved in a matter of conversion (to what extent was he really beguiled?). Sully later even boasts of having done his share for conversion. The written dissuasions of Beza, the spiritual adviser of Gabriel d'Amour and others, were in vain, as were those of d'Aubigné who wanted to make the king understand in conversation that it was "better to be king in a corner of France and to serve God and be surrounded with loyal servants than . . . etc."

Henry IV took Catholic instruction, i.e., a six-hour conversation, and on July 25, 1593, ceremoniously renounced heresy at St. Denis. Crowds of Parisians looked on, in spite of Mayenne's order to close the gates and the declaration of nullity by the papal legate.

Despite his best inner intentions in favor of the Huguenots, henceforth there existed in Henry an ill-feeling against them and their complaints. At the same time, however, he had to take care of them, since now there were various new attacks on them. Sully remained a Protestant, possibly out of arrogance; in general Henry IV very much desired the conversion of others.

The absolution by Clement VIII tore apart the Spanish plans for world hegemony. This had been counseled by San Filippo Neri, Baronius, the Jesuit general Francesco Toledo (although a Spaniard), the government of Venice, and others.

Before the Edict of Nantes there were in France over a hundred *terre chiuse* [closed lands] and about a thousand *parrochie e monasterii* [parishes and monasteries]. Catholic ritual had ceased entirely.

The Edict of Nantes was a necessary and unavoidable confirmation of a state of truce in which all factions were to be included.

To be sure, it marks the beginning of the decline of French Protestantism; its fruitfulness ceases. It exists notoriously as a minority and delimited, and must remain so, but at the same time it must greatly burden itself with secular, political affairs, now methodically and perpetually. In this it remains at an increasing disadvantage with the henceforth very bigoted governments and the clergy.

A paradox: the greatest boon for the Huguenot community was not the Edict of Nantes, but its revocation.

80. Holland

(I) The northern provinces consisted of Holland, Zeeland, West Friesland, Utrecht, Overyssel, Groningen, Gelderland, also of the Lands General, a large section of Northern Brabant, and sections of Flanders. These were always treated as conquered territory, were a sort of common prefecture comparable to the Swiss subject lands. Up to the sixteenth century these regions were little noticed; after their fight against Spanish rule—detachment from Spain and Calvinism went hand in hand—their fame was great. Here was a new nation, a new culture, a new world power; in battle it always seemed to gain new strength. On its success visibly depended the whole fate of Western Europe.

For two decades this entire development hinged on William of Orange; without him neither the rise nor its continuation would be conceivable. Spain itself acknowledged this through the high price on his head. When he was finally murdered, his people had advanced so far and England was so dependent on their salvation that the defense continued most vigorously, albeit amid great new perils, until the fate of the Armada gave the Dutch breathing space.

They were not popular on the outside, having the reputation of being overconfident and harboring unkind feelings toward the Germans in particular (in 1582 people thought they had poisoned the herring). Charles V had practically detached the Burgundian circle from the German empire.

Spain kept regarding them as people committing high treason and deserving of extermination, against whom any methods were permissible. However, the campaigns of Maurice of Orange liberated the northern provinces from the Spanish rule.

Of the powers which had freed themselves from Philip II's grasp, France had already made peace in 1598; England had desired it for a long time and made it in 1604; Holland alone continued to fight for the time being, in even greater danger since Spain's hands were otherwise free, but actually protected by Henry IV. And yet the war had its advantages along with great sacrifices.

Little Holland, which was constantly fighting with the sea, had what may have been the strongest "will to live" of all times.

(II) *On the federal constitution of the Netherlands.* It is the epitome of nothing but practical usage which lives on *because* it is really alive and because people hesitate to replace it with uniform freedom and universal permissiveness whereby the real inner strength might be damaged.

81. Mary Stuart

(I) Mary Stuart is the child of a dynasty which in a poor country fought with a fearsome nobility that in the form of clan chieftains was able to sway the people.

The first four Jameses all died violent deaths, and Mary's father James V at least died of grief in 1542 when the nobility left him at the moment when he was supposed to fight the English. At that time the child was a few days old. James's widow and Mary's mother was Marie de Guise. In 1538 the Guises had succeeded in getting one of themselves onto a throne.

From the outset, all sorts of plans were connected with the child Mary. On his mission to Scotland in 1547, Edward Seymour did not succeed in effecting an engagement with Edward VI, who was her senior by only five years, because the Scots, although at a disadvantage, did not let him extort their princess from them. And now the Guises decided to make this niece, who was already Queen of Scots, the Queen of France. Thus Mary was brought up at the French court and married to the dauphin Francis during the last part of the war of St. Quentin.

Did the adoption of the title and coats of arms of England take place at that time or a little later, only through the will of the Guises or of Henry II? It was *this* deal which Paul IV wanted to decide.

This drove Elizabeth toward Protestantism. Scotland itself, however, was the most unsteady ground for ambitious dynastic plans.

Protestantism penetrated there, and against it the crown and the clergy certainly stuck together. But while the desire for robbing churches might already have been stirring in the Scottish nobility, it had to happen that Scotland produced one of the most ruthless Calvinists who must have made an extremely great personal impression: John Knox. Under the regent, since 1554 Marie de Guise, he had fled, returning in 1559. At the end of May of the same year, the convents were stormed. The loot from this was distributed among the congregation of the nobility, which made any Catholic royalty almost impossible. The regent, however, offered open resistance with French aid.

And now Knox had to do what no Scottish "people's" party had ever done: apply to England for aid. After some scruples, Elizabeth sent ships and Knox's faction was able to maintain itself. Elizabeth made a treaty with the Scottish lords in order to drive the French from Scotland. Shortly before this the regent had died (June, 1560).

(II) A queen in the most insecure position has been on trial to this day.

To some she is the idolatrous Jezebel who conspired with Spain and the pope to make Scotland Catholic again by trickery and force. To others she is the object of infinite sympathy and, especially later, of boundless compassion, and this is where poetry has entered.

In any case, the extent of Mary Stuart's actual participation in events must be greatly limited. The really powerful elements were the Scottish chieftains with their clans, and even Knox had no power over them once they had safeguarded their church spoils. *Why* and according to what inner impulses these people act in each case is as uncertain as it is with savages.

A part of this clique, in association with the expelled Murray, Mary's illegitimate half-brother, murdered Rizzio at the royal table on March 9, 1566. Now there really is proof that Rizzio was the mediator for papal and Spanish contacts with Mary Stuart. But it is madness to speak of the possibility of a Catholic restoration in Scotland in 1566, at a time when the second religious war was approaching in France, and in the Netherlands the great Gueux uprising. The only certain things are that for some reason the clique wanted to frighten and humiliate the queen very deeply, and that Rizzio was in its way.

The motive given for the participation of Darnley is that Rizzio withheld the matrimonial crown from him. That he had knowledge of the plot is almost a matter of indifference, considering his slight personality. The plot against Darnley himself, as it was carried out on February 10, 1567, was, according to more recent students, the doing of the same clique. The queen saw something coming, remained passive, and had to let things happen. It is quite erroneous to believe that she promoted or instigated the death of her spouse because a divorce would not have been feasible on account of the young prince. At any rate, Darnley was not killed merely for his own sake, but because he was in the way of the clique materially.

There followed Bothwell's divorce and marriage to Mary Stuart.

82. On Elizabeth of England

(I) After the battle of Bosworth the Tudors were able to base their power substantially on the nation's repugnance for any further civil war. People were willing to put up with anything but a fight between heads of factions. They gave up parliamentary rights and safeguards against judicial arbitrariness, even the salvation of their souls, if only there was a strong government that steered the ship of state with a firm hand. *Where* it was going did not matter so much. In this sense, actually only Edward VI's reign had been dangerous, because factious heads were fighting again; right after that, the absolutist Mary was again allowed to do anything she pleased.

Through the question of succession Elizabeth not only gets on the side of Western European Protestantism, but also becomes its head. With the Tudors' system of eradicating all possible claimants to the succession in the country itself, the dynasty finally devolves on one person. Besides, the Stuarts of Scotland are undeniably the nearest heirs. But Elizabeth does not want the question of succession to be dealt with at all. Mary Stuart, who has fled to England, is arrested and eventually beheaded; James VI, however, for the time being remains but a very doubtful successor.

Then the old maid, without allies, passes the great test in the form of the Armada. To be sure, we do not know what might have happened without the helpful storm in the Channel. Now her welfare and that of the overwhelming majority of the nation were bound up together.

(II) Elizabeth, who had inherited papal hatred from Mary, was driven to defection from Rome and to the creed of Edward VI by the pope's foolish claims to refereeship and church property.

It was to her advantage that in the name of the queen of Scotland, who was at the same time the dauphine of France and niece of the Guises, claims were laid to England, namely, immediate possession of the English throne, in which Henry II and the Guises played their daring game.

After some reflection, Elizabeth found within herself the strength and the stubbornness of her father. Yet her own religiosity was highly dubious, to say nothing of her creed. She saw through the clergy and knew that it followed her. She counted on an insular and anti-Roman frame of mind, exploited the odium of the Francophile Paul IV, and ventured to decide, although she was in favor of celibacy.

As for the religious creed, complete supremacy was enforced. Elizabeth was the sole fount of truth and every authorization. This made the Catholics who remained Roman guilty of high treason *ipso facto*, even if they kept perfectly quiet. The serious Calvinists, i.e., the Puritans, then realized that the noose they had helped put around the Catholics' necks was now around their own as well. Elizabeth brooked no "deviation." The persecutions did not stop short of the scaffold.

Her coerced Parliament went along with her, and henceforth she had nothing but devoted parliaments, although she let go at them as at a pack of dogs, and the courts and administration were violent and at times truly depraved. England prospered materially and became a great active European power, even with meager help from abroad. Her small standing army proved that even though she was not popular, she was at least safe from internal disturbances. However, it sufficed thoughtful Englishmen to have a government that was strong enough not to become the plaything of aristocratic factions.

Elizabeth's personality was hardly tolerable. One simply was not allowed to laugh. But her main characteristic was a queenly one: strength of soul. When she trembled, at least no one was aware of it. In her one notices as little as in her father that she might have been emotionally dependent on anyone for support and consolation.

Her ministers, above all Cecil and Burleigh, were in the fortunate position of knowing their interests to be generally identical with the queen's. At the worst they would have been destroyed together with her. There existed a veritable complicity, and Elizabeth, for her part, did change favorites, but not workers.

83. The Age of Elizabeth

Between the allegory of Spenser's *Faerie Queene* (1596) and the pastoralism of Philip Sidney's *Arcadia* Shakespeare stands quite alone and also at a great distance from the other dramatists.

His public consisted of only two poles of society: the young nobility and the lower classes. The theater was growing only moderately, considering the size of London at that time; it was already considered not respectable (while, actually, the "respectable" nation was too dull for it). The court gave it only the attention that befitted its position, so that this sort of entertainment might not be lacking. Elizabeth took scarcely any notice of Shakespeare, and *The Merry Wives of Windsor,* which he wrote at her command, is one of his weaker plays. In the provinces there seems to have been no theater whatever, at a time when there were theaters throughout Spain. Shakespeare is a veritable windfall for England. If he had never existed, his age would not have missed him. Soon he was completely forgotten and was not revived until much later.

Rümelin (in his *Shakespearestudien*) demonstrates that Shakespeare's knowledge of life was more divinatory, inwardly intuitive than empirical.

In the key plays the outlook on life is profoundly melancholy. From this somber background there stand out jest, humor, and beautiful fantasy (*A Midsummer Night's Dream*; especially *The Tempest* with its distribution of evil; *King Richard III* and *Macbeth,* too, are quite clearly shaded right into the darkest black; the comedies with melancholy background include *As You Like It*).

From this outlook on life, the characters are all "justified" as long as they stand in front of us and talk.

Shakespeare not merely disposes of the vanity of this world in contemplative verses (although he has these in profusion), like Saadi and Hafiz, but he sketches the great, detailed, multiform *picture* of this world. Would he also have done this as a mere published author? Fortunately he was a theater man and an actor.

There has been endless research on *Hamlet* and on what Shakespeare intended and meant by this work. Every reader sees a different picture in it, and a new one at each reading. And the main thing is that he desires to read it again and again.

Shakespeare had a different key to the nature of man from that of any poet before or after him.

The present-day squabble over whether he was a Protestant or a Catholic is delightful. At any rate, he was not a Puritan.

It was probably of decisive importance that here as well as in Spain the theater consisted essentially of competing private enterprises (in Italy a court theater usually set the fashion with operas, pastorals, comedies in the conventional sense, and in addition there was little more than popular farce in the form of masked comedy). The English theater fortunately was not tied to any pomp.

Englishmen in Germany trained German actors; Jakob Ayrer and his dramas were under their influence. Perhaps one reason why they were on the Continent was that at home they could hardly profit by their art any more.

IV

History of the Seventeenth and Eighteenth Centuries

84. Introduction to the History of the Seventeenth and Eighteenth Centuries (1598–1763)

(I) [May 4, 1869.] The preceding lectures presented the break with the Middle Ages.

The Middle Ages and the beginning of modern times differ in great, essential ways: In the former, there is the endless division of power and the still slight contrast among the nations; in the latter we have concentration of power, the wars of conquest with national development of power at any price, and the crude beginnings of the so-called state system.

In the Middle Ages, moreover, there is a limitation to the European West and to ecclesiastical unity. In the age which succeeded them, the European nations spread over all continents, Catholicism is divided into great ecclesiastical parties whose conflicts threaten to absorb all other conflicts and affinities.

At one time culture was determined by the church and was homogeneous all over Europe, partly because of the church, partly because of the specific spirit of the Middle Ages, and still differentiated by race. But now culture is refashioned out of antiquity and new research into nature, and alongside all ecclesiastical influences it is nevertheless secular in essence, as well as multiform nationally and yet highly individual.

Now there takes place a truly endless crossing and entangling of all these strands. An unprecedented *variety of life* becomes characteristic, and *this is developed further in the seventeenth and eighteenth centuries.*

The ordinary value judgment of history is in the habit of demanding the immediate and complete victory of one element. It cannot stand variety. Clerics of all denominations, fanatics of all denominations and non-denominations, popular philosophers, dynasts, and radical politicians who in history cannot stand the sight of rival forces and their fights demand one thing, completely and immediately, too, although this would make the world dead and colorless until those concerned killed one another out of sheer boredom or produced a new conflict. For it is an illusion to expect lasting contentment with any victory, something for which man lacks the organ anyway.

Of course, man must in this life want and represent something definite, but must reserve higher judgment.

One thing that we need not wish for but encounter as a reality, whether we rejoice at it or deplore it, is *Europe* as an old and new focus of multifarious life, a place where the richest formations originate, a home of all contrasts which dissolve into the one unity that here everything intellectual is given voice and expression.

This is European: the self-expression of *all* forces, in monuments, pictures and words, institutions and parties, down to the individual; the full life of the intellect in *all* aspects and directions; the striving of the intellect to leave behind knowledge about *everything* that it experiences, not to surrender mutely to world monarchies and theocracies, as did the East with its monolithic monarchies. From a high and distant vantage point, such as a historian's ought to be, bells harmonize beautifully, regardless of whether they may be in disharmony when heard from close by: *Discordia concors* [discord becomes harmony].

The old peoples could have founded in Asia still more great, powerful empires, such as Iran and Assyria, one after the other, but every one of these would have had only one kind of strength, spirit, and tone, like other Oriental empires. They, too, had to exist as the soil of certain civilizations.

An obscure impulse may have driven a few branches of the Indo-Europeans to the West, toward the setting sun, because here there were waiting for them a different soil and a different climate, that of freedom and variety, a craggy world of promontories and islands. For it is European to love not only power and idols and money, but also the spirit. They created the Hellenic, Roman, Celtic, and Germanic civilizations, and did so in constant transformations and conflicts which in the periods concerned were always painful, but ever accompanied by the release of new forces, unlike what happened in Byzantium, quite estimable in itself, where for seven hundred years the same revolution of throne and army kept repeating itself. These civilizations are far superior to the Asiatic ones by their being multiform and by the fact that in them the individual could develop fully and render the greatest service to the whole.

The church created a great new framework for European life. Bound and yet infinitely free and myriad-formed, the Middle Ages and finally the transitional epoch rose into modern times, the fully expressive ones.

History should rejoice at this profusion and leave the mere victor's desires to those with an ax to grind. It is the function of history not to deplore this struggle of the European West, but to study and present it. From its vantage point, as high and free as possible, it perceives *discordia* as *concors*. It should rejoice at *all* forces of the past, not merely those that happen to be congenial to a contemporary decade, and regard them as riches. Considering the great violence of the struggles at that time and the desire for the destruction of the adversaries, we humane latecomers could not keep absolute sympathy with any side, not even the one we consider ours.

A concealed supreme power here produces epochs, nations, and individuals of endlessly rich life.

The development of the West has the most genuine characteristic of life: out of the struggle of its opposites something really new develops; new contrasts supplant the old; it is not a mere inconsequential, almost identical repetition of military, palace, and dynastic revolutions, as happened for seven hundred years in Byzantium and even longer in Islam. At each struggle people become different and give evidence of it; we have insight into a thousand individual souls and can date the styles of the spirit by decades, while at the same time national, religious, regional, and other elements add countless spiritual nuances. These things in their time were not pleasant and enjoyable, but struggles for life or death.

Only one thing has always appeared to be fatal to Europe: crushing mechanical power, whether it emanated from a conquering barbarian people or from accumulated local instruments of power in the service of a single state (the ambition of Louis XIV) or of a single leveling tendency, be it political, religious, or social, such as the present-day masses. Against such crushing powers Europe will always gather its last strength, and it has always found its deliverers (William III of Orange).

At that time there were no primitive barbarian forces or invading barbarians, with the exception of the Ottomans, and even they had been at a relative standstill since Suleiman II. Modern Russia was still a relatively small state and separated from Europe by a very large Poland. But the Spanish "world monarchy" did seem dangerous. The fight of all the others against it occupies the sixteenth century and part of the seventeenth. Added to the original elements of power of this world monarchy was its alliance with the strongest old faction, the Catholic church; thus it could hope to break through all merely political opposition.

Under Philip II, once he was involved in the quarrels of the entire West, it became a fight between Spain and its dependencies, which for a considerable period included the Roman See, and the entire heretic world, based especially on the thirty years' powerlessness of France which Philip promoted in every way so that France, too, might fall prey to him.

(At this point a more detailed survey should be added, as an introduction to the history of the seventeenth and eighteenth century and continuing up to the Treaty of Vervins.)

The saviors of Europe were not the greatest enemies of Rome, but the most persistent enemies of Spain: the Dutch, Catholic as well as Protestant England, and Henry IV, despite his conversion. The savior of Europe is, above all, he who saves it from the danger of an imposed politico-religious-social unity and forced leveling which threaten its special character, the varied richness of its spirit. It is a banal objection that the spirit is unconquerable and will always be victorious. Actually, it may depend on the particular degree of strength of one man at one certain moment whether peoples or civilizations are to be lost or not. Great individuals are needed, and they need success. But at moments of crisis Europe frequently did find great individuals.

As the main content of this course of lectures the following might be set forth:

From the beginning of the seventeenth century a growing inflammation from Germany and Austria can be noticed. The greatest individuals, Henry IV and Gustavus Adolphus, fell early, by violent death, at the moment when they saw their greatest ambition within their grasp. Spain, inwardly a corpse, again becomes a world power, just strong enough to interfere everywhere, but not to determine events. In 1612, 1626, and at other times France bows to Spanish policies, and Richelieu who frees the country from this domination is able to do it only through an inhumane regime on the inside, and Mazarin has to fight Spain once more *de imperio* [for the first position]. Italy, politically dead, lives only through its culture and no longer derives any benefit from the decline of Spain, until then its tyrannical master. Germany collapses in the misery of the Thirty Years' War. Sweden and France have it at their disposal. To be sure, alongside this there is the highest flowering of Holland, and the English Revolution breaks out. Even though it was only a thinly disguised military revolution, it left the English people very powerful and inwardly in a condition in which no permanent forcible rule was any longer conceivable.

However, once more Spain arises from the grave, and in its most dangerous guise, as a *Hispanicized France* under Louis XIV. (? The blame for this must no longer be placed on Spain.) The Spanish program is grafted onto a nation which possesses disproportionately more real means and a central location for the gagging of Europe. Once again there arises the danger of a Catholic world monarchy, and the opponents, too, have been infected by "sultanism." The political repulse is accomplished in part through terrible wars whose physiognomy is almost entirely military, political, financial, and commercial, without the psyche of the peoples being clearly expressed in them.

However, *culturally* France was victorious. Louis XIV brought it about that in the eighteenth century French becomes tantamount to European; to him France owes her general capacity for contagion.

In the meantime, while the *heritage* of Spain was being fought for, Sweden, the same great power which had once wanted to form, with part of Germany, a great German-Scandinavian empire, was blown up in the air by a mad hero. Out of and beside the powerlessness of Sweden and Poland there arises Russia, starting with Peter the Great, immediately bent on shaking up and inciting the West and on its own business in the East. And Prussia, the last great power that was emerging with an unspeakable effort from the debris of Germany, after the Seven Years' War must acknowledge itself as the permanent and inevitable ally of this Russia. Meanwhile England puts Holland in the shade as regards colonial and commercial greatness. Finally, with the aid of France, which had been humiliated in the Seven Years' War and was thirsting for vengeance, there arose the beginnings of a future great power, North America.

All this is happening as the great crisis of the entire old system of what we consider authoritarian states and religions approaches perceptibly and with strangely increasing clarity—the revolution.

(II) [May 4, 1871.] The following may be said regarding the justification for the course of lectures as regards its scope, apart from its being recognized academically.

Any limitation is really made only out of necessity. There is always something arbitrary in detaching one sequence or view from the stormy sea of world history, beginning with the most remote past and flowing on into the most distant future, and yet even a painter of seascapes proceeds no differently.

But it is still arbitrary and dictated only by necessity to lift out of the great intellectual continuum of *all* things only one thing, out of all knowledge only one branch of knowledge, and to give it special treatment.

Actually, we ought to live constantly in the intuition of the world as a whole. But this would require a superhuman intelligence that would be above temporal succession and spatial limitation, and yet in constant contemplative communion with it, and, on top of that, in sympathy with it.

And when the starting and finishing points of a course have been established, the most arbitrary limitation has only begun.

To be sure, from presentation to presentation there has evolved a certain consensus of treatment, for large-scale classification, evaluation of data according to their significance or lack of it, but in the main this applies to objective facts only.

Now there arises the question as to the nature and quantity of what is to be imparted, according to what principle the lecturer should include or omit material. There is no uniform standard; in books standards differ greatly, on the platform they are limited. A writer has no necessary limits, but a speaker has.

And this is where arbitrariness inevitably enters into the selection. Of all scholarly disciplines history is the most unscientific, because it possesses or can possess least of all an assured, approved method of selection; that is, critical research has a very definite method, but the presentation of it has not.

It is on every occasion the record of what one age finds worthy of note in another.

Every historian will have a special selection, a different criterion for what is worth communicating, according to his nationality, subjectivity, training, and period.

Nevertheless, the chronological definition of this course has at least a relative justification. The Treaty of Vervins, with which we begin, marks a real intermission for all the chief peoples of Europe, such a suitable one as would not occur in history far and wide. And to conclude before the preliminaries to the French Revolution, perhaps with the Treaty of Hubertusburg, 1763, is imperative if a finish is to be made anywhere.

Starting with the last decades before the French Revolution, events and personalities are of a specifically new kind, even though their origin from what preceded may be quite apparent to us. The classes of men and the number of people that participate in things now become substantially different from what they were previously.

The Peace of Vervins and the time of Henry IV are the intermission between those two great periods of the Counter Reformation which may be named, after their main phenomena, those of the French religious wars and the Thirty Years' War.

Today all merely political and especially military events of the past are reduced in value by the events of our times. If the quantitative differences among events are great, the qualitative ones are especially so.

At that time there was nothing but cabinet politics and cabinet wars. Now there are operative latent or open national movements and (to be sure, technically perfectly conceived and led) national wars and race wars (and in the end perhaps religious wars again).

About the wars of those times one has the feeling, right or wrong, that the rulers could have waged them or abstained from them. Of present-day wars we suspect that they are undertaken in order to cut off revolutions or to channel them, something that need not always be successful, of course. Hence the slight current interest in, e.g., the wars of Louis XIV, with the possible exception of those moments in which a real popular movement is discernible among his opponents or allies— Holland, and Spain in the War of Succession.

The relative contribution of the generals we cannot judge expertly, and we seldom get the expression of a great political tie-up with the military. Therefore anything military should be given only briefly, in the form of results; of the political elements, not every single intrigue should be noted, but only those in which there is expressed an agitation arising from actual conditions, one which has a connection with the past and the future.

It will thus be our main task here to bring world history as close to intellectual history as is possible; there is an abundance of means for this. Viewed superficially, the history of the seventeenth and eighteenth centuries deals only with power relationships, but the intellect is present as well.

To be omitted is the mere external debris of data, especially excerpts from dispatches and counter-dispatches. A subject worthier of consideration would be the cocky humor with which diplomacy and bold strokes alternate, particularly in the first decades of the eighteenth century; those were the times of Görtz, Dubois, Alberoni, and diplomats and courtiers of a similar kidney.

(III) This course is in the nature of an "entracte," or, rather, an "interlude."

In relation to the great beginnings of the modern world epoch after 1450 it is a continuation; in relation to the age of revolution it is only the termination of an earlier age and a preparation for the coming one. At the same time, however, it retains a wealth of specific interest. Not all ages can be of primary interest; the pulse beat of world history is a very uneven one. But here the movements are still powerful enough and the evidence for the entire external and spiritual existence is plentiful and, in part, of the highest caliber.

In relation to the sixteenth century, the seventeenth has been designated as *retarding*, as a *reaction*. There is an impatient point of view for which world history does not move rapidly enough and which holds, for instance, that as early as the sixteenth century complete modernity wanted to appear and should have done so, and that the fight against these forces was nothing but a wasted effort. People simply call something *progress* and then deplore its prolonged failure to appear.

If one asks such people whether they are satisfied with the goals *now* attained, they have a thousand different opinions, especially about the desirability of what has already been attained or is in process of coming into being, and one could invite them to agree for the time being on one opinion in this regard at least. And along with them there are other people, those who want still more.

But for the present, history will do well to turn its back completely on mere desiderata and devote itself to contemplating and depicting as objectively as possible past struggles, conflicts, and multiplicity.

For the life of the West *is* struggle.

As far as he is personally concerned, a historian may not be able to separate himself from the struggle of his locality. As a man existing in time he must desire and represent some definite thing, but as an historian he must maintain a loftier view.

A great many people get beside themselves if someone else has a different opinion and want to convert the other fellow as soon as they see a corner of his coat. But if one becomes silent or continues to express different opinions, one enjoys their hate or their pity, depending on their temperament. To be sure, we admit that forces opposed to our taste are forces *as well*, because they are palpably in front of us, but we do this with unspeakable wailing and abuse.

The meddling of values in world history is as if in the sea of time one wave wanted to shout insults against all the other waves.

(IV) [May 5, 1873.] The character of the spirit in the seventeenth and eighteenth centuries is determined by the classes which were at that time the principal participants, and by the contemporary way of life in general.

Most important, the state, with a few exceptions, is absolutistic or administered absolutistically. It is the time of authority rather than majority. Changes are not easily conceivable. Any striving for change is considered a crime as a matter of course, even in the non-monarchic states; in this respect, aristocracies are just as inexorable. Everything is calculated to last forever. People know nothing as yet of the mutability of all conditions.

The classes are still separated by different rights. The only thing that encompasses all classes, the religions, is even in the eighteenth century somewhat in decline among the upper classes.

Real estate is still generally non-transferable; capital, i.e., disposable values, is still in very moderate supply and of little service to industry.

Despite all velleities toward the mercantile system on the part of individual states, the general tenor of life is still far from being an industrial one (the consequences of what people would like are often not even thought out; e.g., customs boundaries continue to exist within the great states themselves). The biggest business at the time is the overseas trade of some few colonial powers, not yet industry as such, as an untrammeled activity, an absolute material exploitation of the world. And where it does exist it is not yet in control and cannot unleash its fearsome competitive system on the nations.

The middle class as a political force, e.g., in the German imperial cities and elsewhere, had either died out or shrunk completely. In art, literature, and way of life it does not set the tone anywhere, with the possible exception of Holland, but receives it from the other classes, whereas in the Middle Ages it had a culture of its own. And even in Holland the life of the upper classes is not so very bourgeois, but more aristocratic than is usually assumed.

The predominant character of society is determined by aristocratic revenues, ground rents, state and army offices which belong to the particular caste, and ecclesiastical income. In individual instances, especially in weaker states, such an aristocracy becomes subject to corruption by foreign cabinets out of a desire for display (Sweden, at times even England), and in the strongest states it is certainly highly dependent on its own potentate; almost nowhere is it an element of political freedom any more, except for the better times of the English nobility. But its social significance was still very great, greater even than it had been around 1500. For at that time there still existed a bourgeois culture in the North and an aristocratic-bourgeois one in Italy. Above all, this aristocratic society is still Western and not merely national. The aristocrats are still as close to one another throughout Europe as they are to their own states.

Their life is made up of leisure and the activities that are considered aristocratic, like military service, individual heroism, famous love affairs. Despite the often very dissolute living, social intercourse in the eighteenth century is more refined, more generous, and intellectually livelier than it has ever been since. People still have time to read, i.e., for lively intellectual intercourse. They have not yet surrendered to business.

Talent, no matter where it may come from, easily finds patronage, positions, and a wealth of occupations. Here all arrogance ceases, because people really want to have enjoyment.

Scholarship is partly in the hands of secure corporations, partly in those of independent dilettantes.

At length, to be sure, this nobility, because of all its noble leisure and abstract generosity, comes upon liberal principles and begins to take the real institutions of the state lightly. This lends it one last, exceedingly noble resplendence. Meanwhile, to be sure, other strata, together with their "public opinion," have started to take control of matters.

It was for this aristocratic class, in the main, and not as yet for publishers and a mass public, that artists wrote, created literature, composed, painted, and so on. Also, the whole incipient opposition in the state and the innovations in all intellectual matters are essentially in their hands.

Our view must become accustomed to this nature of the intellectual life in those times.

THE STATE

The states are organized along class lines, approximating the so-called constitutional state, with safeguards for the individual in respect to life, property, and freedom of action. The class state was realized in some measure of completeness only in Holland and England, amidst great struggles. Here the opinion prevailed that the internal and external strength of the nation was substantially connected with it.

In Germany at the beginning of the seventeenth century there were very strong revolutionary classes only in Austria. In the other states the class system was already very weakened and the princes were actually close to absolutism. In the Thirty Years' War the class system in both regions really goes under and at best survives formally. Later the model of Louis XIV—people imitated his sultanism at least—and the princely type of the eighteenth century held full sway. Finally we see the most brilliant handling of absolutism in Frederick the Great, as the highest example of what can be achieved with a submissive and admiring people.

Apart from Holland and England, the universal opinion is that only absolutism gives strength to the state and knows how to govern.

In Scandinavia, Denmark becomes an absolutist state out of revulsion against the power of the nobility. In Sweden, on the other hand, the latter maintains itself and in the most depraved form, too, with Charles XI as the sole interruption. There is venality toward the outside and, after the end of Charles XII, complete impotence. In Poland, all "misfortune," i.e., all political powerlessness, is obviously due to the aristocratic government; it is regarded as a model of the way a state should not be.

Italy has a completely absolutist government, with the exception of Venice, which has every reason to remain quiet. Italy passively bears the War of the Spanish Succession, the War of the 1730's, and the War of the Austrian Succession, with all their consequences. Countries silently pass over into the hands of other masters (Italy in consequence of the War of the Spanish Succession, etc.).

Spain is internally absolutist under the last Hapsburgs. In part it is already under the pressure of the approaching problem of the succession. But it is powerless against its own tools and elements; the machinery of the state stands still. Under the Bourbons there appear absolutist beginnings of reform and renewed self-assertion in European politics.

The power of the Ottomans is clearly on the wane after the period of the Kuprili (second half of the seventeenth century) and they are incapable of making new attacks upon Europe.

Finally, Russia before and after Peter the Great. Here there is effective an absolutism which suddenly becomes aware of its potential strength and observes a certain system toward Ottomans and Europeans. For the time being the Russian people with its hatred has been silenced completely.

European politics and the supposed balance of power are characterized by a desire for expansion, but this is not yet done in the name of nations, but for the time being only in order to gain more subjects and revenues. From the conflicts of these absolutisms which mistake power for happiness there emerges the idea of a supposed balance of power.

The major achievement is that France is periodically told to keep within its bounds. This is a typically European matter: against a one-sided dominance all the others rise. Europe wants to remain varied.

Negotiations include tariff problems; in fact, here and there they are already of predominant importance.

The rulers in general equate power with good fortune and the peoples at least equate impotence with misfortune, because it tempts powerful neighbors to invade and constantly steal land.

All states in general, however, are still based on *authority*, even where decisions are actually made by majorities, for these are not yet head-count majorities.

THE GREAT POWER AND INDUSTRY

The first thing everywhere is the desire of the rulers themselves to get money; the merchants and industrialists are supposed to be chiefly tax channels. The Islamitic states of the Middle Ages and the Italian states from the fourteenth or fifteenth centuries laid the groundwork for this; fiscal management has been developed into a science.

Real property gradually ceases to be the sole basis for existence, although it is still enormously predominant and safeguarded. There arise great fortunes and businesses that are independent of it. Trade and commerce gradually lose their rather local character and there begins a greater concern with distant places.

With the oceanic peoples there is added the exploitation of their colonies; these are still regarded entirely as the possession of the mother country. However, it takes a long time for the so-called normal cycle to occur: importation of colonial raw materials and forced consumption of the products of domestic industry by the colonies.

In the seventeenth and eighteenth centuries colonization increases. Great French territories are created in North America and later in India; in addition to this are the Dutch occupations in the East and West Indies. Only England establishes larger English populations in distant areas, because they do not settle in tropical regions and many more Englishmen than Frenchmen emigrate.

Spain fades away, not only because of taxes, the mortmain, the monasteries, and other things, but because of its completely unindustrial mentality in a Europe which was otherwise becoming industrial.

France has its miseries. There rules a king who is terribly wasteful and eager for conquest and devours more than his Colbert can supply him, with the utmost overstraining of the country; and yet he is an envied model for other dynasts. The Colbert system which conceives of industry as an enriching force gains European validity. However, the industrialists are not as yet the ruling class here, nor are they in England.

The French Revolution and its monarchic continuation by Napoleon have pointed up the model of Louis XIV and his system; before and alongside them there existed the imitating states. At the same time, after 1815 the model of England begins to be effective.

Europe becomes the mill for all five continents; industrial and political superiority are regarded as going hand in hand. Through the confiscation of church property, the abolition of mortmain, a huge mass of energy and property as well as the people living there become available to industry.

Machines and mass production gradually rise. The great capital needed for them is accumulated and there is a progressively smaller number of people governing their destiny. Competition and mutual throat-cutting set in.

At the same time, however, with J.-J. Rousseau and the French Revolution ideas of equality and human rights as well as the expression "existence worthy of a human being" begin to have an influence. The greatest political freedom is combined with the largest measure of economic dependence; the middle class declines perceptibly.

An absurdly lamentable addition to this is the fact that the state incurs those well-known debts for politics, wars, and other higher causes and "progress," thus mortgaging future production with the claim that it was in part providing for it. The assumption is that the future will honor this relationship in perpetuity. The state has learned from the merchants and industrialists how to exploit credit; it defies the nation ever to let it go into bankruptcy.

Alongside all swindlers the state now stands there as swindler-in-chief.

INTELLECTUAL LIFE

First of all, *thought and research* (an intellectual situation which is enormously different from today's, but had its *raison d'être* and its style): both are still impeded in many ways by the existing forces, especially narrow-minded creeds, and yet in essence they were not at all so restricted as is believed; a case in point is Leibnitz and the *Théodicée*. This is true if one admits that a thinker's happiness is not yet absolutely bound up with a vociferous preaching of materialism and that the final reasons for existence are not decided by mere individual reflection, least of all with the right to coerce others.

Actually, the study of nature was, despite the story of Galileo, completely free, even in Catholic areas. In Spain, at any rate, it did not exist. In discoveries, to be sure, the nineteenth century and even the end of the eighteenth enormously outdistanced the two preceding centuries; the latter, however, may have had a greater appreciation of the blessings of scientific pursuits, as seems to be indicated by the large number of amateurs in physics and other sciences. Newton and the law of gravitation were of basic importance. In those times people were more disposed toward leisurely contemplation.

The history of that period is set forth in a great number of fairly well written works; it has a predominantly politico-military character and is colored by the nationality of the historian. In addition, there is a wealth of important and excellent memoirs.

Past historical research still follows ecclesiastical or legal interest; a magnificent collector's spirit and often a very efficient critical mind are at work here. A very weak spot is research into origins in every sense. And yet even here there is the achievement of a man like Giambattista Vico.

Geography was still in its infancy; despite colonial life the earth was still known infinitely little as compared to present-day knowledge. But there was a good deal of interest at that time; the eighteenth century excelled in the eager reading of travel books. People were still able to master discoveries and knowledge, and in this area, too, had not yet been caught up in specialized research.

"Man" was known as well as we know him.

Universal knowledge was still possible at that time and in practice, too (Leibnitz). Collections and cabinets still contained, unseparated, objects of natural history, historical curios, and even works of art. The criterion of "rarity" was often decisive. Where the advancement of knowledge as such is concerned, present-day scientific methods are infinitely superior, because of the division of labor and the specialization *ad infinitum*. But today the faculty for all-encompassing presentation is probably found less and less frequently. And those polymaths and amateurs of the seventeenth and eighteenth centuries may have derived more joy from their knowledge than today's specialist does from his.

The secular basis for all scholarship was a teaching position or membership in a corporation which was usually still clerical. For bookdealers the main thing was the very great number of learned libraries, those of corporations as well as of wealthy collectors; the property in both categories was assured and indivisible, safeguarded by entail, among other things. In addition, there was the patronage of princes and important people, with the corresponding dedications.

On the other hand, there was as yet no relationship to an "educated public," no concessions to its sympathies. There was no "critique of the daily press" to go with such a "public," and thus no degradation. Patronage and dedications degraded a man less than do today's concessions to the opinions and tastes of the masses.

Latin continued to be the language of scholarship, with its disadvantages as well as advantages; the latter are stressed especially in Schopenhauer. Think, for example, of the Latin of Francis Bacon. The desire to be effective through the vernacular does not assert itself until Thomasius and Voltaire.

FREE CREATION: POETRY

Here one must start from its premises. A big reading public and a mania for reading either did not yet exist or were in their infancy. Boredom was not yet fought by reading. Thus Don Quixote becomes a ridiculous figure.

In his composition a writer nowhere had in mind his popularity or mass effectiveness, and there was no such thing as yet as a modern publisher who *must* count on these things. There still was no literary industry. All of *Simplizius Simplizissimus* is as though written for the author himself, with no thought of any reading public. The reading public was still relatively aristocratic and exclusive. Here, too, there was patronage on the part of important people and select circles. Women did little reading as yet.

Then, too, a writer did not write for a particular moment, a political or social mood of the hour, and thus did not become subject to the transitoriness of today's productions.

Furthermore, the peoples were not yet being made lustful or terrorized through spiced-up depictions of the imagined life of big cities;

these cities did not even exist in the present-day sense. Thus the picaresque novel was still entirely humorous and highly didactic. All of *Don Quixote* is set on highways and in solitary places.

On the whole, there was no whipping up of the sluggish imaginations of such people as are receptive only to the most adventurous and coarsest things and want to be continually amused or kept in suspense. There was as yet no production of reading fodder, i.e., no consideration for empty and substandard minds.

All in all, this is a truly refined literature, not one that merely pretends to be so; it depicts life in general the way a refined person wants it presented. It portrays people, therefore life among the people. On the other hand, it almost never gives a worm's eye view of life among the aristocrats themselves, as does present-day literature.

This is the literature from Shakespeare to Voltaire, who still wrote entirely for the upper classes and has been understood and appreciated by the middle classes, too, only by virtue of his malice. There are a large number of books from that period which are still at least widely known, although the interest in them is predominantly historical.

In the field of poetry there is already a decided predominance of the theater in England, France, and Spain, with great, richly developed styles.

On the whole, the seventeenth century and a large part of the eighteenth are still times of strong feeling. Frequently, some general moral reservation is directly emphasized, albeit more often in the case of scabrous material.

Antiquity—essentially Roman antiquity—constitutes the general criterion of the excellent. Whoever does any writing knows and esteems it, even though he may betray it only indirectly, notably through lucidity.

The general advantage of that period over ours lies in the fact that it has claimed the attention of perceptive and appreciative people for one or two centuries, while our time faces a future in which perhaps precious little notice will be taken of *anything* past.

THE PLASTIC ARTS

The great main difference from present-day art lies in the obviousness of the subjects and in the homogeneous way of thinking of those who commissioned works of art. This way of thinking is still completely independent of any art journals. All information about the artists during their lifetime was conveyed by word of mouth or by letter. Recommendations from court to court and place to place were the decisive thing. The church painters were almost the only ones to become publicly known through their altar paintings and frescoes, and even this happened only in the Catholic countries. Critical articles on art were completely lacking. Only patrons, independent of anything printed, decided about secular commissions. There were no exhibitions whatever before the Paris Salon of the 1760's with Diderot's *feuilletons*. The accumulation of heterogeneous objects and their mutual murder through bedazzlement were still completely unknown. There was as yet no public and no public taste. The princely collections were not accessible to any "public," but could be used by artists for study.

The subjects were predominantly religious, mythological-allegorical, or those of Dutch realism, especially in genre and landscape painting and allied subjects.

Only in France was there general direction from above and a predominant concentration of art around the court. Other princes were only on a par with wealthy art lovers. But Louis XIV was not even an art lover, because what would he have loved anyway?

To sum up: Nothing but patronage from above, and not by *nouveaux riches*. That way art was better off than it is with today's support from below. There were a lot of painters who rose from the poorest classes through the help of higher-ups. Talented individuals were at least as sure of getting ahead as they are today, and were not nearly so much led astray as they are now when an artist has to devise his own subjects. In those times there occurred an ever new creation of actual given conditions.

MUSIC

It creates two great new forms, the oratorio and the opera. Its social significance varies greatly from nation to nation. Here and there it is no longer entirely ecclesiastical and courtly, but is fostered through associations, as yet only of select people. For on the whole it is still very much regarded as a real art.

From the end of the seventeenth century it rises spontaneously and very mightily in Italy and in the North (here especially Handel and Bach), and in the course of the eighteenth century it becomes the highest power in all contemporary art. The stylistic laws of music which were achieved at that time will, at least in broad outline, remain in force as long as our present tonal system.

85. The Character of the Sixteenth and Seventeenth Centuries

To what extent can the thesis be supported that the sixteenth century was *fanatical*, and the seventeenth *bigoted?* At any rate, there is a spiritual difference between the first and the second phase of the Counter Reformation, between which stands Henry IV. The first period is more popular and lives more among the masses; that is the case especially in France. Then, too, its guiding personalities still have a shade more passion, they still experience the issues directly, while the men of the second period take them over complete and decided, and now administer them mechanically.

For men with a Jesuit upbringing, like Ferdinand II, it was a foregone conclusion that the world must be brought back again by any methods; they never knocked their heads out or wavered about the main goal.

On the other hand, the peoples (the middle-class elements were far less significant than in the sixteenth century) were appreciably more tired and less spontaneous, e.g., the French Huguenots and Catholics. In Germany the great danger did not produce any popular stirring any more, except in Upper Austria and Bohemia. The Thirty Years' War remained merely a matter of the governments long after the populations had been fleeced, and on the Protestant side most of these governments were small and weak.

Afterwards, Gustavus Adolphus with his vigor is in great contrast to all the others. That is true also of the earlier Upper Austrian Peasants' War. Catholicism was at an enormous advantage. As long as it was united (but after Urban VIII it no longer was), it also knew what it wanted; in comparison with Protestantism, which was divided and consisted of mere governments, it had an ecumenical mentality or, at least, basis.

But the behavior of Spain remains symptomatic of the change from one century to the other. Here there is actually a difference between fanaticism and bigotry. Philip II stands spontaneously at the head of all Catholic activity; Philip III (overthrow of the Duke of Lerma) and Philip IV (proclamation of the Netherlands armistice) let themselves be drawn into the cause again only out of *"fausse honte"* [false shame].

A peculiar interlude was Lerma's period. A pleasure-seeking *parvenu* has established himself in the fanatical, world-monarchical state of the Spaniards, to the grief of all those working for the cause, apparently with a very bad conscience toward the house of Austria. To be sure, the high Spanish officials act without him, too, on their own account.

86. The Huguenots Under Henry IV

Henry IV had a much harder time with them than appears at first glance. His optimistic delusion that they would be converted together with him had not been fulfilled, or at any rate, only very slightly. For the 60,000 conversions which did take place were not of much consequence. In this Henry had completely misjudged the Huguenots among the people (middle class and peasants), because he did not know their kind of religiousness despite having lived among them for a long time. But the Huguenot leaders, false and treacherous, stuck to their creed as to a political position; they now remained with it all the more, counting on unrest if the king should die suddenly. Subsequently they and their families all became converted when it was convenient to do so and Richelieu had drawn their teeth. In addition, there was the unreasonableness of the Assemblies which in 1602 and 1607 declared the pope to be the anti-Christ, merely out of theoretical stubbornness. To the parliamentary deputation Henry had said in 1599: *"Il faut que les catholiques convertissent les Huguenots par l'exemple de leur bonne vie!"* [The Catholics must convert the Huguenots by the example of the good lives they lead!] How long did the crown actually give the Huguenots the money for manning strategic places?

87. Gomarists and Arminians

Even Calvin himself with his eternal predestination and eternal damnation of the vast majority is a caricature. Then he much more poisoned his life by suspecting and persecuting the presumably or certainly damned than he transfigured it by guiding the elect. This had to be so and must necessarily repeat itself with all orthodox Calvinist believers in predestination in a cultural epoch which is superior to them through its imagination and irritates them.

As long as there was armed combat in the Netherlands and the theologians receded to the second and third lines, Calvinist doctrine remained inactive. But when peaceful times came and the clergy (to the great detriment of their parties) were able to regain their voices in France, the Netherlands, and especially Scotland, they started operating with predestination again. Damnation was even much more strongly emphasized here than by the Catholics. After all, Calvin assures only the tiniest fraction even of his own adherents.

Now the doctrine penetrates the masses in Scotland and the Netherlands. This was incomparably more disagreeable than had been the debates of the Constantinople shopkeepers over the second person of the Deity in Chrysostom's times.

Yet in the Dutch cities all the educated and more refined people clearly turned away from the abominable doctrine represented by the Gomarists and toward the far milder doctrine of the Arminians. This showed the Gomarists what people basically took them for; at best they were regarded by the educated Netherlanders as isolated zealots. This made them more furious; they incited the masses more and more, and Maurice came and reaped the advantage for himself.

Oldenbarneveldt, as leader of the Estates party, desired that the religion of the individual provinces not be decided by the religion of the majority in each province and that the particular mercenary troops of the individual provinces not *eo ipso* be under the command of the stadholder as commander-in-chief of the whole nation. Maurice of Orange, the stadholder-general, as the alleged "representative of the whole nation," with designs on a monarchy of his own, allies himself with an aggressive religious party, the very same Gomarists, which claims to represent the religion of the whole state against the religions of the provinces. He manages to rescind the sovereignty and arming of the provinces and to destroy the most important opposing statesmen, such as Oldenbarneveldt, while at Dordrecht a council of the vehement religious party, a veritable parody of Trent, sharpens the dogma.

88. Powers and Society in Europe Before the Thirty Years' War

The three powers which had defended themselves against Spain in world-historic struggle were the following:

France. It was highly problematical how long beyond Henry IV's lifetime it would be able to maintain an independent policy.

England. It was capable of remaining neutral in a great new contest.

Holland. It alone would *have* to participate on the Protestant side if war broke out again. On the seas its opposition to Spain had already become a colossal business.

The North was still dormant. Did anyone at the outbreak of the

Thirty Years' War have any inkling of the impending world position of Sweden?

Only one thing was to be foreseen with certainty: when war among the political and religious adversaries began, *Germany* would be the object and the chief battleground.

If one examines the Catholic-Spanish forces one by one, they seem scarcely adequate for a great contest. Neither in strength of inner impetus nor in resources would they have been at all equal to the opposition if the latter had stuck together. But there, too, the inner impetus had been extinguished, and there was no unity.

A branch of the Hapsburg dynasty, allied with many Catholic individual interests and the house of Bavaria, then finds itself strong enough to risk the combat.

To what extent were the Protestant countries principally dominated by middle-class culture and outlook, the Catholic countries mainly by aristocratic culture and mentality? The difference between the two was not as great as it seems to have been.

The seventeenth century is substantially aristocratic on the Protestant side, too—more so than the period 1500–1550 had been.

The more middle-class character of the sixteenth century had given way before a reaction of the privileged. Italian private life, in particular, had been Hispanicized. The middle class existed everywhere, but no longer with a culture of its own; it now adopted modes of living and ways of thinking more from the upper classes. Even in Holland the life of the upper classes was much more aristocratic than is believed.

89. Italy in the Seventeenth Century

Italy was Hispanicized and immobilized. Its sterility manifested itself in its political death and intellectual decline (the latter, however, must be taken with a grain of salt). Economically it decayed while its needs increased. Sismondi (*History of the Italian Republics in the Middle Ages*) breaks out in especially great lamentations over the general practice of married women having a lover (*cicisbeo*). This practice had emanated from the court and come into being as a contrast to Spanish jealousy; it was a reaction to it. In the end, no one any longer knew in any respected Italian family whose son, father, or brother he was. At the same time, it was an excellent remedy for the general depression of spirits.

But Hispanicization also took the guise of "noble leisure." The bankers and businessmen invested their fortunes in real property with *entail* (I am not shedding any tears over the banking houses that went out of business). People generally were doomed to become idle—the earlier ones because they were arrogant, those born later because they could do nothing about it. For the latter, the *cicisbeo* practice came to be their chief amusement.

Two rules were in force here: No lady may appear in public unescorted; no man may escort his wife. Morals had been no better before this, but only now was adultery declared harmless. (Who said so, anyway?) For the most part, incidentally, this practice was innocuously boring. To what extent did the practice spread to the people? Sismondi says: *"Ces moeurs nouvelles . . . imitées par la masse entière du peuple"* [These new customs . . . imitated by the entire mass of the people].

In any case, the ruin of commerce was caused by the disappearance of the industrialists and the withdrawal of capital. On top of this, Hispanicized Italy was steered in this direction by the monopolies and the absurd trade taxes which smacked of Alcavala.

Something else that can be traced back to Spanish influence was the increase of pomp as a matter of social position, at the expense of real needs and the comforts of life. People began to live purely for display.

This is true also of titles and ceremony, beginning with the wrangles over precedence at the courts (Este, Medici, Savoy, Farnese, and others), which, after all, were all in the pockets of Spain or France, and of the cardinals who only now (1630) became Eminences. This reached so far down that people wound up addressing their cobblers in writing as *"molto illustre"* [very illustrious]. Everyone simply became more and more discontented about the titles that were still denied him.

The father of a family, who had originally been married off without his own consent, was not honored by his own (or other men's) children. Half of his brothers and sisters were in convents, the other half were enjoying free board at his table. He was considered only the administrator of the family estate, while all the others were secretly bent on their own pleasure. He could no longer augment the property; on the contrary, it was decreasing through taxes, misfortune, and extravagance. (? Then there would long since have been nothing left!) He could neither mortgage nor sell it; creditors could reach only his income, not his property. (Am I not right, *citoyen* Sismondi? Everything should have got into the hands of the speculators even then. For it would *not* have got into the hands of the peasants.)

"Pour chaque besoin imprévu il prenait sur le fonds déstiné à la culture" [For each unforeseen need he drew upon the funds earmarked for farming], which he should have spared; *"il ruinait ses terres, parce qu' il n'avait pas droit de les vendre"* [he ruined his lands because he had no right to sell them]; the tenants suffered along with him.

Added to this were the indolent or venal judiciary, the secret enemies and informers, the *tribunaux arbitraires* [arbitrary tribunals].

People let themselves go and had as much fun as they could.

This description of "Hispanicized" life actually applies also to most other European peoples of the time.

Yet Italy lived on in its fashion without declining further. Sismondi is the mouthpiece of utilitarianism. The race did not degenerate.

To be sure, in those days people were a long way from the present-day utilization of manpower and of the earth. Periods of so-called lying fallow, materially speaking, have a value of their own.

90. Richelieu

(I) He is the great accelerator of France's later political development, for good as well as for bad.

Alone with his idea of the state, which he completely identifies with his person, he confronts a world of egoism.

He must constantly control himself in order to employ the methods necessary to deal with and subdue this mountain of malice. In this he is aided by his satisfaction in the toppling of every single traitor. He is absolutely indifferent to morality in his methods. If he catches the nobility fighting duels, so much the better, as far as he is concerned.

His regal manner becomes manifest through the splendor of Richelieu Castle, through the city of Richelieu, through his domination, which seemed natural to him, of a literature which has become lacking in purpose, which he severs from its *"Air de Spadassin"* (*Les Grotesques*) and prepares for its future reign.

As for his relationship with the royal house, the latter has a deadly hatred for him, yet he cannot and will not do without it or replace it. He works only for people who would like to have him poisoned or hanged, i.e., for the idea of which possibly only these people or their successors will be the bearers. He is in an infinitely less favorable position than Henry IV, who was a king and commander in battle. But Richelieu is merely the most hated of all ministers and is allowed to be present at military campaigns only because without him everything would be disjointed.

He has to be friendly at all times to Gaston, the brother of Louis XIII, the heir presumptive to the throne or possible regent for Louis XIV if the king should die soon, and he must take all his *pater peccavi*'s [Father, I have sinned] as cash payment, although he knows what Gaston would do with him if he became king. He resigned himself early to Gaston's utter infamy as well as the meanness of the two queens. He does not waste any energy on moral indignation, but goes on ruling.

The king belongs to him only in the sense that he distrusts others even more than he distrusts Richelieu and that Richelieu supplies him with pocket money. Louis XIII gradually gets the feeling that Spain and high treason against him are one and the same thing. The constant danger to Richelieu lies only in the fact that the king feels himself overshadowed by him and must confess to Richelieu time and again that he has wanted to dismiss him.

(II) Let us once more survey the thoroughly rotten situation out of which Richelieu had to pull France, indeed, Europe.

His opponent was Spanish-Hapsburg politics which was, at the same time, a way of thinking, Catholic propaganda, and as such carried its compass within itself, while the French courtiers and leaders had increasingly become separate appendages to this Spain.

Richelieu was obliged to begin by breaking one single element of French strength which was drifting along between these storms, that is, by subduing the Huguenots. It was his intention that they should henceforth be treated decently, but should no longer form a state within the state.

From then on Richelieu was stamped as a good Catholic to the extent that now the French clergy was allowed to support him without reservation; several orders sought his protection; the Jesuits (at least the French ones, for those in Hapsburg lands thought more along Hapsburg lines, something that was winked at in the Gesù in Rome) took his side. Urban VIII was able to enter into an alliance with him; he called him to Italy, was privy to the Swedish-French alliance, gave no money at Wallenstein's reactivation, and at Gustavus Adolphus's death spoke of him in edifying terms.

But in domestic politics Richelieu had to defend by the most fearful means the welfare and the independence of France against those who ought to have been the born protectors of the state. Thus France became subject to general pressure, and Richelieu became *"le dictateur du désespoir"* [the dictator of despair].

Where independent action might still want to assert itself, it did so in a manner harmful to the community, e.g., in the case of the parliaments which wanted to debate Richelieu's just decisions. If Richelieu had wanted to keep France free of strife, he could actually have done so only by taking the attitude *"je mourrai en la peine ou je réduirai ce royaume au gouvernement d'Espagne"* [I will die in agony or I will reduce this kingdom to the condition of the government of Spain]. For his king he procured pocket money, but he also lectured him, as for example after the capture of La Rochelle.

When the German war continued, a war from which the king would never have found a way out without Richelieu, he *had* to keep his minister.

(III) In France the spirit of the nation or the state is personified more than in other nations. It does not always have to be the person of the king; Joan of Arc, e.g., was the embodied spirit of the nation. In Richelieu we have the embodiment of a certain idea of the state—it is the idea since then approved of by France and almost all of modern Europe—at a moment when one may hardly ask how things would have turned out without him.

For this it took a man who, completely against his own safety and comfort, exercised a tremendous will which appears to have been stronger than he himself.

Richelieu's methods were utterly unscrupulous. He was sure of his tools only if he never faltered. Typical of his tools was tricky Père Joseph. He had his spies everywhere, even in the Val de Grâce. He defended the good of his country against those who should have been its guardians. But he was not able to proceed nearly as systematically as his memoirs would have one believe.

Richelieu enforced a system of universal obedience. Any independence, inherited from earlier times, expressed itself only harmfully; this includes the parliaments which knew nothing about affairs of state. For Richelieu the purpose of the state takes precedence over everything, unaffected by compassion or favoritism. Failure to punish appears to him to be the greatest crime against the public welfare. The state must neither forget nor forgive. For political crimes the mere probability of guilt is sufficient.

Richelieu stands alone with his idea of the state. He constantly has to control himself in the face of scoundrels; he beats people down one by one and does not care about the methods: he catches the nobles dueling. He works for people who would like to hang him. He is no king, but only a hated minister. He acquiesces in Gaston's explanations and the wretchedness of the two queens.

He has no sunny disposition, like Henry IV. He wins no hearts, but conquers people by force only. He is not a king, but he is more than a king, namely, the receptacle of the conception of state which without him would perish because of the dereliction of duty on the part of all those who ought to be its promulgators, but instead commit treason against it.

The thing that especially ennobles Richelieu and makes him invulnerable in history is the constant presence of mortal danger. This he has in common with Henry IV.

91. On Germany's Situation Before the Thirty Years' War

The German Empire was a community whose parts had just enough connection with, and influence upon, one another to arouse the utmost mutual indignation, but not enough to subdue one another easily. Basically, all these elements tended to diverge and desired sovereignty; but then each did try to assert a will of its own through separate alliances with one another and with foreign countries.

The entire period of Charles V had been spent in taking advantage of the Reformation either to weaken the emperor and the Empire to the utmost or to get the central power into other hands.

In our unenlightened judgment it would have been the most desirable thing for people to leave one another alone. However, people so much enjoy forcing their will upon other people, and the religious mentality of all factions is so bent on compulsion that this would have been inconceivable.

Through the confiscation of church property and entire ecclesiastical sovereignties all the wrangling had the character of offended and contentious *jura quaesita* [vain quest for rights]; next to and above the issue of creed everywhere there was a material and political issue.

To this must be added the insufficiency of the peace settlements of Passau and Augsburg, in fact, of *any* conceivable treaty. Certain struggles may be declared at a standstill for a while because of exhaustion, but nevertheless their continuation will be quite inevitable, until they end with the decisive victory of one party or the dead exhaustion of both, as happened in this case. It is fruitless to grumble that the opposition is still in existence.

92. The Swedes in Germany

It is correct that at first glance German Protestantism seems to have been saved only by the appearance of the Swedes; to be sure, one has to put up with the subsequent conduct of Sweden, its armies, and other things. (The Swedes came; Protestantism lived on. Now the two things *seem* to be causally inseparable.)

However, the question is permissible whether German Protestantism would not have been helped without this horrible remedy, too. (Any miserable government had long ago become accustomed to seeking foreign intervention for whatever cause.)

In the first place, it is scandalous for a creed, no matter whether it is Catholic or Protestant, to place its salvation above the integrity of the nation. Thus Germany could be torn to shreds for metaphysical reasons. If one approves of such behavior, one must also approve of the fact that the popes led the German princes to weaken the Empire.

Secondly, no German government or faction helped to call Gustavus Adolphus; it was, rather, foreign countries—Richelieu and his followers, Holland, to a slight extent England as well. But it was Gustavus Adolphus himself who had the strongest desire to force himself on Germany. The Duke of Pomerania was immediately horrified at his arrival.

Well, if one imagines things without him:

Either Wallenstein would have remained at the helm and asserted his command over North Germany in his own spirit as we know it, involving non-observance of the Edict of Restitution, parity, even a *coup d'état* which would easily have been possible for him because of his army's indifference to creed; or, as actually happened, after Wallenstein's dismissal his army, too, would have been greatly curtailed, i.e., made incapable of continuing to enforce the Edict of Restitution even if it had wanted to.

And finally: even assuming a completely tenacious imperial army and government, would it not have been better and more desirable for the whole future if the North German *people* had at least done what the Upper Austrians did with infinitely slighter prospects, namely, fight a national fight for their religion?

But people were not prepared for this, because in the sixteenth century the Reformation had been accomplished so very easily, with people actually receiving it as a gift. In Magdeburg some real desperation finally made an appearance.

Because of that, people now had to submit to a foreign king who stepped on imperial soil, intending to deprive the Empire of the entire Baltic coast. Scandinavia desired a slice of Germany. Christian IV, at least, was still a German prince, on account of Holstein, when he directed his greed at Hanseatic cities and ecclesiastical lands and then waged war in Germany as the head of the Lower Saxon Circle. Gustavus Adolphus had no connections whatever with Germany.

The religious situation here was as follows:

If Ferdinand II had quite forcibly and cruelly made all of Northern Germany Catholic only about as far as the Elbe, but had left the rest unmolested, Gustavus Adolphus would have stayed at home. If, on the other hand, a Protestant emperor, or a Wallenstein turned indifferent to creed, had subjugated, or wanted to subjugate, the southern coast of the Baltic Sea, Gustavus Adolphus would have set out against him.

The Swedes, no less than the French, simply could not bear to see German imperial power gain strength in any way.

93. On Wallenstein's End

The main excuse that he wanted to avoid war with France, in which the Empire was to become involved for Spain's sake, is an empty and worthless one, for the French were already inside the Empire, and, as long as the war continued, France probably would interfere anyway.

Then, too, there are his inordinate desires. Ferdinand II was supposed to look on while Wallenstein, with imperial resources, established within the Empire a big hostile state which he wanted to set up for himself with the aid of parity and toleration.

Now there set in the accidental development of the crisis because of the desire of the Cardinal-Infante Ferdinand of Spain to lead German troops from Milan to the Netherlands through the Empire. To be sure, Spain wanted not only the Netherlands, but also its military road which the French had broken through in places. But if Wallenstein was against it, this was surely not due to abstract enthusiasm for the integrity of the Empire, but because *he himself would have liked to have the Palatinate, among other things.* Here he pitted his will against that of Spain, which had previously, including in 1632, helped to boost him. At the same time, he let the League's interests in South Germany suffer bitter distress, so that, e.g., Regensburg became Swedish in November of 1633, and he was stationed in the emperor's own land rather than outside. He had demonstrable immediate designs on the crown of Bohemia, with the aid of France—and for his reluctance to fight against this same France he is given so much credit. Finally, because of the sentiment in favor of the Infante he threatens to "abdicate," i.e., he starts agitation among his officers, and this is inevitably the beginning of the contest between the emperor and the general for the army. Then comes the

12th of February, 1634, at Pilsen, the banquet and the signing of the declaration by his lieutenants; the rest is the consequence of the latter.

For Ferdinand II it is simply a matter of outbidding Wallenstein with the generals, or at least of reassuring them as to their credit and other things. The two manifestoes contain nothing about an assassination, although the second one does mention qualified high treason. In addition, there was Piccolomini's orally transmitted instruction to Butler to bring in Wallenstein alive or dead. When at the publication of the second manifesto not a soldier stirred in Prague, it was shown how empty the power of such a *condottiere* is at bottom. Wallenstein's final machinations with Bernhard as well as his movement toward Eger were mere attempts to save himself. He no longer would have brought the Swedes an appreciable number of men.

If Ferdinand had let him have his own way and had lost all his crowns in the process, he would have reaped, by way of thanks, the mocking laughter of half the world.

Wallenstein's assassination was of great benefit to the emperor. He suddenly became the master of his army which was now an imperial army, and remained so in the future. Then, too, Ferdinand got rid of a financial obligation to Wallenstein which he would hardly ever have met after a peace. The military leaders, with their prospects of Wallenstein's estates and more, given the alternative of betraying Ferdinand or Wallenstein, were able to betray the latter with more safety and fewer pangs of conscience. Not one foreign cabinet accused Ferdinand of a wicked deed or defended Wallenstein against the charge of treason.

Does the fondness for Wallenstein, apart from Schiller, stem from Friedrich Förster? (*Later addition:* No, apart from the hatred for Ferdinand it has a general reason. Wallenstein, like Magdeburg in 1631, had become a trump card in the game of the Protestant faction.)

Why did the electorates of Saxony and Brandenburg not want to listen to him in the autumn of 1633? Was it perhaps because they already knew too much and because Ferdinand II, in the final analysis, was more agreeable to them than this Wallenstein?

94. The Great Elector

He is the great-grandfather of Frederick the Great and a sixth-generation ancestor of Emperor William. The subsequent growth of Prussian power dazzles our evaluation of its beginnings.

His main characteristic, similar, perhaps, to that of his great-grandson Frederick the Great, is his *hardness of soul,* a special characteristic of rulers, which cannot be replaced by mere majority decisions of chambers or assemblies chosen by mass democracies.

95. England Before the First Revolution

The crown was not by any means so much the only support of the nation as it was in France. Its insular location was still more important to it. Unity was never disturbed through the issuing of provinces to branches of the royal house as hereditary individual fiefs to the extent that it was in France. Thus even the greatest hostility within the house of Plantagenet was not capable of splitting the kingdom apart. There are no princes of the blood, no secondary dynasties with secular possessions ruling individual regions, let alone any with the permanent custom of conspiracy with foreign countries. To be sure, from time to time there are foreign alliances. The Plantagenets and Tudors have died out, the Stuart line has almost run out. There are no princes of the blood, and certainly no mutinous ones.

In comparison with the French Estates General, Parliament has the advantage of periodicity which is never interrupted for long, and of the compatibility of the two houses because they are aware of their mutual interests. The Lords do not declare the commoners to be beneath contempt, as did the French nobles with the Third Estate at the Estates General of 1614. Rather, the theory of the lower house that it should be exalted grew beyond the control of the upper house. The English Parliament also possesses the advantage of an old, firmly rooted tradition and conception in people's minds according to which the crown and the people are in a contractual relationship to each other.

England had not been unified and saved through the power of individual princes, as had repeatedly happened in France. Except for a brief period in the age of Elizabeth, it had not been obliged to stand in the breach against the Hapsburgs on behalf of all Europe; thus there had been no need for it to get accustomed internally to situations that were always violent. The middle class had long since developed more than it had done in France, although with a lesser culture; it had Protestantism within itself.

The Puritan mentality, with its only really justified protest, that against the royal supremacy, was one that pressed onward and upward and was inevitably republican in its consequences. Even with the crown acting quite correctly it would have ventured to make its bid for control, out of its exalted view of its own importance. It cannot bear to see or tolerate alongside itself anything at all that is different from it. All such things it calls idolatry and presses for their destruction. Added to this was the horrible arrogance of belonging to the "elect." It is *this* party, rather than the Anglican-royalist and Arminian, that works for the downfall of Catholicism in England, and in this quite natural way the kings are driven to protect it. This was foreseeable, however, and the royal protection of the Catholics later became the main leverage for the overthrow of the crown. This party is not an element *with* which a clever ruler could have governed as with an "available force." Royalty was not to its taste because it had not emanated from it. Even the Lollards once said that *populares* [commoners] were allowed to *corrigere* [straighten out] a prince who neglected his duties.

The true core and main moving force of this party is the Independent mind which subsequently throws aside its previous guises (Presbyterianism, etc.) with a few vigorous motions.

The parliaments under the Tudors had put up with anything, and the genuine parliamentary tradition had been cut off. But now it is not only resuscitated, but puts forth new growth. Think of the decisions of 1621.

Parliamentary method had never been forgotten, because it had lived on in smaller spheres (the administration of shires and cities, etc.); added to this was the Puritan element which now supplied will and strength.

96. English Royalty and Its Task

Under the first Stuart ruler the parliamentary system again raises its head and seeks to set up its boundary posts as far inside the region of royal power as possible. But it is able to do this only because it has allied itself, in large measure even become identical, with a religious-moral view of life which long ago had become powerful and at the same time has increasingly turned into a sect; this is Puritanism. But the crown had to represent the *entire* people and afford equal protection to all, including the Catholics, who were no longer a menace in England and existed as an excessive majority only in Ireland; but it was in England that the Puritan screams about idolatry were the loudest. Moreover, the crown had to protect the remnants of popular enjoyment and fun still left from Elizabeth and her Poor Laws (the legislation relating to paupers and mendicants), as well as the drama (Shakespeare, died 1616; period of Massinger, Beaumont, Ben Jonson), and, in general, all of higher secular culture, including the world of Francis Bacon's thought (ousted 1621, died 1626).

For Puritanism, at bottom, wanted to tolerate only itself and what issued from it. Everything else was "idolatry." But the crown did not derive from it, and Puritanism more or less consciously sought its downfall through litigation.

Subsequent English historical thought, to be sure, is not interested merely in rights, but asks: "Can you govern England?" The answer is: "Yes, indeed, and Scotland and Ireland, too." And they tried it with the full arrogance of the elect and the awakened, until about 1644 they became aware that the helm had actually been seized by a most violent faction within them and by a powerful individual within this faction.

The decisive moment came in 1625 when parliament denied the new, as yet completely inactive, king tonnage and poundage, i.e., the resources for any kind of government.

It became the doctrine of the parliamentary party that everything that any parliament had ever wrung from the crown must become the permanent law of the state.

97. Cromwell

(I) How would things have happened after 1645 *without* Cromwell? To be sure, the Presbyterians and the classes of the people who needed peace would have sought to make a peace with Charles I. However, the question is whether they would have had a chance to do this (instead of the Independents, would not others have seized the power?), because with the exhaustion of the "good people," the revolutionaries, the "Jacobins," who had got the floor through these same good people, would have seized control. Because of the fact that Cromwell represented them and at the same time controlled them he is a *sauveur* [deliverer], after all.

(II) In 1648 Cromwell becomes a *sauveur* against anarchy which, to be sure, would not have become dangerous without his actions. (? I have my doubts again; with the exhaustion of Presbyterianism a destructive kind of radicalism would have had a chance if Cromwell and the army had not been there.) He presently brings the Levelers to their senses with his sabers, and soon he thunders the loquacious Presbyterians to the ground through his enthusiasts.

(III) Why did Cromwell and the Independents alone hit it off so well together?

This anarchic sort of people inconvenienced him the least. They were communities which rise like water bubbles from a boiling pot and can vanish again, too. In that way he got rid of the entire previous personnel of the Revolution, those Puritan and Presbyterian notables who had been thinking that things would not work without them.

Only in the Independents did he find that mixture of fanatics whom he could take in and scoundrels whom he could make use of. Only with the Independents was he able to be the religious leader as well; only here was he able to appeal to inspiration at all times and to choose his own texts for his sermons before battles and other great moments. The arrogance of the Independents toward all other people and the army was enormous. Of course, this could not go on forever, and it had to be Cromwell's further task to make out of the Independent army one loyal to him personally.

(IV) It is in England's urgent interest to think of him as great, mythical, portentous, for it is too humiliating when the *real* Cromwell is recognized, a man who spoils for the other English parties their politico-liberal attitude and their ephemeral sectarian nuances of creed, and who with *his* army simply puts the English Revolution in his pocket as he goes. Thereupon they make out of him not only one of the most gifted Englishmen (for he was that), but a genius of the highest rank and a national hero.

There are people who are born rulers, and he was one. But it is a nice question whether a nation that has produced such a man should abandon itself to a special feeling of exultation. His authority consists of two elements, his greatness and the baseness of the vast majority of those who obeyed him.

The modern appraisers of Cromwell can be classified as follows: There are those who believe that they serve the English view, and even the nation, best if they elevate the whole phenomenon to unmeasured heights; then it is easy for them to proscribe as pedantry the mention of, or emphasis on, "individual shortcomings." Once this kind of opinion gets in full stride and, through the press and other media, takes hold of large semi-educated and ignorant parts of the population, blind jubilation can take possession of the people, as with Victor Hugo's corpse.

There are those who regard Cromwell as a basically pious spirit, albeit one afflicted with great weaknesses, and all in all a religious, or at least pietistic, tool of God.

There are those who have at certain moments clearly recognized in him the hypocrite and crown hunter and have taken a general dislike to him. They consider him an out-and-out dissembler. But since they do not deny his great talents and actual lordship, in their accounting the English nation of the time must appear all the more stupid and cowardly.

Then there are those who explain him analogously to the way Mohammed is explained: From an earlier, more or less fanatical period and accustomed reverence a general style is left. In the meantime, the profession of ruler has highly developed all the specific endowments required for it, primarily a lucid intellect which necessarily and inevitably fights pious narrowness. In the course of successes there then develops a kind of secondary piety and honesty which, to be sure, deems the most horrible blows at the heads of others permissible. Then, too, Mohammed's devotional character is less offensive than that of Cromwell the dictator in whose mouth the Puritan expressions sound truly scandalous and yet seem comical. Caesar did not have to preach to his soldiers, although he at least was *Pontifex Maximus.*

But at bottom it is true that Cromwell is *terrible,* in this respect: he *destroys* what is in his way or could some day stand in his way, from Charles I to the Irishmen of Drogheda and Wexford.

(V) The difficulty in our evaluation of Cromwell is this: Though in theory we have a very high opinion of power politicians (of whom Cromwell was one), in fact they often seem to us inadequate. For we do not see the many individual elements of power as well as of resistance which they have to take into account, but give rein to our armchair politician's views, composed of imagination and impatience.

Cromwell, who, above all, wanted to rule and had to rule, tried to make this clear to the nation in a great variety of ways.

His real weak point was that everything inevitably had to stand and fall on his personality and that he could never *seriously* think of being succeeded by his family. He was aware of all who were waiting for his death, and death by assassination could occur at any moment. In such a mood he continued to rule at home and abroad, powerfully and often magnificently. The English state under him was more powerful than ever before and for a long time afterwards.

One of the strongest ideas in people's minds at that time was that valid taxes could be voted only by a parliament.

But Cromwell's basis still was his army which he seems to have maintained at full numerical strength despite all periods of peace. And between this army and any kind of parliament there was an inevitable antagonism.

Had he lived longer he would probably have been obliged to use this army for foreign wars, presumably in the spirit of a Protestant-Independent crusade. For to dismiss it or to keep fattening an inactive army in England was equally dangerous. They would probably have set out against the "idolators," i.e., gone to war and committed depredations and all sorts of acts of violence against Catholic peoples. At any rate, Cromwell's threat concerning the pope betrays a thought of this kind.

It is questionable whether Cromwell, as Protector with the civil power, would have waged such wars in person or have left them to admirals or generals. Toward the Catholics still in England he was and remained cruel and would not tolerate any of them in the country. His was a regime which, to be sure, for long years dealt daily and deadly insult to the convictions and especially the tastes of innumerable people, but a regime under which people were able to live and engage in business.

98. The Fronde and the French Aristocracy

In France the princes of the blood, the bigwigs, and all the other nobles after the Middle Ages were incapable of forming a true aristocracy.

The crown, which long ago achieved a *de facto* absolutism (the fight with England had made French royalty a war royalty), either is strong enough to keep everyone in check or to make them take what it gives them, or it is weak, and then everything breaks down into egoistic factions. No organic form for a permanent, legal counterbalance to royal absolutism has ever been able to take shape. Out of turbulence again and again the power of the crown rises to the top, and again everyone eats at its table.

The Fronde was noteworthy as the last clear occasion for the nobles to show themselves capable of forming a true political aristocracy which would have become a lasting force for legal freedom, a genuine organ in the life of the state. Independence here never manifested itself as law, but as the privilege of a caste and prerogative of the individual.

However, instead of true political effectiveness as a group, every individual only wanted to create or preserve "importance" for himself. The relationship of the Fronde to the Paris *parlement* and especially to the *peuple* was a ruthless or scurrilous one. Under intelligent leadership the whole movement could have used the favoring wind which undeniably was blowing over from the English Revolution.

99. The Fronde and the *Parlement* of Paris

Any truly legal shaping of public affairs was hardly conceivable in those days. Between ruthless *seigneurs* and a dangerous city mob there was maintained the highly dubious legality of an authority like the *parlement* of Paris. Even if it was allied with all provincial parliaments and in all of France the *noblesse de robe* behaved blamelessly and harmoniously, it nevertheless was only one class against which all the others would have conspired. And it was a curious class to rule, too, what with its filling of offices through purchase and inheritance.

The critical moment is January, 1649, when the parliaments called in the *seigneurs*, who, after all, were well enough known! With the *seigneurs* they inevitably opened the door to the old Spanish conspiracy against the French state as such.

From that point on the entire parliamentary system along with the whole question of relief of the people is only an appendage to the struggles of the mighty, in which, oddly enough, the "people," too, take an interest, for or against. No matter how loudly Condé, e.g., may in all phases of the Fronde voice his naive contempt for *parlement* and Parisians, the people and the *parlement* nevertheless help to demand his release.

Although in the 1640's the mere threatening of parliamentary councilors had caused great outbreaks, afterwards any act of violence could take place with impunity. Especially in 1651 the *parlement* was egged on to the most extreme and most foolish decisions only in the interest of the *seigneurs*. It persistently joined in the clamor that Mazarin must never be allowed inside the country again.

Condé had become so blindly set in his arrogance and his contempt of Mazarin that gradually whatever vestiges of royalism were still within Frenchmen had to turn against him.

French royalism of the time is described thus (in Hiob Ludolf, *Schaubühne der Welt*, Frankfurt, 1713, III, 395): "For this praise must be given to the French: whether their king may do them good or harm, act justly or unjustly, they still stick by him and always speak well of him."

A very base thing was the last union of Condé, in the spring of 1652, with Gaston, the uncle of Louis XIV, who brought with him the Duke of Lorraine.

In the affairs of the Faubourg St. Antoine, Gaston's daughter, Princess de Montpensier, helped to save Condé, and the *parlement* ruined itself for all time by "conferring" upon the two conspirators (who were now openly allied with Spain) the two highest powers of the state—and this in the face of the king who had attained his majority. All this was done only out of rage against "le Mazarin," the foreigner, the extortionist, the tyrant, without their stopping to realize that they would hardly have acted better toward any possessor of the supreme state power.

And now there ensued what always happens at some time in unpredictable phases of a movement: the peace-loving elements gained strength.

Later, in February, 1653, when Condé was a fugitive, the royal uncle Gaston was semi-pardoned, and Retz was in prison, Mazarin was able to move into Paris again and manage a satiated despotism without any longer having to speak politely to the *seigneurs*.

100. On Mazarin

(I) After the terrorism of Richelieu who had had at his side an adult and, at least later, completely docile king, ruling was difficult for the female regent of a five-year-old child and for a minister, no matter who he might be. And in the beginning Anne of Austria, importuned from all sides, resisted Mazarin and sought to make shift with the Bishop of Beauvais. Her background is a blind predilection for her homeland, and as recently as 1637 she had carried on a dangerous correspondence. Richelieu, however, had virtually bequeathed Mazarin to the dynasty by using him for the most difficult and secret matters. Just as people would not have known how to carry on without Richelieu, now they cannot get along without Mazarin.

(II) This remark reveals the main traits of his personality: *"Je ne suis pas esclave de ma parole"* [I am not a slave to my word]; this also goes for all other active participants at that time. No matter how things stood: in the Fronde, Mazarin was the standard-bearer of the French state's strength and independence of Spain. He could not be reached by bribes from the outside, like the Russian ministers of the eighteenth century, if only because he had learned how to make France tributary directly to himself. And for the French he has that abysmal, at times scarcely concealed, contempt which in his dealings with every person makes him ask only about his price and confiscate lampoons in order to have them sold at a high price. To be sure, his opponents can apparently not be bought—but only for as long as ambition and vanity are involved. It was Mazarin's task to find the moment at which an individual was to be had. With the individuals whom he wanted to use, he asked, in addition to their price, about their happiness, their luck—e.g., in the case of a general: *"Est-il heureux?"* [Is he happy?].

101. Styles of Life and Art Around 1650

The peoples with strong feeling are the Romanic ones and the Catholics. The Hollanders are the realists and the bourgeois. England does not count in this period, and Germany has, for the time being, salvaged only its scholarship from the Thirty Years' War.

The emotional peoples: Their style of life and fashion still follows the Spanish prototype, even in the higher Catholic circles of Germany and especially at the imperial court.

Art and literature are shaped by the Catholic church, the old Roman culture (still without an idea of the Greek); literature is also partially influenced by Spanish literature, which was being widely translated (Corneille's *Cid*).

The baroque style of the three arts is derived from Michelangelo in architecture, in sculpture and painting mostly from Correggio and Titian, through the Caracci family. To what extent is it realistic? Its main goal is the great, stately effect. This is the time of Bernini and Pietro da Cortona, of Rubens, Van Dyck, and their school, of Velázquez and Murillo. In this art there is life and coloring, with relatively little attention to the deepest aspects of the subjects.

For the less stirring moods, we may mention, first of all, elegiac themes, pastorales, and landscapes, then realistic secondary genres. Here, too, there are Bambocciads and the like.

Lyric poetry is heroic-pastoral and lyric-elegiac. In Italy and Spain there is artificial lyric poetry. Representative of those two forms of poetry are Marino's *Adone*, Tasso's successors, Chapelain. In addition, epistolary literature and satire are practiced. As for the drama, in France it is either heroic or comic, in Italy only comic or non-existent, in Spain by turns sacred, heroic-tragic, intrigue, comedy.

Finally, in Italy the opera has its start and is transplanted to all the courts; this is the beginning of the modern stature of music generally.

The realistic and bourgeois peoples: They, too, express themselves through knowledge and feeling, and in this are indebted to antiquity and the Romanic peoples. But side by side with this there prevails Dutch realism in genre painting and the elegiac reaction in landscape painting.

Moreover, an obeisance to the sacred element is made in the form of Biblical painting, which, of course, was in the hands of Rembrandt and his school.

The highest level in the free treatment of Biblical material is represented by Milton's *Paradise Lost.*

102. Sweden Under King Charles X Gustavus

Vivitur ex raptu [people live on stolen goods]. The inner restlessness of a nation brutalized by great successes coincides with a king from a new family who is already known to the nation as a bold general and now acquires unlimited finances. A mere domestic government is hardly conceivable with someone like Charles Gustavus. Then, too, Sweden's artificial hegemony over its outlying lands could best be maintained *fataliter* [by destruction], by the conquest of further outlying lands. All of Sweden's neighbors considered themselves at an unfair disadvantage because of extorted peace treaties. Sweden thought it would be most useful to keep powder-smoke constantly under its neighbors' noses.

Of these neighbors, the non-Swedish Scandinavians, namely the Danes and Norwegians, were actually the most hated. If these had been able to unite themselves with the Swedes right at the beginning of the Thirty Years' War, a very large part of Germany probably would have become their permanent booty.

The "Pyrrhus of the North" was in tune with his men in their boldness and a rapidity of movement which seems adventurous. Moreover, he appears to have been no drunkard, but rather constantly capable of diplomatic duties. At a decisive moment he was able to intone, say, a Lutheran song. But at table, where he ate a lot of butter, he always drank his first toast to all cuckolds, and that presumably put him in tune with the temper of his surroundings.

103. The Age of Unlimited Princely Power

The age of ecclesiastical dispute is definitely at an end, but appearances still deceive insofar as intolerance continues and there are isolated notable conversions.

Within the different creeds it appears that religious ideas no longer dominate the world. A wholly secular cabinet policy has not only taken the place of spiritual motives, but, with the exception of England, overmastered worldly-constitutional class forces. The nobility has little use any more for political effectiveness and everywhere seeks only dispensation and display.

It is of little moment that Rome, too, has again secularized itself. Since Alexander VII the popes have lacked any European stature; they are no more important than the church state is able to make them. Even against the Peace of Westphalia Rome has only a feeble protest. It is of little importance, further, that the Jesuits are now only bent on possession and power and are inclined to take the side of the individual countries in which they reside. Even if things were different, cabinet despotism and sultanism would carry the day and take into their service art, splendor, and every higher form of life, on the Protestant as well as the Catholic side. (Unfortunately this does not prevent intolerant actions in individual countries, nor the attitude that uniformity of faith is politically convenient. This is part of negative religion which essentially consists in hating the others.)

Given this absolutist state of affairs, the primacy of *one* state was inevitable, in keeping with the inner necessity of despotism which in addition to power at home also demands power abroad.

Just as surely as Spain had formerly striven for this position, *France* now had to do it, a country which at that time was infinitely more powerful, relatively speaking, than it is today, with by far the strongest army, conservatively estimated at 120,000 men. Russia and North America did not yet exist as far as European politics were concerned, Brandenburg was as yet no more powerful than Saxony, Austria (and for a long time England as well) had been bought by bribing the ministers, and Spain was mortally weak.

Internally, the princes, the clergy, the nobility, and parliament had hitherto passed themselves off as the state, and the middle class, let alone the masses, could *not yet* pretend to be the state. Any attempts at group action, special privilege, political organization, and so on had regularly fallen before ruthless monarchs. Then Louis said, *"L'état c'est moi."*

The *creed* does not matter. Except for England, the Protestant *rulers* have become as despotic as the Catholic ones, and in matters of creed they are fully as intolerant. For the Catholic rulers' authorization of perjury and other questionable things they have substitutes of their own.

The Protestant *nobility* for its part (Sweden and elsewhere) squeezes the people dry, like their Catholic counterparts, and even more ruthlessly.

104. On Louis XIV

He engages in the *enlargement* of power and property if only for the sake of their preservation, but later as an admitted personal predilection. With his fearsome power of all of France's resources at his disposal, Louis of necessity reached the point of striving for a universal monarchy.

Characteristic of Louis is a statement which he made in his later period, in 1688, intended for Maximilian Emmanuel of Bavaria. He said that the Elector should use the opportunities presented to him by fortune for his *aggrandizement,* "the worthiest and most beautiful aim of a prince."

105. Louis XIV as Lord of the Church

(This is by way of introduction to the revocation of the Edict of Nantes.) There are clear manifestations of a period in which the main impulses of Catholicism no longer emanate from the papacy, but are now and then even directed against it. Thus, these impulses now originate rather from the cosmopolitan Jesuit order in its period of externalization and orientation toward power, and then from the French king. In the latter there reigns a mixture of mania for territorial power, which will no longer brook any differences, and of stupid bigotry which wants to do penance on other people's backs and strikes out all the more blindly and fanatically because at the same time the pope is being hurt and the Turks and Hungarians are being used against Austria-Germany.

In the Catholicism of France and other countries, more refined and more intellectual currents sought to maintain themselves and to prevail, laboriously enough, in the fact of the cold lust for power, the bad confessional morality, and the coarser piety of the Jesuits as manifested after 1675 in the cult of the *"sacré coeur"* [sacred heart]; cases in point are Jansenism, constantly persecuted from Richelieu's time on, then mysticism, and quietism, as practiced by Molinos.

The crown had the French Jesuits completely on its side, and on the subject of Molinos Innocent XI himself had to submit to a hearing before the Inquisition. There also arose a quarrel with the pope over the royal prerogatives, which was intensified up to the formulation of the Gallican Articles of 1682. Later, in 1687–1689, there was added the quarrel with Innocent XI over diplomatic immunity.

But along with all this the dominating realities were the resumed persecution of the Huguenots and the revocation of the Edict of Nantes. For this price the clergy sided with the king against the pope.

The church of the Counter Reformation, in its form of Jesuitism, was much more sensitive to matters of dogma and hierarchy than the earlier church, which would have endured or ignored movements like Jansenism. The papacy would have let Jansenism and quietism pass unnoticed but for the French Jesuits. The Jesuits, however, feel jeopardized by any deeper view of the concepts of sin and grace.

Even mysticism, which the earlier church tolerated to such a large extent or even placed in its service, soon became suspect.

And the Huguenots were destroyed as soon as the state power was compliant enough to the church and great and unscrupulous enough to do this.

For all this France was the proper soil, for the reason that it was the active country. The Jesuit church and its friend, the state, still found people to fight. Louis XIV had taken possession of a France full of self-willed minds. In the beginning, the spirit of the Fronde still lived in many. People did not realize immediately how much it would cost to want to be something special under this king.

In this connection should be mentioned Louis' low esteem for the members of the French clergy. Specifically, this is clearly reflected by the tone of *Le Lutrin*. Boileau would not have ventured such persiflage if the king had not been pleased with it.

106. The French Spirit of Uniformity and the Huguenots

The French spirit of uniformity in the monarchy and the restlessness of French Jesuitism at the slightest breath of anything different brought about an initial persecution of the Jansenists, who could certainly have been overlooked, as well as a persecution of quietism to the point of defiance of Innocent XI. The Jesuits simply have their patented mysticism in the form of the *"sacré coeur."*

Gradually this French spirit of uniformity and Jesuitism quite consciously takes its stand against the great and universal Catholicism. On the occasion of the disputes over the royal prerogatives it solidifies into the Gallican Articles; added to this are the brutal acts which Louis orders committed in the matter of the asylum of the French-curial legations, and the occupation of Avignon. Later there is contrasted with this, on the approach of the War of the Spanish Succession, Louis' retreat, the written revocation of the Gallican Articles, and, finally, the papal bull *Unigenitus.*

The *Huguenots* were the principal victims of the spirit of uniformity and Jesuitism. An intelligent king would have spared such useful and loyal subjects under any circumstances and let the clergy scream and the idle castes grumble.

And if the French crown had wanted to be great and powerful by any means, it could have become the most exalted in the world if it had been the *only* one in all of Europe to give the example of equality for both creeds. Louis XIV *could* have supplied such an example simply by observing the Edict of Nantes.

107. Louis XIV Prior to the War of the Spanish Succession

[Inserted after the summer vacation, 1869.] Every situation of power is dominated by greed for more and "rounding off," as soon as the internal situation permits it. It attacks small adjacent lands with insecure governments and may assert that annexation is necessary for their own good. In those days people claimed hereditary rights, rights to compensation, and the like. There was also this excuse: If we do not do it, someone else will. One creates an opportunity and then says that he must use it. In this sense every real power is evil.

Louis XIV, however, had already ventured forward astonishingly far at home and abroad, in theory (in his arrogance) and practice (in his sacrilege). Everything that ran counter to his concept of power was pulverized. He found himself bound by no law. Internally, there were exploitation, bondage, and the most heinous religious persecution; on the outside, wars of conquest were undertaken on the emptiest pretexts.

At the Peace of Nimwegen Louis had secured for himself Franche-Comté, the southern edge of Belgium, and actually almost all of Alsace; inside France no voice was allowed to be raised against the royal concept of religion, which was at the same time the royal concept of power.

But how were things to go on like this? Holland had emerged from the war in splendid shape, and thus Louis had already failed in his main purpose in the war. Moreover, he became short of resources; unscrupulous extortions could help here for a long time, to be sure. More serious were the facts that there developed a shortage of men, that Louis himself began to work with ministers who were essentially only clerks (Louvois died in 1691), and that promotions were made increasingly on the basis of tractability (on the whole, these were made according to seniority).

And now the problem of the Spanish succession gradually approached, already pregnant with a great war for which good alliances were needed. Instead of this, all Europe was stirred up and full of hatred. For the time being it was probably helpless, for the Great Elector was in alliance with the French, the emperor was ensnared and busy with the Turks, and the house of Stuart was on the throne in England. France with its central position was able to carry out the most ambitious projects.

Yet against his will Louis had elevated to power an *adversary,* William of Orange, whom he should have known by then because he had again and again appeared on the battlefield after lost or indecisive battles and rejected all of Louis' overtures. But Louis may have hoped to stir up sufficient opponents for him within Holland itself.

The degree of Louis' arrogance after the Peace of Nijmegen, apart from the revocation of the Edict of Nantes, becomes clear from the political outrages from the reunions on.

108. On the Second English Revolution

(I) Concerning the lofty talk about this second English Revolution: It was enough for the conspirators to know that the nation would not stir. It was indolent and preoccupied with business. Its hatred for the king was not yet great enough for it to overthrow him, but it just sufficed for it to stand by and watch others overthrow him. Afterwards it watched what the army was doing and ran or crept behind it. Since the engineers of the Revolution were clever and lucky enough to give the whole matter the appearance of a mere change within the royal family, the people let it pass.

The nation certainly had an antipathy toward Holland's friendship, but its hatred for France was probably even greater. However, the *active* pursuit of those who were truly active was, for Whigs as well as Tories (to the extent that both participated), the saving of Anglicanism from the dissenters. And even so, most of them did not participate until William was there. But this reproach sticks with England, that *it took a Dutch army to make England really reform herself.*

In addition to the well-founded concern of the ruling Anglican caste over the rise of the dissenters due to the Toleration Acts, there probably still existed as well a *vestige* of fear of the *vestige* of Catholicism. The masses, to be sure, were averse to it and alienated from it by a hundred years of disuse; but, after all, this time the masses had no say whatever. At any rate, with real and complete freedom, Catholicism would have achieved an appreciable stature along with the dissenters, though less because of court favor than in spite of it. But the dissenters, who had become even more powerful in the meantime, would then have started a war of destruction against the "idolators."

(II) As to the shabby course the Revolution took, the English view consoles itself with the well-known idea of how very well God finally dealt with England and how execrably with other nations.

But the real achievement of England (which, being an island, got away with many things with impunity), something that no continental

country could have achieved at that time, was to produce two aristocratic parties which not only took turns governing, but were really
capable of governing, i.e., possessed the necessary credit with the rest
of the nation and, through the parliamentary elections, were dependent
on the people. A safeguard against destructive activities was the rather
restricted electorate, numbering 200,000 for England and Wales.

To be sure, in the beginning the Whigs were not yet completely separated from the Republicans, nor were the Tories from the Jacobites. At
first a large Jacobite party survived, which, given the dubiousness of
the new succession, could very well hope to rise once more. Here everything hinged on whether the new, anti-Jacobite England would
prosper in the decisive decades. And it did produce a splendid prosperity, in its political influence on Europe, in acquisitions, in industry
and commerce.

Thereupon the Jacobites withdrew into ever narrower circles, became
easier and easier to count, and finally became extinguished. They had
had the better right on their side, but one day they were no longer
there.

109. England's Defense Against Militarism

When William III ascended the throne, public opinion was
charged with hatred for Cromwell's military despotism and the threatened military measures of Charles II and James II. Therefore Parliament
stipulated for all time in the Declaration of Rights (January 22, 1689),
which called William to the throne, that the sovereign must not maintain any standing army within the United Kingdom in peacetime without the permission of Parliament. In the spring of 1689 the Mutiny Act
sharpened this further by making the right of the crown to hold courts-
martial for mutinous soldiers dependent on the *annual* consent of Parliament. Parliament was authorized to fix the number of officers and
soldiers subject to martial law and stationed on British soil each time

it passed the budget. The army that was approved at that time numbered 10,000 men (?).

The fact that English military institutions were not wholly dissolved is attributable only to the traditional political moderation. In almost 200 years there has been no parliament which tried either to paralyze the government completely by refusing it permission to maintain its instruments of power, or to force it to violate the constitution.

William III had to send his Dutch guards, the companions of his glory and the saviors of England, home over the Channel. On the other hand, Parliament has always granted even the most unpopular governments enough troops, though a modest number, to maintain internal peace and external security.

110. On the Characteristics of the Seventeenth Century

Before the War of the Spanish Succession leave must be taken of this seventeenth century with its bad and good points.

In comparison with the sixteenth century, to what extent was it a retrogression politically?

On the basis of the many original minds which it produced we have too splendid a general conception of the sixteenth century and are too quick to believe that the world at that time wanted to merge directly into an age that was completely modern, i.e., in tune with our preconceptions, and that this was prevented only by the Counter Reformation, worldwide monarchism, and other things. The sixteenth century may well have been more "modern," as compared with the seventeenth.

But the seventeenth century was wholly aristocratic at least. Apart from the two great states in which the aristocracy was in direct control, Holland and England, it was substantially in control in the despotic states as well.

Both centuries have their advantages and disadvantages as regards higher intellectual life. In both periods political and religious conditions are firmly established. At first the Catholic and Protestant churches have almost everywhere established the closest contact with the state and middle-class society. Scholarship is subordinated to the church, research is dependent on its permission. Dissenters must remain silent or leave the country.

But in the seventeenth century individual thinkers gradually collect a following extending into the ranks of the mighty and even influence the theologians. Their influence is European, cosmopolitan, no longer national. There is a regeneration of epistemology in general (Bacon). Philosophy frees itself from religion (Descartes). Necessity is understood as causality (Spinoza). Skepticism becomes universal (Bayle). Reason appears as the mistress of religion (the English freethinkers). Applied to the state, this means that it is no longer founded on divine right, but on reason and expediency and a presumed contract. The groundwork for this way of thinking had been laid by the uprising of the Dutch in the sixteenth century and the English Revolution in the seventeenth. Gradually there comes into being an atmosphere of Western enlightenment.

For the time being, however, the seventeenth century is everywhere a time in which the state's power over everything individual increases, whether that power be in absolutist hands or may be considered the result of a contract, etc. People begin to dispute the sacred right of the individual ruler or authority without being aware that at the same time they are playing into the hands of a colossal state power.

111. Russia

Up to that time the Romanic and Germanic nations of the West had had alongside them in the East the Turks as an antithesis and archenemy. They were a purely destructive element which allied itself with the West only in time of war, and then only with the side that seemed to have the upper hand. Otherwise they maintained their exclusive

Mohammedan-Tartar culture and looked down upon Western civilization. The influence of the Turks upon Europe was exerted only through conquest and external force.

Now there arises in the East a state which appears to be most eager to attach itself to European culture, but in order to dominate Europe by any means! It utilizes foreign brainpower, but shuts out foreign ideas.

If the *nation* in question had its way, it would remain racially as Oriental as possible. In addition to the culture it is forced to adopt, it has preserved its old native customs with extraordinary tenacity, so that a startling contrast between the two prevails.

Meanwhile, however, in the hands of a "government with a definite program" it has for 150 years constituted one of the most powerful machines ever set in motion for *world* dominion.

For, in addition to possessing its old traditions it is thoroughly *drillable* and, on top of that, from its store of healthy barbarism it continually supplies a wealth of elemental strength for the purposes of the government. The Russian element at least *can* flow into European civilization, because it has no Koran.

Could the Russians have remained secluded barbarians? Certainly not in the long run. Even tyrants of moderate stature, e.g., Ivan IV, managed to develop power and culture from this talent for being drilled and to make themselves terrible to their neighbors. In the office of the czar there seems to have been a permanent temptation to do this; the world experienced its strongest and definitive outburst in Peter the Great. It has ever been thus with barbarians; their strong rulers are invariably conquerors.

The tragic element in the subsequent destiny of Europe lies in the fact that the Western peoples, while engaged in constant transformations and revolutions from within, are at the same time affected by an almost wholly mechanical force from without which has virtually no share in their joys and sorrows, their mind and higher aspirations, yet constitutes a major weight on the scale and helps to stabilize or revolutionize, according to its convenience. (N.B. In most recent times this has become different. What has been won so far is beginning to take revenge and hit back at its master.)

In their methods of ruling, the czars are completely unconstrained and capable of things that the West with all its Caesarism no longer has the heart to do.

The Russians attain to one of the highest positions in world history with utter abuse of their own character and profound inward unhappiness for the greatest part of the nation.

Whether without Peter they still would have fallen into all sorts of evil and dangerous ways, only of a different kind, we do not know.

And even if the Russian nation does want to be great and powerful, i.e., bad, toward the outside, like other great nations, it may still have the goodness to recognize the excellence of Peter and his institutions.

Will the fate of individualization, that is, the atomistic revolution, ever reach the Russian people, and if so, how soon? And will this render it ineffective or all the more influential for Europe?

112. England After George I

Broken forever was the crown as an absolute authority, and the royal church supremacy as well. The political advantage of the latter now devolved upon the cabinet minister of the moment. It was he who from then on had substantial control of ecclesiastical job patronage, which naturally strengthened his party.

In the beginning the sympathies of the crown even veered toward the dissenters, as long as the high Anglican clergy still had Jacobite leanings.

England and Scotland were now completely united; but opposed to the Anglican church in England there existed a hostile Calvinist-Presbyterian church in Scotland, which likewise was a state church.

To England Hallam's words apply: "The Supremacy of the legislature is like the collar of the watch-dog," which the state puts on a church endowed and raised to a state institution by it, as the price for sustenance and shelter.

On the other hand, in time all sects or religious associations which are already formed or are to come into being in the future govern themselves in complete freedom.

What had been achieved was religious freedom, i.e., freedom not to belong to the state church (likewise Protestant), and this achievement was in conflict with the principles of original Protestantism. What had been won back was civil liberties, part of which had been destroyed by the Protestant state church of the sixteenth century; these were now extended, too. Protestantism in its previous official form had been a mortal enemy of civil liberties. In its later state of further fragmentation, in its secondary forms (sects), it actually had some share in their restoration.

Not that they were tolerant willingly and themselves gave evidence of freedom. Each would have liked to suppress the others and impose its yoke of views and institutions upon the whole nation.

The Presbyterians in England dissolved themselves completely and were supplanted by other new sects.

Since the eighteenth century the crown has been a powerless phantom; instead, there is rule by the majority of the lower house.

In 1715 Addison wrote that the nation had become a nation of statesmen, each age, each sex, and each profession had its own list of ministers on its lips, and "Whig" and "Tory" were the first words a babe babbled on its mother's breast.

113. Frederick the Great

The change in his character, his final maturing, must have come about as the consequence of his attempt at escape in 1730. This marks the beginning of his inevitable contempt for people and undoubtedly his particular contempt for everything that existed in the Prussian states, while through his father he got to know the enormous fist of royalty. This time the methods of utter debasement had been applied, not *in anima vili* [in a spirit of wickedness], but to him as the successor to the throne, when Katte had been killed before his eyes and he had then been locked up with a Bible, a songbook, and Arndt's *True Christianity*, and besides had been permitted to study the archives of Margrave Hans. In opposition to the king's semi-Lutheran view of universal grace, Frederick took up with "Calvinist" predestination (William III of Orange had also been a vehement predestinationist). As late as 1737–1738 Voltaire most urgently remonstrates with him in behalf of human liberty as against his fatalism which, he says, hardens hearts.

Frederick's sojourn at Küstrin had the great value of breaking his narrow orientation toward intellectual pleasures, which would later have impeded his great political development. He learned the knack of administration and military command in miniature. Then came the forced marriage to Elizabeth of Brunswick-Bevern, with whom he lived at Rheinsberg for the sake of appearances.

His adherence to things French is sufficient evidence of his desire to live separated from his state and people, above his people. If intellectual things had come his way in German, he would have been in danger of having to respect Germany.

On the very first day upon receiving the news of Charles VI's death, his decision to get control of Silesia was made.

If he had foreseen all those with whom he would have to deal in consequence, if he had been older and more experienced, he probably would hardly have risked it.

Through his first martial act, the necessity for a *personal dictatorship* to the end of his life was determined for Frederick II.

V

The Age of Revolution

114. Introduction to the History of the Age of Revolution

(I) [November 6, 1867.] The time at which this course of lectures is given modifies it each time, for it is unlike any other course. It concerns itself with the beginning of that which is still active and will continue to be so, with that world age whose further development we do not know as yet. At this very moment events are being shaped, and on the horizon, in the near or distant future, there is a great European war as a consequence of everything that has gone before.

That is why in this case objectivity of presentation is even more dubious than usual. And yet the man who presents this age must give a general account from his vantage point.

The lack of judgment which contents itself with assigning to each individual moment of the revolution its relative *raison d'être* as an evolutionary stage is shallow and inadequate. For, in the first place, not everything is necessary by any means, but many things are accidental and personal doings, and secondly, the worst judgment is easily substituted for the supposed absence of judgment, namely, the approval of the *fait accompli,* the *succès.*

Above all, the revolution has had results which now completely shape us and constitute an integral part of our feeling for justice and our conscience—things, therefore, that we can no longer separate from ourselves.

All previous situations involved states in which the nobility and clergy were organized as class forces only here and there, to be sure, but enjoyed the greatest personal privileges, tax immunity, exclusive eligibility for higher offices, and great real property which was tied up in estates subject to mortmain and entail—states in which industry was exploited by the government and frequently bureaucratized in the most senseless manner, in which state religions with exclusive rights at best tolerated those holding different beliefs, and a show of unity of faith was preserved as far as possible.

On the other hand, these were the results of the revolution:

Complete equality before the law, including more or less equal eligibility for offices, taxation, and inheritance.

Complete or almost complete disposability of real property, with mortmain and entail greatly reduced.

Freedom of industry, theoretical conviction of the harmfulness of any state interference; enormous increase of the science of economics; the necessity of industry's counsel for the state; enormous increase of material civilization, bound up with rapid exploitation of the earth's surface.

Equality of religions, no longer merely of the Christian creeds, through the creation of tolerant states with a paid clergy, and state indifference; further, a tendency toward separation of church and state, with complete dominion of the latter over the former.

Beginnings of absolute political equality; the examples of America and Switzerland as more developed democracies; universal suffrage in several places; also, general standardization.

However, it is doubtful whether the world has on the average become happier for all this. The two components of happiness are the conditions themselves and the degree of satisfaction with them.

The chief phenomenon of our days is the sense of the provisional. In addition to the uncertainty of each individual's fate we are confronted with a colossal problem of existence whose elements must be viewed separately and as *new consequences and tendencies arisen from the revolution*. These are the following:

THE NEW CONCEPT OF THE STATE

This is not the philosophical concept (Hegel!) which would pass the state off as the realization of morality on earth, something that is not the business of the state but of society, whereas the state is, after all, only a protective shield. Rather, it is here a question of the new concept of the extent of the state's power.

In the preceding century, sultanic despotism had reigned to the extent that it was able to prevail against privilege. In the crevices there nested all sorts of special existences.

Then came the revolution and unfettered, first, all ideals and aspirations, then all passion and selfishness. It inherited and practiced a despotism which will serve as a model for all despotisms for all eternity. Another essential feature of it was the secularization of the church. Part of this general process was a *lawless centralization* which had arisen in a time of "danger to the fatherland." This centralization has existed in complete form even in the monarchies only since the revolution, having been created partly for purposes of defense, partly as an imitation.

The concept of equality is a two-edged one here. It turns into the abdication of the individual, because the more universal any possession is, the fewer individual defenders it finds. Once people have become accustomed to the state as the sole guardian of rights and public welfare, even the *will* to decentralization no longer helps. Governments no longer entrust their provinces, cities, and other individual forces with any real matters of power, but turn over to them only those trials and tribulations which the governments absolutely can no longer cope with—something that the smaller units hardly desire. In general, despite all the talk about freedom, peoples and governments demand unlimited state power internally.

The Revolution left France in a condition for which at first a cure was sought in world conquest; then, after a deep humiliation, the country was filled with nothing but demands and accusations. Coupled with the complete extinction of the awareness of constitutional and international law, this condition pressed toward periodic revolutions, in consequence of which Europe is again imperiled, up to the sudden shift of 1870. But the others have also learned how to threaten, and governments and peoples agree on the necessity of being powerful toward the outside.

The consequences of this international situation are an immeasurable increase of militarism (since Frederick the Great there have been huge standing armies, usable at home as well as abroad) and also a colossal increase in state debts, which is in striking contrast with the general mania for money-making and the desire for high living. What is perpetrated thereby is then called cabinet and dynastic despotism, but soon also acquires the name of great national necessity.

To what extent are the dynasties still in control, to what extent only the managers and messenger boys of mass movements? They devour or drive out their own kind, their cousins and other relatives, as soon as the moment impels them to! And dispossessed sovereigns then trade their claims for sums of money or pensions. The feeling of divine right has deserted the governments—and how should the belief in it still be present in the feelings of the people! Belief in invisible, immemorial foundations of existence, politico-religious mysticism is gone. The dynasties will come to an end, if only because only special talents will be needed. Would adopting heirs help? Our sympathy for the elective empires of past times is foolish, while all Europe is drifting toward something similar, whether it be special personalities or adoptions or something else, when people will not even be able to vote any longer!

In the end the people believe that if the state power were completely in their hands they could fashion a new existence with it.

But in between occurs long, voluntary servitude under individual leaders and usurpers; people no longer believe in principles, but from time to time they do believe in saviors. A new possibility of long despotism over weary people presents itself again and again.

RELATIONSHIP TO THE NATIONALITIES

The Revolution and its wars first summoned the French, then other nationalities as well, to activity in love and hatred, stirring them out of dismemberment and separate territorial life or at least to keener national consciousness, if the nation was already united.

Reflective thought might reply that common nationality by descent and language was something long since outmoded. The French Enlightenment and later the French Revolution talked very big about "humanity," and there was also a refined "cosmopolitanism." Or it might reply that culture, which was European, and the community of experiences, interests, and aspirations were a stronger bond, and that not nationality, but a healthy state was the homeland and lord of the emotions.

However, in unhealthy situations botched by parliaments one falls back on his descent and language as a saving solution of the intolerable, until one finally gets his way, without his being better off for it than before.

Then, too, where power already exists, nationality is used as a further means of agglomeration. (Or a revolutionary party uses the desire for reuniting the nationality as chicanery, like the Italian irredentists.) Princes and peoples are agreed on this. Resistance is hated. Foreign elements already under one's power are crushed. The imminent eradication of the German element in the Baltic provinces is a popular notion in Russia.

Since the revolution, and despite the interim of thirty-three years, people have become accustomed to every conceivable change in their boundaries.

PUBLIC OPINION

The crusades and the Reformation are well known as earlier eras in which an intellectual atmosphere dominated an entire people, not just particular classes. But the revolution exerts such a dominance in a far different sense; since the revolution this control has been permanent, and in this there has been a European solidarity. Here the fluctuations are enormous, and they are the more contagious the greater the increase in the rapidity of all communication and in the homogeneity of European culture and the daily press. The latter is by far the predominant—indeed, almost the only—reading matter of entire classes and countries. The great experience of 1789 was that public opinion forms and transforms the world—once the traditional powers were too weak to prevent it and once they started to make deals with individual currents in the stream of public opinion.

In all matters of high significance, division into parties and the corresponding double theory now run through all European peoples. *Public opinion,* i.e., the passion of entire peoples, is indeed irresistible.

But the real success of the press today lies more in the leveling of views than in its immediate effect. What is recommended and demanded most loudly and most generally is often the last thing to happen. For, at times the press screams so loudly for the very reason that people are no longer listening. Some of the opponents may be people who do not read newspapers anyway. Then there is the public opinion fabricated by those in control and by small parties, a venal press, and the like. The rulers, on the whole, are much less uneasy, let the boldest remarks pass because they are ineffective, and completely forgo censorship in the old style, although they do reserve sudden indirect action. (Since then they have again become much more uneasy. After all, public opinion *can* descend to the street overnight and turn into an uproar.) Meanwhile, the rulers have discovered the true counterpoise of the press:

BUSINESS AND COMMUNICATION

As soon as the great wars were over, the example of England caught on. Since 1815 a progressive industrialization of the world has been taking place, beside which the great landholdings recede completely. Machine labor has far outdistanced all older techniques; capital is accumulated for the building of factories, human masses for their operation; at the same time credit is enormously expanded. Machines are also used in large-scale farming. The railroads, steamships, and telegraphy place themselves in the service of communication. All goods can travel far; a European adjustment comes about; all local character of production ceases where it is not a question of immediate consumption of the products of the area concerned. Added to this are, finally, commerce, speculation, and, later, gain from stocks and securities. Money becomes and remains the great measure of things, poverty the greatest vice. Money is the successor to birth, but it is more equitable than the latter, because it does not remain long with incompetent heirs.

Intellect and culture are appreciated, to be sure. But literature has unfortunately become an industry as well in most cases. Alongside it, the literature of the eighteenth century appears all to be written with the heart's blood. Today very few things are still produced out of inner necessity. The *raison d'être* of the vast majority of creations is the honorarium or the hope for a position. The most famous writer is the one most likely to turn manufacturer. As for scholarship, popularizing for payment overtops even the tremendous amount of research.

Hurry and worry are spoiling life. Through universal competition everything is forced to the greatest speed and struggle for minimal differences.

But at the same time, through the influence of big cities, there arises the mania for getting rich quick, *l'amour du million*, because this simply is the measure of existence. A naive concession to this may be noticed everywhere. "Respectable living" is jacked up to the point where it is hard to afford; at least the semblance of wealth is required. Cheating of all kinds is inseparable from these phenomena and conditions.

In any time of crisis a lot of card houses collapse. But those who are unable to establish themselves and get rich, as in 1849–1853, lament pitifully [since then the crash of 1873 and its consequences]. If those times had continued, the most terrible crises would now be here because of mere cheating and overproduction; for experience teaches us that people do not restrain themselves. [This subsequently happened in 1871–1872 and was punished in 1873.]

And all this takes place while fermentation from below penetrates over and over again, something that is currently, e.g., terrorizing all of propertied England (and since then other countries as well); while people have no scruples whatever about changes of any kind, something to which the French Revolution has accustomed mankind, particularly the malcontents. At the same time there is utter uncertainty as to the legal limits of majority decisions, while the darkest clouds move up. The great continental war which must destroy all weaker state structures would in any case entail the influx of the great social problem which would appear all by itself with the cessation of industry and credit. [This has happened, but quite differently from what we expected; France went through it with the Commune of 1871; elsewhere the illness remains in the body as a creeping one.]

Here things depend on how well our generation can stand the test. Times of terror and profoundest misery may come. We should like to know on which wave in the ocean we are floating, but we ourselves are the wave.

However, mankind is as yet not destined for downfall, and Nature is creating as graciously as ever.

However, if in misfortune there is to be some fortune as well, it can only be a spiritual one, facing backward to the rescue of the culture of earlier times, facing forward to the serene and unwearied representation of the spirit in a time which could otherwise be given up entirely to things mundane.

(III)* [November 6, 1871.] In regard to the name of this course it may be remarked that actually everything up to our day is fundamentally nothing but an age of revolution, and perhaps we are, relatively speak-

*Misnumbering of sections in the original. (Translator's note.)

ing, only at the beginning or in the second act. For those three apparently calm decades from 1815 to 1848 have turned out to be a mere entracte in the great drama. But this seems about to become one movement which is antithetical to all the known past of our globe.

To be sure, in those three decades in which we were born and grew up it was possible to believe that the revolution was something completed, which therefore might be described objectively. People also believed—and the high point of these illusions was the spirit of 1830—that they possessed the bridge between the old and the new in the form of the constitutional monarchy. A few "achievements" spread more and more homogeneously throughout Europe, albeit in part only as something sought after, and were regarded as "benefits" of the French Revolution. These were: equality before the law, equality of taxes and division of inheritance, equal eligibility for offices; disposability of real property, reduction of mortmain and entail, as well as a more productive cultivation of the soil, with a quicker exhaustion to a certain extent; freedom of industry, dominance by business and communications; fixed capital overtaken by liquid capital and itself made liquid; equal rights of denominations, something that has become inevitable especially in quite mixed states; in places, state domination of the church, also a tendency toward separation of the two; a great influence of public opinion on all events; widespread currents of public opinion transcending anything national; the modern press.

At that time appeared those books, well written even though not classic, which tried to present a general view of the years 1789 to 1815, as of a completed age—not impartial, to be sure, but trying to be fair and quietly convincing.

Now, however, we know that the very same tempest which has shaken humanity since 1789 bears us onward, too. We can asseverate our impartiality in good faith and yet unconsciously be caught up in extreme partiality.

But in any case, the period 1789 to 1815, with its preliminaries dating from the middle of the eighteenth century (the Enlightenment, the beginnings of reform by governments), constitutes a kind of self-contained whole for practical consideration, with at least the facts and their causes passably well established.

If one wanted to proceed strictly, history itself, from its beginnings, would be only a very dubious source of pure knowledge, because even to its earliest reports sympathies and antipathies of the present can attach themselves every time. Even with ancient Greek and Roman history, with Egypt and Assyria, one can completely lapse into partisanship and interweave jabs at the present.

But let us nevertheless venture the academic presentation of that *first period of our present revolutionary world age.* A good scholarly justification for this would lie in the facts that so many figures and events of that time have had a typical significance for subsequent developments and that the ritual and imitation of the first French Revolution are an element of the present movement and thus necessary for its understanding, if only historically.

(II) [November 1, 1869.] First we encounter the period of reform from above, with its enlightened rulers and ministers. At that time a public opinion is coming into being, guided by an important literature and poetry, partly negative, partly imaginatively positive, which proceeded from the premise of the *goodness of human nature.* It is a public opinion which, for the time being, still expects everything to come from above. But a great external event, the liberation of the North American colonies from England, appears as the general prototype of all emancipation. At the same time the important constitutional fights in England itself work in this direction.

But the great despotic reformers are at the same time revolutionaries, to the extent that they are annexers and conquerors; thus Frederick II, Joseph II, and Catherine II. The first great example of the confiscation of an entire country and people is Poland.

Then, on the occasion of a profound financial upheaval, the French crown calls on the already fermenting nation for counsel. All ideals and desires explode in the *cahiers* which are unique of their kind. This is still the time of visionary hopes, which afterwards returned only for brief moments, and this mood also radiates over Europe.

In the Assembly itself there is a quick turning against the king. Immediately all organs of the old state structure dissolve themselves; *anarchie spontanée* sets in. Any agreement between the old concept of power with its methods and the new attempt at a people's government, an agreement from which the establishment of general happiness is demanded and expected, becomes utterly impossible. Human rights are the great moving force which speaks not only for France, but for the world. The two camps must be regarded not as two contending legal parties, but only as two phenomena.

Now there appears the rift in the alleged goodness of human nature. Its engineers are J. P. Marat and *suspicion,* which was at first directed against the king and the royalists (*émigrés*), then against all who are not unqualified members of one's own party. The most dangerous elements of *Paris* assume the helm of the Revolution. Paris becomes fatally significant, much more so than Rome at the time of the Civil Wars. Rage acts out of fright. The Parisian spirit takes the leadership in the existing state of anarchy; Paris prescribes not only action, but thought as well.

The September massacres may be regarded as the real beginning of the Terror. The foreign war started and waged by France is countered by the Prussian campaign directed at the Champagne and by the subsequent Wars of the Coalition, which keep alive the feeling on which the government of terror subsists. Meanwhile, at home, the government carries out its executions against federalism. The Terror turns from the royalists to the comrades, as it turned in the Spanish Inquisition from the Jews and Moors to the Spaniards.

The Revolution now passes through the characteristic phases with a regularity and rapidity unmatched by any other revolution. It presents by far the most complete picture of a revolution in a very cultured period with all the illustrations one could wish for from the arts and literature.

And since foreign invasion is staved off with relative ease, due to the most vehement internal dissension among the Coalition, France has time during all the Terror to grow a new skin; after Thermidor it is plain to see.

There is a new society, a lot of new property owners who desire no class privileges whatever, in fact, hardly any political rights, and would only be embarrassed by any sort of association; a lot of released manpower is available. All these elements desire only peace and security. The concept of property has outlasted all other principles and values. The difference is that, for the most part, it is in new hands.

The Directory tries to keep the surviving participants of the Revolution in power and honor, without the principles of the Revolution in which hardly anyone believes any longer. Financially it makes shift by founding and plundering so-called daughter republics, and, politically, by reverting to terror in any straits. But in the meantime militarism grows, too. However, since the generals are no longer beheaded, but allowed to become ever more famous and powerful, Napoleon seizes power on the 18th Brumaire.

His is the most instructive type of Caesarism. He is, at the same time, the savior of the new French society and a world conqueror. People would have settled for a much lesser man.

Internally a complete taming takes place. Fourteen years of mute obedience follow; the government and the legislation become national. This Napoleonic state has a great significance as a model for other European states. The Revolution had centralized almost exclusively by destruction. This state added order and a purposeful organism.

Abroad, Napoleon is a terrorist, of the school of 1793–1794. And yet he may be the foremost general of all time. With utter moral unscrupulousness he has at his command the greatest military ability.

It is his mission to trample the peoples down for the time being, but at the same time to awaken in them all their future strength, in part by using and training them, in part by enraging them.

The peace with England, which has scarcely been concluded, he breaks after one year; he gains ground in Italy, Switzerland, and Holland.

He sets up his empire, and, after threatening England, he wages war against the Third Coalition which he encounters for the first time at Austerlitz. Then comes the move against Prussia, which has unhappily remained neutral, and against Russia; the great chapters in this conflict are Jena, Eylau, Friedland, and Tilsit. But henceforth England remains the chief adversary; Napoleon plans a stand-up battle, but after Trafalgar he has to content himself with an indirect one.

It is impossible for Napoleon to pause in this course. The peaceful submission of other states no longer suffices him, because, as long as there is an England, they could still come under its influence; hence the Spanish war. The latter is used by Austria to break away; for this Austria is again crushed, although this time with more difficulty.

The tragedy of Napoleon lies in the fact that the politician carries on in such a way that the military commander can no longer keep pace. Napoleon is incapable of making out of those conquered anything but subjects or vassals, of somehow gaining them as allies through reconciliation. By this he provokes a profound inner revolt of the peoples, who thereby really get to know themselves for the first time and put up with the greatest inner transformations, as, e.g., Prussia after 1808.

The goal which is apparently beckoning from near at hand becomes the overthrow of England, with which he fights for power in such a way that his sphere and the English one are two worlds completely apart. Once he can force Russia to let French customs officers officiate in St. Petersburg, England must give way.

Making his way over the snarling peoples of Europe, with overtaxed resources, he undertakes the Russian campaign and finally there follows the colossal three-year judgment. Its main significance is the fact that a new order of states is brought about, not, perhaps, through the sudden death of Napoleon and an agreement among the governments, but amidst the very greatest national excitement of the peoples, especially in Germany, Russia, Spain, and England. *In this way* peoples which have been aroused by the French Revolution and the Wars of Liberation never again go to sleep, despite all their need for rest, and henceforth have a different standard for their whole existence and will never be satisfied with the said new political order.

From this there follows as a main consequence the spirit of *eternal revision*. Napoleon himself had temporarily held this spirit in check: *"J'ai conjuré le terrible esprit de nouveauté qui parcourait le monde"* [I have mastered the terrible spirit of novelty which was running loose in the world].

(IV) [November 6, 1871.] During the following three relatively peaceful decades the great new storms are clearly getting ready, in accordance with the most profound principle of the revolution, one which differentiates it from all earlier such events: eternal revision, or, rather, revolution.

The decisive new thing that has come into the world through the French Revolution is the permission and the will to change things, with public welfare as the goal. This new thing manifests itself in the equality which here places the decision for change in the hands of universal, or at least very extensive, suffrage. From this there results a change in all forms as soon as a new content makes itself felt.

Therefore state power has since then been present either only qualifiedly, constantly endangered by the desire for revision, or as a despotic reaction with a breaking down of political forms.

Power is theoretically nowhere a hereditary *jus quaesitum* [sought-after right] any more. Hence, if the moment does require its existence, it is produced temporarily through a *coup d'état*.

Universal suffrage is the logical antithesis to divine right and the old authority. The revolution proclaimed it and falsified it almost from the beginning. Its limits are indefinite. Created for elections, it can be extended to all matters of state and finally any desired sphere of existence. In the end one would arrive at the communal will of a beehive or an ant heap.

All political freedom *before* universal suffrage is specifically different from that *after* it. Even in England it was confined to a limited number of voters. Only political freedom *after* universal suffrage, based on the theory of equality, possesses or arrogates to itself the authority for eternal revision. Only since then have constitutions constantly been in question and the form of state been subject to constant change.

Equality and participation in the government through universal suffrage have become equivalent ideas (until, perhaps, one day some despotism will show us that there can be equality before *it* as well).

The driving force in all this is a great *optimistic will* which has suffused the times since the middle of the eighteenth century. The premise is the *goodness* of human nature, which, however, is a mixture of good and evil. That optimistic will hopes that changes will bring about an increasing and definitive well-being and in every crisis believes it to be quite close at hand, like a mountain height in a warm, dry wind. One nation, class, level of culture after another has been gripped by it and has believed that once what was desirable for *it* was achieved, the world could stand still for a while. People did not suspect that their *own* desiring gave all others, present and future, a right to want things *also*. People were too ready to forget how far Rousseau had already set the goal with his talk about the *"genre humain"* which could be made uniformly *happy* through a return to simple, ideal conditions. But the overwhelming majority of the desires are *material* in nature, no matter how they may disguise themselves as ideal, for by far the greatest number of people have no other conception of happiness. Yet material desires are in themselves absolutely insatiable, and even if they were continually gratified, then they would be all the more insatiable.

Idealistic minds, to be sure, let their desires and fantasies batten upon a radiant vision of the future in which the spiritual would be reconciled with the material, religion, thought, and life would be one, there would be no dichotomy between duty and inclination, and an epicurean life and morality would be compatible—and all this in the highest sense, with everything being all knowledge and yet simultaneously all beautifully figured. Actually, to date only culture has increased, while human goodness has not, and happiness has certainly not. For happiness depends on two things: the conditions themselves and the degree of satisfaction with them.

It is conceivable that a shifting of that optimism to pessimism may take place, such as already happened at the end of antiquity, and there are isolated indications of this; but the "whether" and the "how soon" remain in doubt.

Schopenhauer adds his voice to the political pro and con and speaks of the misery of this world, which had better not exist at all.

And Darwin's theory of the struggle for existence in Nature is now applied more and more to human life and history as well. That struggle has always been present, but with the slowness of political, national, and industrial life it has been far less perceptible; now, however, it is terribly alive and is accelerated by national wars and deadly industrial competition.

It is also possible that by this blind will to change (which prevalent optimism superficially terms "progress," as well as culture, civilization, enlightenment, development, morality, and other things) there is intended something permanent (that is, relatively so), that something stronger and higher is exerting some *will* in and with us. Some future time, historically surveying this our century of crisis as a whole, may then realize this, while at the same time it may be as blind about its own life and actions as we are about ours.

(It is a moot question how long our planet may still tolerate organic life and how soon its solidification, the exhaustion of carbonic acid and of water, will be coupled with the disappearance of tellurian mankind.)

Our task, in lieu of all wishing, is to free ourselves as much as possible from foolish joys and fears and to apply ourselves above all to the *understanding* of historical development. To be sure, as stated above, the age of revolution makes this objective understanding the most difficult for us. As soon as we become aware of our position, we find ourselves on a more or less defective ship which is drifting along on one wave among millions. But one could also say that we ourselves are, in part, this wave.

But with some effort a serious interest may be taken.

These are epochs, countries, groups, movements, and individuals in which some specific spirit and a force and passion applied to it manifest

themselves eloquently and by turns as instructive and as tempestu-
ously moving. Out of the jumble and confusion we shall win a spiritual
possession; in it we want to find not woe, but wealth.

The age of revolution is particularly most *instructive*, in contrast to
everything older and earlier, on account of the rich mutability of things,
the multiformity of modern life as compared to earlier life, the strong
change in the pulse beat, and, finally, through the great notoriety of
everything connected with it.

From this alone we know (certainly not by our own merits) much
more about the general life of humanity than did the greatest minds of
a hundred years ago. While their ancestors did not undergo much more
than wars, the last three generations have experienced an infinitely
greater variety of things, namely, the formulation of new principles for
existence, numerous new state formations, rapid changes in all mores,
culture, and literature. As a shaking up of life, the age of the Reformation and colonization, for example, is a trifle compared to ours. We
even have a knowledge of earlier times which is very different from
that of our forefathers, because the age of revolution has opened up to
us an appreciation of historical driving forces where our ancestors
knew only acting individuals. We now see in the history of all epochs
to a much larger extent great waves of necessity and regard the individuals as mere tools.

The two greatest changes are the new significance of nationalities
and the new concept of the state in connection with new social programs.

THE NATIONALITIES

The French, as well as all other nationalities, through both resistance and contagion, became much more conscious of their own
selves than they had previously been; especially those whose states
were dismembered yearned for an end of their isolated territorial existence and for a communal existence and unfolding of their strength.

With such prospects Napoleon I tantalized the Poles and Italians, and they believed him beyond his death. There developed the ideal of a national will which might be able to assert itself outside the country as well as in relation to one's own ruler. To be sure, in this context belong also the subsequent national *wars* and their character; *militarism* is their consequence.

THE STATE IN THE NEWER SENSE

The state is to be coterminous with this nationality, i.e., expand until it encompasses all who speak the same language. Nationality is to serve it as a further means of agglomeration, or vice versa. Foreign elements already within the state are crushed; externally the nationalistic state can never be too powerful or can hardly be powerful enough.

But this applies also internally, and here political and social interests write the most extensive programs for the state, with scarcely compatible contents. On the political side these postulates are made: the greatest freedom of all action and movement, universal voting and decision-making; the national will (no matter how it is determined) is to be the master, the *ad hoc* organs will turn up; all institutions are to be kept provisional and flexible. The origin of this political program is the *theory of revolution*, not its practice.

On the social side an all-powerful state is postulated throughout. For it is not expected and hoped for that *society* will of itself realize the desires concerned, which is the way it really ought to be; that is why these tasks are passed on to the state, which has the necessary means of coercion or will create them on behalf of a pretended universal benefit and thus needs an unprecedented wealth of power. The careerists, however, want to take this omnipotent state in hand and guide it. The origin or, rather, the basis of this social program lies in *Caesarism*.

The French Revolution was social from its very beginning in 1789. In the rural regions the transfer of property was immediately the driving force without which the peasants would not have participated. Moreover, the persecution or destruction of those property owners who had hitherto been at the same time the holders of official power were also effective here. Added to this was the freedom to postulate all sorts of things, as though the world were a *tabula rasa* (clean slate) and everything could be enforced through well-devised institutions. Those tendencies were represented theoretically by Saint-Just who, as a consistent follower of Rousseau, wanted to leave only swords and plowshares, and, finally, by Babeuf tagging along behind.

The period after 1815 then took up that development and carried it on. Only now, through the peace, were revealed the consequences of a released colossal real property and an industry hitherto really shackled and only relatively free. With England as the model the age of absolute, ruthless *acquisition and communication* began (Goethe to Zelter: wealth and speed); modern industry came into being. Beside the national wars there appears national competition which is equally murderous, as well as fights along national strata and class lines—beginning with large-scale wheat growing by machines, continuing with the crowding out of household industry and handicraft by large industry and the factory system, mainly producing for mass consumption, then for everything. (Hellwald, *Machines and Misery*, p. 783. N.B. This is true not merely of transitional periods.)

In the most striking contrast with political equality are misery and physiological deterioration (brain formation). To be sure, misery constitutes "a component of every phase of civilization," but formerly it was not concentrated and yet politically without a voice. Now it makes a noise; it simply wants to be misery no longer, and we are, after all, in the age of eternal revision.

It is under such circumstances that, alongside all the other proclaimed equalities, the only kind of inequality—but the most sensitive of all—is supposed to maintain itself, namely, the inequality of property—and this precisely when it is most strongly on the increase and the entire middle class obviously on the decline.

Thus socialism with its series of systems appears. It strives to gain control of the state, and at the same time the state tries its hand at social experiments.

As factors intensifying the danger there are the dissolution of the smaller units of living, unrestricted settlement and business establishment, as well as overpopulation—and all this with increasing demands made by the state.

Fortunately our consideration of history is not concerned with the future, unlike certain philosophers, e.g., Herr von Hartmann with his two kinds of prophecies. Soothsaying is dead, to be sure, but it is a fact that our time in general provokes *calculations* and *constructions* about the future.

One prophecy (Hartmann, *Philosophy of the Unconscious,* pp. 348, 351 f.) speaks of the breaking up of the world into republics which together will form a republic of states with common legal protection.

In social respects, Hartmann foresees free association, with uniform organization of production and worldwide marketing, by which the riches of the earth would also grow in much faster progression than now, *provided* (!) that it is not paralyzed or outdistanced here, too, by the increase in the population. (So here even philosophers can see no connection.) The final goal would be for everyone to lead a comfortable life, one worthy of a human being, with a work schedule allowing sufficient leisure for intellectual improvement. (But then who is to load garbage and perform similar chores?) Materially, man would then have the possibility of finally fulfilling his positive, real mission.

Hartmann's other prophecy (*op. cit.,* p. 337, esp. 341 f.) is as follows. After colossal self-praise of philosophy and philosophers and other pretty speeches there follows (in connection with Darwin) a vision of the future which may harmonize with the above as best it may (p. 343: this is also where he admits that his perspective is *horrible* from the eudemonic standpoint). It is the struggle for existence. This, he says, takes place among men according to natural laws as inexorable for men as for animals and plants, i.e., eradication of the inferior *races* of mankind, of the savages as remnants of arrested developmental stages. To be sure, the faster the whole earth is occupied by the most highly developed races, the whites, the more quickly the fight among the various *tribes* within the races will break out; because these are far more evenly matched, this fight will be much more terrible, bitter, and prolonged, but all the more beneficial to the progressive "development" of the species (yes indeed! into depraved devils!). According to Hartmann, the form of the struggle does not matter, whether it be war or another form of competition, squeezing dry by commerce, or other methods. Thus the earth will become increasingly the exclusive prize of the most highly developed peoples, which will become ever more civilized. Of course, even within these peoples further development will be able to come about only through a grandiose struggle for existence. (And what about the above-mentioned comfortable life, one worthy of a human being?)

We shall do without such historical decorative endpieces. Instead, we have a request to make of fate—a request for a feeling of duty for what lies before us each time, submission to the inevitable, and, when the great problems of existence confront us, a clear, unambiguous statement of these; finally, a request for as much sunshine in the life of an individual as is necessary to keep him alert for the fulfillment of his duty and his contemplation of the world.

115. The Period of Reform from Above

Absolutism, which had formerly lived primarily for the enjoyment of its power and its goals of greed, basing itself on divine right, begins to concern itself, as sultanism, with *public benefit,* or at least pretends to do so, partly in the spirit of great causes, partly as the benevolent father. For this it needs and demands another increase of its power over the privileged classes, including the *church,* and regional differences and special privileges.

Public opinion had already been set in motion by a French-European, partly negative, partly imaginatively positive literature and poetry and had as its basis *equality* or at least *uniformity*. In this it aided absolutism to the extent that it, too, considered that state as the best-ordered in which the privileged classes were allowed mere advantages and had as little corporate power left as possible, where there was the smallest possible number of differences. Poland and Sweden, kingdoms ruled by the nobility, were regarded as the most unhappy countries. According to this view England constituted an exception. At the same time, public opinion increasingly espoused the *"Enlightenment"* in general, i.e., the abstracting of all primeval and invisible foundations of existence.

The reform had on its side unqualified centralization; the Enlightenment included enmity to everything traditional. The enlightened, i.e., absolutist, state strove for complete inner unity and complete availability of all forces; public opinion strove for the breaking down of all barriers.

Socially, the upper classes were still in high favor everywhere, and only they were eligible for the higher offices in the state and partly in the (Catholic) church as well, but inwardly they were no longer sure of their special privileges and were already strongly affected by the new developments.

If the state now no longer derived its authorization to omnipotence from divine right, but from the concept of public benefit, it inevitably had to run the risk of passing from the hands of the dynasties into other hands. It just did not know yet how close this moment was. Everyone believed himself capable of governing in the spirit of public benefit.

This double origin of the modern state from the complete centralization of power and the Enlightenment has since then been constantly apparent. Thus the political tradition in France is woven together out of the Revolution and Napoleonic despotism.

In keeping with this general state of affairs, Frederick II's instruction to the General Directory of 1778 reads: "Our interest is identical with that of the people." In Frederick the Great's view a prince had long been *"le premier serviteur de l'État"* [the chief servant of the state] (Testament of 1752?). To be sure, during his regime the "public benefit" is replaced by the concentration of all forces on war and readiness for war, as well as his inevitable and permanent dictatorship. Only a very small part of his nobility were true aristocrats, the overwhelming majority being Junkers.

116. Absolutism in the North

Gustavus III's task was to save the country through the overthrow of an oligarchy very similar to the one from which Charles XI in 1681 took the usurped crown lands and rights. Gustavus' *coup d'état* was a genuine royal revolution in the name of the whole country against an insolently encroaching part.

In Denmark, on the other hand, there was royal rule in abundance, but a bureaucracy of kinsmen participated in the rule without outside support (here there were no parties of the Caps and Hats, as in Sweden), merely as a matter of custom. The arrogant, vain Struensee, a real professor, strikes into this nest of abuses in the name of Enlightenment and progress and then has to move forward step by step until he is heard panting and is overthrown. His entire story is only of pathological interest, as evidence of the prevailing fever of progress as being equal to rulership in a debased spirit. The monarchy remained about the same after him as it had been before him.

117. On the North American Revolutionary War

(I) Once the Americans truly believed that America existed for their sake and belonged to them, it did not even take the doctrine of "no taxation without representation" to bring about their revolt as soon as they were strong enough. Actually, however, the moving spirits wanted to break away from England, and the tax business was only the most welcome pretext.

A very characteristic thing was the prolonged preservation of the semblance of legality in the rebellion.

There was a striking disparity between the great personal freedom and political rights of the Americans and their commercial tutelage and exploitation up to that time.

Only one thought is impossible and inconceivable in that period: that England should have given these colonies their freedom without being admonished, on its own initiative. After all, only a short time previously it had triumphantly had new territory in America transferred to it. Too, England might have had to defend these areas at a later time if some other sea power wanted to establish itself there, e.g., the same France that later sided with the colonies.

And so the most powerful politicians and political economists of the world of that time simply had to pay dearly for experience, too.

To be sure, without foreign aid the Americans would initially have been defeated, but hardly for long. And then, the very fact that they found and accepted such foreign aid is a characteristic of people such as they were.

The originally so divergent backgrounds and political and social difference, as well as the non-English, Dutch, and refugee elements, had already been largely smoothed out.

(II) Without French aid and the European naval war North America would certainly have been subjugated. Thereupon the whole political and economic life of England would have had to be oriented toward the permanent suppression of America. England would have become a sort of military state. However, the French Revolution, which would have come anyway, probably would have induced America to rebel again, but presumably so soon that England would have had to take a stand long before 1793 and join the Coalition. Anyway, in England itself the military state would have had to defend itself against a revolution. The America (United States) of 1783 had only one and a half times the population of New York today. It surely had no inkling of its future reciprocal relations with Europe, although people must have known immediately that the successful revolt had a moral meaning for Europe generally. And this state had inscribed into its founding documents the "pursuit of happiness" as an aim of the life of peoples.

118. England

Here there exist a state structure and an economic life which are able to keep completely aloof from the contemporary continental zeal for change and so-called reform through their own great political strength and the ability of individuals.

No Montesquieu and no Rousseau could do the slightest harm to the English, and even the influence of the French Revolution was completely rejected at home. After great victorious battles England passed over into the nineteenth century the way it had been before, as the most glorious among all opponents of the Revolution and of France. It goes through its internal crises without outside countries being able to interfere through disturbance or invasion, let alone permanent conquest. Its public opinion rises above the fluctuations and reactions of the Continent's. Everything is settled on the island.

England had entered modern times, from 1763 on, with high splendor (Peace of Paris) and in general had been almost persistently on the ascendant since the War of the Spanish Succession.

Its upper class possessed in the highest measure the two capacities which the French nobility lacked: through its two parties it was able to govern the kingdom, and at the same time it ran its counties as regards justice, administration, and military command, all without pay.

119. On Small States

[Regarding German conditions.] Petty princes and counts were especially numerous in the Westphalian, Upper Rhenish, and Franconian areas, and particularly in Swabia, all with little courts and a complete administration in miniature. If they had only contented themselves with being country Junkers! Instead of this there prevailed courtly and military dilettantism. Reforms almost never penetrated there. Contemporaneously with the reformers of the larger states there existed here little Nimrods and peasant baiters, surrounded by adventurers and indulging their mania for governing. The small states all exist only as long as no stronger man lets another stronger man have them.

The small state has meaning and life only if it is a republic, a genuine one, and changes and preserves only as much as is commensurate with its active strength.

120. On the Dissolution of the Jesuit Order

A curious thing is the anonymity of the entire order in its decline. Did not a single Jesuit once more appear as a personality to face powerful personalities like Pombal and others? In this last hour of the order one misses at least a book which might have made a plea for the order from the viewpoint of power and expediency. [*Later addition:* Such a book would have availed nothing.] To be sure, there were no later "revelations" either.

121. The Intellectual Situation Prior to 1789

An essentially materialistic explanation of the world, an equally irreligious doctrine of man's nature, a hatred for Christianity (and not just for its external embodiment of power, the Catholic church) *combine* with a growing criticism and scorn of the particular French state system, with the ideal of the constitutional state, with new views of national economy, and *cross* and *coincide* in part with a doctrine of the goodness of human nature in its supposed natural state, with the drive toward a radical change in mores as well as in the state. All this, in all its phases, is conveyed by an irresistible literature which beyond France sweeps Europe away.

There is a general susceptibility to contagion. The need for emotion has been aroused and exists, with compassion and a feeling of virtue being especially required for it. It becomes the fashion to trace the psyche of one's fellow men; the great document of this is Lavater's work on physiognomy.

The need for emotion in the direction of visionary enthusiasm and enlightenment is exploited in Europe outside of France by secret societies, in France itself by miracle-workers and charlatans.

A general victorious and reassuring *feeling* predominates, one which is fed by the great travels, nature descriptions, and discoveries in the natural sciences.

122. German and French Intellectual Development in the Eighteenth Century

The French mind takes cognizance of things almost only *ad probandum* [for the sake of arguing], any more, in order to derive some proof of the reprehensibility of everything up to then.

The German mind, on the other hand, exists *ad narrandum* [for the sake of reporting], i.e., it has an infinity of things to report from within as well as from the world viewed through new eyes. It has a decided capacity for becoming absorbed in itself and in the world.

Conclusive evidence of this is supplied by the treatment of music in the two countries at that time. Since it has nothing to do with the *probare*, the sole activity of the contemporary French mind, it plays a small role in France, Grétry and Méhul notwithstanding. In poetry, too, no really great work is possible in France because of this tendentiousness.

The German spirit, by contrast, is positive, rich, multifarious, exploring itself in all directions and enjoying its treasures, oriented toward understanding and intellectual happiness.

Nowhere among its greatest representatives is there a trace of the general dissatisfaction or of the scornful tone with which France flies in the face of *everything* past and present. Individual feelings predominate, but where the general does appear, it is patriotism of the enthusiastic rather than the embittered variety. Instead of bitterness there prevails here buoyant enthusiasm in a great variety of endeavors.

123. On Rousseau and His Utopia

(I) Rousseau's utopia had already spread widely from the educated circles down to the semi-educated. This utopia was composed of, and sustained by, the following premises. Human nature was assumed to be good once the barriers were taken down; in connection with this, virtuous feelings, compassion, and the like were extolled and the praises of primitive man were sung at the expense of civilized man; arguments or actions were advanced transcending individual nations, in the name of mankind; the assumption was made of an original contract into which things could be put at will (the more cautious spoke of a tacitly made contract); then, from the "social contract" there were derived *liberty* and *equality*, the latter assuming that all men should possess something, but none too much; finally, the *volonté de tous* [will of all] and the *volonté générale* [general will] were to be balanced, without its being stated who was to determine the latter.

The French were familiarized with the idea of a leap into the uncertain; the general need for emotion played its part here.

(II) It is strange that Rousseau makes no use of the real, concrete life and sorrows of the French common man whom he must have known so well, but remains a theorist, a utopian. Was this perhaps done so as not to scare away his only possible readership at the time? The new views had ample time over a period of two generations to gain acceptance.

(III) J.-J. Rousseau remained a plebeian. His warmth of heart was only apparent. The *Confessions* are characterized by an effect of astonishment, a melancholy-rebellious tone, an unnerving dreaminess, and virtuous feelings rather than virtue; there is something un-French about them.

124. The Political Situation in France Before the Revolution

The pressure on the lowliest was the greatest; it made life barely livable. The manorial and clerical pressures hardly counted compared to the pressure exerted by the state. The peasants were in secret ferment.

The budget was greatly overloaded. In addition to the expenses of bureaucracy, of debt and interest, of the tax rents and what they involved, of the army with its enormous officers' budget, and of foreign affairs, the court and all that went with it was an especially great expense, notably the enormously endowed aristocratic court society and the pensions involved; this waste was still on the increase. It was as though the kings wanted to keep not only their relatives but every one of their retinue tremendously wealthy and had to compensate them quite disproportionately for every loss—and all this in the face of an increasing deficit. And yet this high nobility was utterly powerless politically and unaccustomed to any real contact with the people. It gave itself up to salon life and its amenities and isolating effect.

The Third Estate had already gained so many privileges that it wanted the moon and was getting impatient. It was not satisfied with easy elevation to the nobility and the many offices open to it. Since 1614 it had been without any political contact with the nobility; in its municipal offices it was frequently abused; it was devoid of any old municipal spirit. A bourgeois was received by the nobility socially if he had talent or fame (the *gens de lettres*, men of letters), or if he helped to amuse people or to play host to them if he was wealthy. In business the Third Estate pushed ahead and it was acquiring wealth as well as being already greatly affected by the leveling culture.

All classes were still strictly separated from one another, to be sure, even the city dwellers from the peasants, but there was more integration in culture and customs than elsewhere, and the theory, supported by the reading of the time, was essentially leveling.

In this, the influence and absorptive power of Paris was of basic significance.

All this confronted the government which was still completely caught up in the spirit of arbitrariness, even though it now had moderated its use of the *lettres de cachet* [warrants of arrest] and in general was *modéré et faible* [moderate and weak] and exerted a will to action and progress. Through its absolutely centralistic behavior it prepared the Revolution (cf. Tocqueville's statements).

125. The Destiny of the French Revolution

What fated this Revolution was that according to old tradition the crown considered itself entitled to use any means, especially deception, for which, however, it had little talent; for instance, it would surely have taken back any pledged word, on the ground that it had been extorted from it, as soon as it could have done so. In the face of this, the revolutionaries presented a constitutionality that was entirely new, so that of necessity everything seemed like treason to them. The crown could not possibly submit or adjust itself quickly to this new morality. Besides, there was the feverish and furious attitude of the opponents from the beginning, the aspect of revenge on the existing king and nobility for a thousand years of injustice. The Revolution was unconditional in its demands. The crown, those who had been privileged up to that time, and presently all propertied and educated people no longer knew with whom they were dealing and how far Paris would go as the mistress of all conceivable assemblies.

126. On Mirabeau

(I) Mirabeau's studies and writings were many-sided. He had a talent for always seeing in his own case the general case and France. His knowledge of foreign countries—England, Holland, Prussia—was unmatched by any contemporary Frenchman's. Even though his genius and his gift for ascendancy were great and he was in his full maturity at that time, one nevertheless must despair of his success if one becomes acquainted with the cancer which gnawed away at the insides of the French Revolution from the outset. Misunderstood by the court at the beginning of the crisis, Mirabeau even had to participate in the disintegration.

(II) Mirabeau's program was such that it was almost impossible for it to succeed; at any rate, it presupposed an unparalleled capacity for hope and boldness. This explains his early moments of utter discouragement. For the program to succeed the court would have had to entrust itself completely to this apparent member of the opposition, while the Revolution, which still had ahead of it such an immeasurable amount of fuel to consume, would have had to be blind enough to let itself be beguiled by Mirabeau. If Mirabeau had not demanded action at any price, he would have been left without hope for any success. It is a fate characteristic of those times that the most highly gifted man shocked those whom he wanted to save with his notoriety so long and so profoundly that they waited till it was too late.

In 1790 Mirabeau made enormous concessions, especially in all clerical matters, just to remain on top. (Cf., among others, Taine, *La Révolution*, p. 235, Note—on clerical marriages, etc.)

He is the most interesting Frenchman of his time. Lafayette and Company look like a bunch of blockheads beside him, but he could no longer be of help after the *anarchie spontanée* set in in the summer of 1789.

Even if, for example, Louis XVI had on July 11 chosen Mirabeau as his minister in place of Necker, and the Assembly had eagerly accepted him, Mirabeau would no longer have been capable of creating that quiet and order which would have been required to refashion all institutions of the state. The quick decay had already progressed too far, and Mirabeau could no longer have prevented Paris from sharing in the government; to escape it was his advice even later. For the time being he could not have changed the fact that the Assembly voted under sharp external pressure and also that its decisions remained ineffective in the face of the actual organic disintegration.

Mirabeau wanted to save the monarchy, which in the beginning kept repulsing him, however. At the end of June, 1789, he said to Lamarck that it was not his fault *"si on le forçait, pour sa sûreté personelle, à se faire le chef du parti populaire"* [if they forced him *for his own safety* to make himself the head of the people's party]. He had to be popular, he said, if only to benefit the monarchy—but also for his own sake. (And in time he had to join in the shouting, just to retain any influence at all.) A good thing about him was the fact that he never sided with the Orleanist party. In the midst of his actions he always realized that he was aiding in the rush toward the abyss. The 5th and 6th of October filled him with the greatest consternation.

Mirabeau's view of the French is expressed in a letter to Sieyès, dated June 11, 1790: *"Notre nation de singes à larynx de perroquets!"* [Our nation of apes with parrots' voices!].

127. The Clergy

The new egalitarian state hated everything about the clergy: that it was a corporation and thus immune to the general pulverization; that it was opposed to equality (which at that time was abolishing the old provinces and their classes, the parliaments, and all guilds and associations); that its vows of obedience were in contradiction to the rights of man; that it had independent superiors and was completely pervaded by the principle of authority, in religion as well as in life as a whole. The *philosophes* regarded Christianity as an error and Catholicism as a plague.

The Legislative Assembly abolished the communal properties, then all corporations, including the charitable and educational ones, and the National Convention, quite logically, did likewise with all academies and literary associations; then it also confiscated all properties of the hospitals and other charitable institutions.

The tithe, whose abolition was of advantage chiefly to larger property owners, had actually amounted to one seventh of the net yield.

The confiscation of the four billion immovable estates positively caused the greatest damage, because it gave rise to the belief that there was no bottom to this barrel. For religious worship, charity (hospitals and the like), and schools—matters that had hitherto been taken care of by the clergy—almost nothing was spent. Now the political communities were supposed to take care of this sort of thing. Everything went into the maw of the assignats. The pensions to the deprived clerics and corporations were scarcely paid after 1790.

128. The Legislative Assembly and the Clubs

Any assembly, inasmuch as it has to preserve forms and recognize principles and is inwardly heterogeneous because it is elected by an entire country, must necessarily bow to ruthless club bosses who seem to represent the matter at issue much more directly, because they are representatives of the most violent forces, i.e., the movement itself which is still progressing; besides, they are quite unscrupulous as to general means of pressure and have the organized services of the rioters of a big city.

Despite all this one must concede to these club leaders a high degree of that ruling spirit which is not worried about the bottomless and purely temporary character of its creations (which last only as long as the Terror).

To be sure, they were favored by the fact that (through the club's will) they were able to rule because there was no longer any other government. Their counterparts function down to every village; and it is open to argument whether it can still be called *governing* when every matter is quickly and subjectively settled through the imposition of terror on entire cities by a certain number of individuals.

Against such forces the Assembly will, with the tide rising, come off badly, because, for one thing, the former's personnel is renewed and always suited to the moment, whereas the Assembly was chosen at a much less advanced moment. The misery of such an Assembly lies in the fact that it must give in constantly in order to keep the appearance of still being at the head of the movement.

The club leaders, on the other hand—Camille Desmoulins saw in the clubs *"l'aristocratie du poumon"* [the aristocracy of the lungs]—only needed to give themselves up to the spirit of the rising passion to be certain of acting correctly for the moment. The way in which they gained control of the Paris sections in the summer of 1792 was fundamentally an obvious one. They frightened them into silence, as they did with the Assembly on a large scale, until nobody but their own men could stand it there any longer.

In time the terrorists gained important experience and style in their task of producing power through terror at any cost.

The Terror here was substantially tantamount to controlling the Assembly by the negative forces of Paris.

The significant fact is that the latter were able to unite with an identical mode of action in specific things, a homogeneous procedure. To be sure, this was the only thing they could do and had to do, but others might *not* have been able to unite and would thus have collapsed right at the start.

An infamous thing is the attitude of Jacobin historiography toward Louis XVI who wanted only to be rescued, and not even that unconditionally. The Jacobin historians are an echo of the Jacobins of that time who had an interest in painting Louis as guilty and dangerous, making murderous threats against him in the papers, and passing off the handful of royalist rowdies for an army of *chevaliers du poignard* [knights of the dagger]. Louis had already been obliged to bring the request for war before the Assembly. On May 25 they took away his *Garde Constitutionelle.*

129. On the 10th of August, 1792

A great deal still depended on the personal conduct of the king. If he had had the expected sanguine courage and furnished an example of defiance of death, he would have found a great many more defenders, or those he did find would have been better able to help him. If he had only inspired the still loyal National Guard through word and deed and given the Swiss precise orders instead of having them defend the Tuileries only when he was no longer inside! But why risk everything for a sovereign who will risk nothing himself? Barbaroux, too, thinks the king could still have won. If there had been even a little of Henry IV in him (apart from his bonhomie), if he had mounted a horse, he could have turned the blow planned against him to his advantage.

Napoleon was in Paris as a captain of artillery on the 20th of June, the 10th of August, and then also during the September massacres.

130. On the September Massacres

(I) The main connecting force was Marat's thirst for blood and the need to cover depredations and irregularities by a great deed of terror and by exerting the greatest possible influence on the Convention elections.

When some saw that something horrible was about to happen, they joined in and put themselves at the head, so that it would not happen without them. Thus Danton placed himself beside Marat.

Only those who participated now could have hopes of continuing in control once terror had been grafted onto the Revolution.

Paris has three dates of this kind: 1418, 1572, and 1792, not counting 1357–1358 and 1381–1382.

However, the murdering of numerous common criminals and accused indicates that this time, except for a number of aristocrats, Swiss officers, and the *insermentés* [the unsworn]—those to whom Danton made the cross at the edge—no specific vengeance was sought, but bloodshed per se, in order to give the Revolution its true temper. On the other hand, that moral indignation was not involved here is borne out by the fact that prisons were opened and rogues were released, so that for a week nobody was safe from robbery in the streets. Both things were done so as to have prison space available for new victims.

Once more the scepter was to be secured for the Commune of Paris through the Terror, and, if possible, permanently. Since they were and remained a small minority and knew it, they had to stick together.

What is desired is *murder per se,* which from now on is to become the temper of the Revolution.

(II) Regarding the elections to the Convention: The Commune of Paris wants the new Assembly to be elected in *its* spirit and to have a Paris complexion.

The disclaimers of premeditation (Villiaumé, Louis Blanc) do not realize the inner barbarism they betray in exculpating the secret committee and accusing Paris as such, and in forcibly welding together the murders with the defense of the fatherland. Paris had to do these things, so that Marat, Robespierre, Billaud, Danton, Manuel, and others may come off passably well. The September massacres inspire the Revolution with the *murderous temperament.*

The September massacres simply mark the beginning of the Terror, i.e., the general *aplatissement* [crushing], and no matter how political things may appear at times in the Convention, actually the fear of the Commune and its henchmen is always there.

The September days, just like the 31st of May later, are another *Par-*

isization of the Revolution. Paris brings the Terror into the Revolution, first of all in order to produce elections of this complexion in the entire country.

The main effect was in the direction of the evil development of the Revolution. The guilty ones had to destroy those (the Girondists) who made accusations against them because of it.

131. Before and After the Dissolution of the Convention

[January 3, 1868.—January 4, 1870.—January 4, 1876.] With the current unprecedented increase in militarism and industrial crises another look back to the origins of the Revolution is indicated, especially in view of the uncertainty of all rights and existences in face of the power of threatening governments from above and mass ferment from below. Our task is not to prophesy, but to show the harmonies from the beginning of the Revolution on. We want to know on which wave of the great storm-tossed sea we are drifting.

The Revolution was prepared by an enormous literary movement which, optimistic about the future, questioned everything, and by a situation of property and power in France which was in more or less conscious disharmony with this movement. Besides this was the premise of the goodness of the human heart and people as such.

The financial distress of the moment exerted pressure for the Estates General, and the *cahiers* acted as a great sheaf for the fire. Instead of constitutional ideas, for which they had relied on the Estates General, they demanded the rights of man and substituted the concept of "man" for that of "Frenchman." The magnitude of the idea caught on, and thus we make the acquaintance of the "political" man of Europe as of 1868. Then, too, many abolitions and equalizations were demanded.

Since the Estates General could not become an assembly of humanity as yet, they became, for the time being, a National Assembly. Their great moment was the 20th of June, on which day the Third Estate took an oath on the Tennis Court to give the country a constitution. But in those days tumultuous Paris took the helm of the Revolution, and the National Assembly was in a royalist mood as early as the 23rd of June. Upon the *coup d'état* on the 11th of June there followed the storming of the Bastille on July 14th, the first major action of the Parisians. In the provinces the old state came crashing down; the cities suffered from a shortage of wheat; in the country the castles were burned. The 4th of August put the seal on it, when the nobles renounced all feudal rights and the clergy gave up the tithe. While Paris and the provinces were preparing the realm of violence for decades to come, the National Assembly occupied itself with the rights of man; even Mirabeau's requests had not been able to prevent this. Then the constitution was deliberated in a spirit of mistrust of the legal power to be set up and with a limited right of veto for the king. This took place while illegal force merrily throve in Paris and elsewhere, the National Guard barely maintained external order, and artificial bread-prices and jobs were supposed to help the situation.

Finally, on the 5th and 6th of October, the king and the Assembly were taken to Paris as prisoners. People wanted to take revenge on the current representatives of everything past, far beyond its mere abolition. The new *départements* were now introduced and the elections from below were carried through. Actually the impotence of the government was replaced by the superior power of a homogeneous club mentality. Next the church properties were gobbled up, which is customary in all modern crises, and soon the new ecclesiastical constitution came into force. This brought about a collision of the Revolution with the age-old sacramental foundations of existence which had been riveted fast in the Middle Ages. The nobility was abolished; the army disintegrated because aristocratic officers became an impossibility, while a general hostility to foreign countries became increasingly apparent. The new France made constant threats and in the main tried to spread the Revolution. The Civil Constitution of the Clergy revealed the decided incompatibility of the king with the Revolution; hence his attempted flight and his subsequent treatment as a hostage while they openly sought to overthrow royalty.

The other countries, which had become reactionary but were most disinclined to go to war, were wantonly provoked. The *émigrés* had to serve as bogy men. A universal rage against them sprang up, stimulated by their foolish acts. Like the Assemblies generally, the Legislative Assembly and the Gironde were used up quickly and purposely. The Gironde wanted to eliminate the crown by war, while Narbonne wanted to save it by war and military dictatorship. In those days Dumouriez was the first to represent the view of the natural boundaries of France.

Meanwhile, internal conditions grew worse. There were rumblings in the South; Avignon fell prey to a reign of terror; there was strife because of the continued decline of the assignats; the problem of the clergy kept unrest alive; club rule expanded. On April 20, 1792, war was declared on Austria, and fighting began in Belgium and Savoy. In the interior the battle increased in fierceness. Louis protested against the banishment of the *réfractaires* [intractables] and the summoning of the *fédérés* [federates]. Danton, who wanted only loot out of the Revolution, and the Cordeliers destroyed the Girondists' support through the test day of June 20th. This meant that Paris once more took control of things. It won over the arriving *fédérés* who were completely wrested away from the Girondists; and thus in this witches' caldron France was made Parisian over and over again. In the Assembly there began, in connection with the war situation, those debates which finally declared the country to be in danger. In the midst of this fearsome ferment there came the Duke of Brunswick's manifestoes with their calamitous effect. The demand for a third assembly was raised.

During the night of the 9th of August the new Paris Commune was formed out of the Paris sections. A corollary of this is the storming of the Tuileries and the imprisoning of Louis. All this the Legislative Assembly watched inactively and decreed a new Assembly, the National Convention. It had been intended to serve merely as a drop curtain.

Would the National Convention now fare much better? It never did govern as a true national representation, but only as an organ of forces outside it.

After it had judged the king, Paris wrested its real political component, the Girondists, away from it; the remainder degenerates into mutual execration of the extreme parties.

The Revolution as a whole kept sacred none of the legal forms it created. This is its worst legacy: the authority to improve things by constantly changing the forms—indeed, by the mere desire to get different individuals to the top.

Its driving force for the time being was still volcanic, determined by the mob of Paris, by lust for loot, and other passions of leaders and parties for the enormous properties that had become liquid, and also by the peasants, who were afraid that the real owners might return.

Meanwhile, in the fight against the European Coalition, there rose anew from the bottom those armies and generals who soon had to pass over from defense to rule of the country. Because in the meantime the political minds had guillotined one another.

A frightful exhaustion had come over the nation which nevertheless was still there and *grew* into a strange new condition: *without respect, but without will power,* the way modern nations often are now.

Militarism was pushed to the highest point by Napoleon, and an artificial will was put into the nation's soul.

And when, after his overthrow, the economic-industrial forces which had become available only through the Revolution were unfettered and Europe, following England, turned into the general industrial mill, there arose the fourth estate, whose inner ferment has had a hand in determining everything since the 1840's. It and militarism from above are now the two clamps of the vise. There is a profound distrust of all forms and, along with it, a readiness for any change, while industries chase one another from country to country to the point of dead exhaustion for the sake of minimal differences in production prices and tariffs. (And things have certainly not improved since 1868.)

132. On the Trial of Louis XVI

[Based in part on Edgar Quinet's *La Révolution*, I, 425 ff.] Like Charles I, Louis was engaged in the crime of *laesa revolutio* [treason against the Revolution]. And like Charles, Louis had also grown up with the idea of a different law according to which he was infallible and not accountable; this was the only law of which he was conscious. Therefore he was punished according to a law that was alien to him.

The trial was highly characteristic as a measure of the revolutionary quality of the parties. The Girondists proved that they were not the truest personification of the Revolution. Only the most violent could be this, at a time when audacity was identical with power.

When was it that Billaud-Varenne proposed taking the king across the border "under sufficient escort"? And would there still have been sufficient escort? At any rate, it would have had to take place long before December 26, 1792.

No dynasty has ever been overthrown through the execution of one king. The decapitated return, with the aid of vast sympathy, in the shape of their successors.

The monarch was beheaded by the Jacobins; but the monarchy slipped away from them, and the rest of Europe felt more revulsion than fear. The consequence was an endless, irreconcilable struggle, to wage which *"on se redonna un maître"* [they gave themselves another master].

A Louis XVI roaming about abroad would have been a hundred times less dangerous than the beheaded Louis with the martyrdom of his family. The perpetrators are supposed to have assumed that no *versatilité* [fickleness] need be feared among the people, that it had broken with royalty forever. (No, worthy Quinet, they did not imagine that.)

The Napoleonic Count Sieyès and the Duke of Otranto must be counted among the small majority which decided in favor of unconditional death.

Louis' death was inevitable, because alive and in a French prison he could always have been used by a more moderate party or by reaction; his death really was part of the complete rule of the Jacobins.

If he said on the scaffold, *"Je pardonne à mes ennemis"* [I forgive my enemies], he was the last one to speak thus; later ones usually died *avec les passions et les fureurs de la terre* [with the passion and violence of this world].

The next consequence was war with England, Spain, and Holland. Finally there arose a new royalism and the longing for some master.

For the time being, to be sure, the alternative was victory or downfall. The enemies sharpened their methods with their hatred, and the French did likewise.

What would have happened if the plebiscite had pardoned Louis? He would probably have been murdered in the Temple. Those who dared the September massacres would have forced this murder through as well.

The spiritual survival of the monarchy is comparable to the sensation in an amputated limb.

The parties, which were now wrangling over power rather than principles, each gave themselves up to a special savage suspicion; each charges the other with monarchist ideas and conspiracy against the republic. And force and tyranny were indeed elements in all of them. No one seriously believed the republic to be established, and this drove them to frenzy and despair, so that all compassion ceased.

133. Girondists and Jacobins

Earlier presentations of the French Revolution have followed more closely the history of the great state assemblies, the Constituent Assembly, the Legislative Assembly, and the National Convention.

But since Taine we have known that through the rapid decay of the old state, starting in 1789, the *country* had in large measure escaped any central direction and that the social revolution had everywhere followed the political one. But the major part of the nation, the losers as well as the winners, wanted to retain monarchy.

However, the Legislative Assembly and its chief orators, the Girondists, press toward the republic out of abstract hatred and declare war on foreign countries, mainly in order to topple the crown—from April 20 to August 10, 1792.

And only now, particularly between the 2nd and the 4th of September, does it begin to surprise the Girondists that right beside them there has come into being a far superior new power, one that mocks at their enthusiasm, a *true* power: the will of Paris clubs in their connection and close correspondence with the club members in the provinces. Its components are the sections and the Commune of Paris, the hired thugs, the Jacobins and Cordeliers, and, as a *bureau d'enregistrement* [registry], the Convention under the pressure of the tribunes, as well as the local clubs in all of France.

This force deprives the Girondists particularly of the exploitation of the foreign war as an instrument of internal rule; it forces them to vote in favor of the king's death; it simply outdoes them in everything that looks bold and wicked, and brilliantly masters the now recognized terror, after the Girondists, too, had formerly threatened with the sanctity of the people's wrath.

With the extremely faulty conduct of the war and the intentional disorganization of the army these Jacobins are able to appear as the saviors of France from foreign countries, especially since the people do not know how deeply disunited the cabinets of the Coalition and their conduct of the war really are. And the Jacobins do govern internally, albeit dreadfully, i.e., the old resources of existence are consumed, the assignats run into the billions, the actual and potential adversaries of each class are driven out or imprisoned.

This sort of thing does not last long, but it does last needlessly long enough to extinguish the light of the *beaux diseurs et gens à procédés* [fine talkers and people with programs]. But the Girondists still do their deadly enemies the favor of participating, until the end of May, 1793, in a lot of decisions devised for their own perdition.

134. The Omnipotence of Utterly Unscrupulous Parties

[Concerning the Jacobins and Their Army.] A party which is not afraid of letting culture, business, and welfare go to ruin completely can be omnipotent for a while.

135. How a Government Becomes Exceedingly Strong

[Concerning the Period of the Committee of Public Safety and the Terror.] A government which abandons business prosperity together with all the culture connected with it can be exceedingly strong and unconstrained.

136. Socialism? Communism?

(I) In those days people wanted to be neither communists nor socialists, but new owners of stolen goods.

(II) Of course, people were as far away from communism as could be, if only because the peasants wanted above all to preserve their new "property." Nothing but individual property is involved, but there is a total change in the distribution of it.

(III) In any case, it is not a question of communism and socialism, but only of new individual property which has been won by depredation or is to be created, regardless of whether Robespierre and Company realized this.

137. The Innermost Core of the Revolution

In his book on the Revolution (Vol. 2, The Jacobin Conquest, p. 69, note), Taine discusses the social views of the terrorists. Antonelle thought that in order to consolidate the Revolution there was needed *"égalité approximative des propriétés"* [approximate equality of property] and for this it was necessary *"supprimer un tiers de la population"* [to suppress one third of the population]. The fanatics, according to Taine, were all of this opinion; Jean-Bon Saint-André even speaks of over one half. Guffroy even wanted to leave France only five million inhabitants.

Here the new France is clearly revealed. Not communism or socialism is intended, which would only lead to an average general misery and equality of enjoyment (whereas equality of rights is desired, with the secret reservation of becoming master over the others), but people want only new private property, approximately equal, but available in plenty. And so that this elite may be well off, great masses have to die. It is the modern French *gracious* living as a goal.

138. Rousseau's Concept of Music and the Destruction of Churches

J.-J. Rousseau said about music that all contrapuntal combinations, particularly fugues, were only *sottises difficiles* [difficult nonsense] which hurt the ears and could not be justified *rationally*, remnants of barbarism and corrupt taste, just as the portals of our Gothic churches deserve to be preserved only to the shame of their patient builders.

From this to the destruction of churches was not a big step.

139. On Robespierre

(I) What makes Robespierre's figure so insufferable is his utter impotence in trying to seize the dictatorship; he presumably took this impotence for virtuousness. To be sure, he can no longer see anyone above him or beside him without feeling an envious destructive rage.

But he does not even himself desire to rule because he has no positive program and his agrarian project is not even meant seriously.

(II) Camille Desmoulins wrote (around the autumn of 1793): *"On a dit qu'en tout pays absolu c'était un grand moyen pour réussir que d'être médiocre. Je vois que cela peut être vrai des pays républicains."* [It has been said that in every absolutist country a great way to be successful was to be mediocre. I see that this can be true of republican countries.] (This would fit Robespierre and also apply strikingly to certain republics.)

(III) Periods which face the alternative between anarchy and some government, no matter how wretched and violent it may be, do choose the latter.

140. Before the 9th Thermidor (July 27, 1794)

Under the pretext of defense of the fatherland the Revolution had rushed out enormously far beyond any reasonable goal, to the point of projected eradication of all individuals with a close connection with earlier conditions and a complete transfer of property. The Convention had long been only an appendage.

The Revolution had become a big business matted together out of many deeds of violence, a business in which the directors and stockholders sought to give one another the air and the smallest possible number strove to remain the masters, while their guarantee would have lain in the greatest possible number of participants.

The fallacy prevalent then as well as in subsequent Jacobin historiography is that the Revolution as a concrete-abstract thing must be "spared," or represented historically, *en bloc*, otherwise reaction would be promoted.

At that time, inherent in this fallacy was the desire to go along with the most violent and most active faction, for to stand still might be tantamount to downfall, because the capable part of the nation had been offended to its very fiber.

At the same time, however, mutual destruction kept decreasing the number of participants, and now Robespierre rises to make vague threats against all who are left. There follows the 9th Thermidor, and subsequently the saving at any price of the compromised personalities through the sham continuation of the Revolution, until a conqueror took it on his shoulders, saved the *citoyens* further effort, and sent some of the worst ones packing.

It is impossible to say how things would have gone without the guillotine, with the mere exiling of the adversaries, and without the arrest of the 200,000 to 300,000 suspects and the universal fright, especially with regard to the great change in property which would hardly have taken place the way it did if all the former owners had lived on abroad.

But *with* the Terror things went about as badly for the freedom and future of France as they could have gone. (For, they had the people of 1789 and not the Terror to thank [hm?] for the emancipation of agriculture.)

In the last days before Thermidor, while there were fifty to seventy executions each day, conditions in the committees and the Convention must have been utterly unbearable. Robespierre had made more or less indefinite threats in every direction, which made possible the incredible alliance against him between people like Collot, Billaud, and the Dantonists, and men like Durand de Maillane, Boissy d'Anglas, Champeaux, and others.

He was really lost when on the 8th Thermidor in the Convention he was told *"Nommez ceux que vous accusez"* [Name those whom you are accusing], and would name no one.

141. On the Mutual Destruction of the Revolutionary Factions

If those people had had even the faintest notion of real governing and a little true ruling spirit, they would not have treated one another the way they did. But their background was that of *gens de lettres* and lawyers, their ambition was to orate and to write, their most rabid desire to be right exclusively, because their literary or legal backgrounds had taught them nothing different.

Terrorism is essentially the rage of *literati* in its last stage, at least in the cases of Robespierre, St. Just, and others.

142. On the 18th Fructidor (September 4, 1797)

The Terror had proved useless; exile would have sufficed for the French. The absurdity of the tragic guillotining in the cities, the terrible suppression of the federalists and the Vendée in the provinces and the destruction of the best republican minds finally produced the 9th Thermidor, the overthrow of Robespierre, and the reaction which threatened to swing to royalism. So the men of the Convention were condemned to remain on top and go on ruling if they wanted to live. Thus they forced themselves upon the new Directory Constitution of 1795, and two-thirds of them had to be taken into the Council of Five Hundred and the Council of Ancients. However, the counter-revolution was in some way imminent if those whose lives would be threatened by it were not left in power. A nice Convention which had successively worn all colors and now wanted to live on notwithstanding! And later, when the Parisians refused to acquiesce, there followed the 13th Vendémiaire and the first military victory in the field of politics under the command of Bonaparte.

Thus the regicides continued to rule, arbitrarily and with proscriptions, with military campaigns designed for money-making, the furtherance of political credit, and the maintenance of internal power, and with utter assignat bankruptcy, total transfer of property, and universal insecurity.

Then it had to happen that of all the generals one became the chief object of the nation's imagination—Bonaparte, who was just about to

conclude his Italian campaign of 1796–1797. Should people have foreseen the future dictator? But they really did want an overlord, i.e., the
dead-tired nation, including the revolutionary faction, was completely
disillusioned. The nation with its vast number of new property owners,
who had bought church and *émigré* lands and discharged their debts
and rents by paying in assignats at face value, wanted, on the whole,
not Louis XVIII by any means, nor Louis Philippe nor a Spanish infante,
but *any* government to safeguard peace and the enjoyment of property.

If the Directory could accomplish this, it would be all right with the
nation for a long time; otherwise it did veer toward rule by one individual. People were not royalist, but gradually, and in part unconsciously, became monarchist. The only apprehension was that for the
time being the Bourbon royalists would exploit the situation in favor
of Louis XVIII.

Participation in the new elections for the councils and officials was
slack. Thus the royalists would be able to secure for men of their per-
suasion sudden possession of the majority of offices or gradual possession, if people did not pay attention. The regicides, who were splashing
about violently and uncertainly—they had to try *d'être pris au sérieux*
[to be taken seriously]—were concerned over the new elections. For, as
soon as the constitution was permitted to function in earnest, the result
was bound to destroy them. The press was already substantially royalist; many *émigrés* had returned home; the Club de Clichy had a royalist orientation. And in the new elections of 1797 it actually happened
that the majority in the Council of Five Hundred consisted of royalists
in a narrow or wider sense; in Paris and in the councils there was
violent ferment in the period from May to September, 1797.

But besides those who had hitherto ruled in Paris someone else had
worries: the victor of Italy who at that time was traveling among the
magnificent villas around Milan. The 18th Fructidor, the 4th of September, 1797, was the wretched rescue by the soldiers of a republic which
was no longer protected by the people, in favor of a man who still had
to wait and was very quick to find out how little thanks people wanted

to give him. On the day of the ratification of the Treaty of Campo Formio, which he had concluded rapidly so that the Directory would not
make it, the Directory appointed him head of an Army of England, in
order to get him away from the Italian army.

143. Bonaparte and the 18th Fructidor

There necessarily was a new Vendémiaire in the offing, if the
Thermidorians, the regicides (and henchmen!) were not to face a harsh
reckoning. They would have liked to avoid the *coup d'état* if they could
have done so. Treilhard's statement to Dumas, addressed to the Cli-
chyites, moderates, and royalists, is characteristic for the situation: "Just
declare that in January, 1793, you would have voted in favor of Louis'
death!" For them it really was not merely a matter of ruling, but of life
itself.

Despite the greatest inner excitement, Napoleon had sufficient self-
control to realize that this time the fruit was not yet ripe for plucking
(this is what he said to Miot at Montebello). Perhaps, too, he had an
immediate desire for a campaign in distant, exotic places. He was
young and for the time being had to follow his specific talent as a
general.

Although he deeply despised the Directory, for the moment he saw
himself as its necessary ally. For what he loathed more than anything
else was the royalist movement whose victory would have brought a
lot of unpredictable people, circumstances, and privileges onto the
scene. Waiting for the courts of Vienna and Turin was certainly also
very repugnant to him.

The degree of his indignation may be gauged by the methods he
employed in the Italian headquarters: the club system and his series of
addresses to his soldiers. He would surely not have resorted to that
except in an extreme situation. It certainly did not take the *Portefeuille
d'Entraigues* to teach him how matters stood with royalism. Rather, he

must have known at first hand from Paris, and perhaps he fabricated the *Portefeuille* in part.

If Hoche had saved the Directory, i.e., staged the *coup d'état* for it, Napoleon could probably have put up with it. In fact, he might have preferred this. Later, when the Directory was on the point of being overthrown on Brumaire, he could have said: "It was not I who saved you then." But considering the dissension between Hoche and the Directory, he had to send his Augereau. Thus the 18th Brumaire or September 4th, 1797, took place.

Immediately afterwards, Napoleon, who had remained just far enough behind the scenes, evinced great independence of the Directors and obviously enjoyed the odium which the pursuit of their victory netted them. He himself later became the peacemaker of Campo Formio.

To him the Fructidor was highly valuable because it dealt a mortal blow to the Constitution of *l'an III* (the Year III) and the directorial government. He was now able to leave them to their further *coups d'état* and symptoms of mismanagement, and even to derive, for the time being, financial advantage from their further predatory wars (against Switzerland, Rome, and other states). Then, while he was in Egypt, the Second Coalition was formed.

To appear as a rescuer *now* was an undertaking which promised direct control.

144. How Aristocracies and Princes Succumb

Aristocracies abdicate, but do not flee, as princes do.

145. On the Invasion of Switzerland by the French

After Paris one had to have Peter Ochs, because La Harpe was not capable of sketching the new constitution by himself. Ochs, who went to Paris only a few days after Napoleon had passed through, must have received suggestions from Napoleon in Basel.

The only explanation for the behavior of the more gifted "levelers,"* provided that one does not want to call it wholly depraved, is this: From the spirit of the century they had worked up a veritable indignation at everything varied and different and yet had no hopes that any substantial change would ever emanate from Switzerland. This at least is the explanation for those who themselves belonged to the ruling classes. Ochs is guiltier by far than La Harpe who at least was a hardened refugee.

What is the source of the hymn to the variety of Switzerland which Hormayr reprints in Volume 2 of his *History?* Is it not from Johannes von Müller's *History of Switzerland,* Prefaces? To what extent is our hectic, industrially efficient nineteenth century, which everywhere insists on simplification, capable of making a judgment?

The most terrible guilt of Ochs and La Harpe is expressed in the fact that subsequently they forced their way into the Swiss Directory instead of hiding their faces from the people.

Nevertheless, Switzerland would hardly have escaped the fate of becoming a battleground of the Second Coalition (1799).

(I believe less and less that Switzerland was considered at the Treaty of Campo Formio. Both signatories had all the greater interest in avoiding any mention of Switzerland as the matter surely was on the tip of their tongues. Thugut certainly foresaw, and Napoleon certainly already desired, what happened soon afterwards. But both were interested in having a respite and shuffling the cards anew, and for the time being Napoleon wanted to shine among the French as a peacemaker.)

An astonishing thing is the crudity of the French republic at that time. In order to steal forty millions, the Treaty of Campo Formio is actually jettisoned.

---

*Manuscript reading [*Yenken*] uncertain in original. Meaning suggested by German editor. (Translator's note.)

146. Old Bern and Why It Is Hated

Ever since the Swiss contingents moved out as the French approached Bern on March 4, 1798, because Bern was as good as lost, part of modern Switzerland has had a bad conscience about old Bern and hates it all the more. Here there are no parties, but only people who put up a defense and people who did not. All constitutional talk is nothing compared to one spark of that temperament which at least defends itself against bands of robbers.

147. On the 18th Brumaire (November 9, 1799) and the Consulate

Actual military rule had of necessity arisen from the preceding exertion of force, through terrorism at home and wars abroad.

Napoleon's rule was at that time the least humiliating of all imaginable regimes. It really seemed as though France were rushing into the arms of a guardian angel. Napoleon had the great good fortune of soon being able to cap it with the Marengo campaign.

It is futile to shed any tears over the Constitution of the Year III and the persons involved. They are in part the residuum of 1793, artificially maintained against the continually onrushing genuine majority by the *coups d'état* of Vendémiaire, 1795, Fructidor, 1797, and Floréal, 1798.

And France wanted to be no longer dependent upon deliberating assemblies; it had had enough of them. People urgently desired concrete, permanent results of the Revolution rather than its prolongation by parliaments and clubs.

Even without any Brumaire the Constitution of the Year III was long since doomed and could have continued to lead a semblance of an existence only through the customary violent measures.

Property (i.e., the beginning world epoch of industry and communication) issues a call for order, and particularly the property arisen from national estates calls for a complete cessation of all further movement.

The great problem was the monarchy without the Bourbons. In the final analysis, even Orléans was too much of a Bourbon. From all Bourbons people at bottom feared less the restoration of the burdensome past than the necessity of adopting a false position toward them after all that had happened. They had been insulted too terribly. People might have been ashamed before them and thus had to continue being emotionally brutal toward them (Enghien).

Given the wretchedness of public affairs, there was absolutely no other possibility of forestalling the restoration of the house of Bourbon but by elevating a quite different ruler who soon would have to adopt royal prerogatives.

148. On Napoleon

(I) Any attempt to give a picture of Napoleon's true being from contemporary sources which have recently become available (Jung, *Bonaparte and His Times;* the *Memoirs* of Madame de Rémusat; the *Notebooks* of Metternich) must necessarily produce one-sided results. The great and unique things about him are not made manifest here—the combination of an unparalleled magical will power with an enormous, all-mobile intelligence, both directed at the production of power and continual struggle, and finally at the entire world outside of France.

(II) Napoleon had a sixth sense in all military matters and a seventh for everything serving for the production of power.

His deadly enemy, like that of all such people, was impatience; it brought his later career great disaster.

149. Napoleon I and His Russian Campaign

The whole world was *dreadfully disarranged,* to the point of an unprecedented state of violence. But this is what Napoleon wished to complete and then leave to his son. Everything was to be so firmly established that even the son's mediocrity would not have done any harm. In this there was at work a giant egoism, devoid of any moral scruples as soon as goals were at stake. The absolute *sense of power* was the decisive thing, accompanied, to be sure, by a tremendous personality, but still degenerating into a gambler's passion. The furies of the sense of power were imagination and impatience, but *not* madness, certainly not Roman imperial madness, which arises from hedonism and fear of conspirators. Within the scope of his great, false goals Napoleon acts not only rationally, but with genius, to the extent that the false ends do not rub off on the means. His intelligence and energy were not on the decline; in the campaigns of 1813 to 1815 he often appears in his full stature. Nevertheless, there were moments of weakness. But the false *political* goal quite frequently and in decisive situations brings perdition to the *field commander,* and in the Russian campaign this is the case from A to Z. He feared adverse effects on the rest of Europe if he did not capture Moscow, but rather took up winter quarters in Vilna, Vitebsk, or Smolensk. And even when he had Moscow, nine-tenths of which was burned, it became his undoing all the more because he wanted to preserve the semblance of possession for as long as possible.

The Russian campaign is the most foolish thing that Napoleon decided upon in his passion and then carried out with the most colossal intellectual and material resources. Even if one grants him his mission to rule over all of Europe, he should not have done *this.* To be sure, Thiers believes that if Napoleon had persistently continued the Spanish war and the Continental system instead of the Russian campaign, he would have subdued England and thus disarmed Europe, too. That way he would have gained time as well as the sense to make at the peak of his power the sacrifices necessary to make his regime bearable and therefore permanent as well.

But it was precisely in the *Spanish war* that the *crime* was avenged. Napoleon had a distaste for this war; it no longer was a pleasant subject for his imagination. He could not get quite stubborn about such matters; he did not want to go there himself again after his brief visit in 1808–1809. Besides, what others have, or are supposed to have, already spoiled has no attraction for people such as Napoleon who like to undertake new things but not to straighten out something that has been botched. His sense of military artistry rebelled against this.

Of course, *employment and financing for the army* could have been found in Spain just as well as in Russia. The marshals and the common soldiers would certainly have liked to stay at home, and the remaining, ambitious components of the army were not even a secondary cause of the Russian campaign. At any rate, this sort of thing was amply counterbalanced by the fact that every war aroused the hopes of the dissidents at home and with Napoleon's life put everything in doubt.

The most plausible idea may be that Napoleon was plagued by the *idée fixe* that *after his possible early death Alexander would be at the head of a coalition against the French power.* However, Napoleon could have frustrated this in another way, by humane and even friendly treatment and consolation of Prussia, Austria, and Sweden.

It is an entirely vain question what he would have done with Russia if he had succeeded to the extent of occupying Moscow, St. Petersburg, and other places, and perhaps forcing Alexander to flee to Kazan or Astrakhan. For Alexander was much safer with flight than surrender. To be sure, Napoleon misjudged him as well as the Russians.

He believed that he had all princes in his net, because they were afraid of the *democratic inclinations of their peoples* (which was the case in Austria); but he would not hear of these peoples' despair and rage which were directed against *him* and which *had* to sweep along the princes, depending on the circumstances. In general, he no longer put up with any alternative proposals to his plans.

Index

This book is set in Palatino, designed by Hermann Zapf in 1948. Like all of Hermann Zapf's many typefaces, Palatino combines beauty, legibility, and distinction without eccentricity. Palatino is an old-style face, intended as a commercial display type, yet it is equally successful in book work.

Printed on paper that is acid-free and meets the requirements of the American National Standard for Permanence of Paper for Printed Library Materials, z39.48-1992. ♾

Book design by Sandra Strother Hudson,
Athens, Georgia
Composition by Impressions Book and Journal Services, Inc.,
Madison, Wisconsin
Printed and bound by Worzalla Publishing Co.,
Stevens Point, Wisconsin